OTHER MCGRAW-HILL BOOKS BY H. JAMES HARRINGTON

THE IMPROVEMENT PROCESS: HOW AMERICA'S LEADING COMPANIES IMPROVE QUALITY (1987)

BUSINESS PROCESS IMPROVEMENT: THE BREAKTHROUGH STRATEGY FOR TOTAL QUALITY, PRODUCTIVITY, AND COMPETITIVENESS (1991)

TOTAL IMPROVEMENT MANAGEMENT: THE NEXT GENERATION IN PERFORMANCE IMPROVEMENT written with James S. Harrrington (1995)

HIGH PERFORMANCE BENCHMARKING: 20 STEPS TO SUCCESS, written with James S. Harrington (1996)

THE COMPLETE BENCHMARKING IMPLEMENTATION GUIDE—TOTAL BENCHMARKING MANAGEMENT (1996)

ISO 9000 and Beyond

*From Compliance
to Performance Improvement*

ISO 9000 and Beyond

*From Compliance
to Performance Improvement*

Dr. H. James Harrington
Principal
Ernst & Young LLP
&
Dwayne D. Mathers P.Eng.
Braxton Associates
Deloitte & Touche Tohmatsu International

McGraw-Hill
New York San Francisco Washington D.C. Auckland Bogotá
Caracas Lisbon London Madrid Mexico City Milan
Montreal New Delhi San Juan Singapore
Sydney Tokyo Toronto

McGraw-Hill

A Division of The McGraw-Hill Companies

1 2 3 4 5 6 7 8 9 0 AGM/AGM 9 0 1 0 9 8 7 6

ISBN: 0-07-026777-4

The sponsoring editor for this book was Philip Ruppel. Production was managed by John Woods, CWL Publishing Enterprises, Madison, WI. It was designed and composed at Impressions Book and Journal Services, Inc., Madison, WI.

Printed and bound by Quebecor/Martinsburg..

McGraw-Hill books are available at special quantity discounts to use as premiums and sales promotions, or for use in corporate training programs. For more information, please write to the Director of Special Sales, McGraw-Hill, 11 West 19th Street, New York, NY 10011. Or contact your local bookstore.

Contents

Appendixes

I dedicate this book to Joseph Cronin, who showed me that life has three sides: work to give me a way to measure my success, a family to give meaning to life, and fun to make all the work worthwhile. I am sure that his voice has made the choir in Heaven a little sweeter, and his laughter has brought a smile to the Heavenly Host.

I also dedicate this book to all the people at Ernst & Young who helped me put it together. Renée Irons and Debi Guido, who converted and edited endless hours of dictation into the finished product; Loria Kutch, who followed the manuscript through production; and Richard Rosenbloom, who created the multi-media package. I want to particularly thank Lee Sage for his encouragement and support of this entire project.

H. James Harrington

Acknowledgments

I want to acknowledge the efforts and contributions made by the many professionals that played a role in developing the ISO 9000 family of International Standards. It was a pleasure serving on a number of working groups through the development of the 1994 editions, and in the strategic planning process for the next set of revisions. In particular, the following individuals have made a significant contribution to envisioning the future role and application for the ISO 9000 standards:

- Pierre F. Caillibot
- Ian Durand
- Yoshinora Iizuka
- Dr. H. Kumi
- Don Marquardt
- Klaus Petrick
- Jim Pyle
- Thomas Szabo, and of course
- Reg Shaughnessy

I want to acknowledge the fellowship and support of the following future business leaders, who accompanied me on the journey through an executive MBA program, and acted as a sounding board during the development of this book:

- Bill Currie   (Canada Trust)
- Bob Hillstrom   (Schneider Canada)
- Nick Hendrick   (Uniroyal Chemical)
- Roger Henriques   (Realmax Realty)
- Rob Young   (Hewlett Packard)

But, most of all, I want to acknowledge the support of my wife Debbie, and family, Brent, Blake, and Kyle.

It is important to note that my earlier book, *The ISO 9000 Essentials,* co-authored with Robert Marshall, Pierre Caillibot, Malcolm Phipps, and published by the Canadian Standards Association, contains an in-depth review and interpretation of all the clauses within ISO 9001. As a result, this was not repeated. This book applies the concepts of system development, process improvement, and change management to the implementation of ISO 9000, thereby going significantly beyond the basic concepts described in *The ISO 9000 Essentials.*

Dwayne D. Mathers

About the Authors

Dr. H. James Harrington is one of the world's quality system gurus with more than 45 years of experience. Over the past 45 years he has been involved in developing quality management systems in Europe, South America, North America, and Asia. He serves as a Principal with Ernst & Young, LLP, and is their International Quality Advisor. He is chairman of the prestigious International Academy for Quality, and Emergence Technology Ltd., a high tech software and hardware manufacturer and developer. He is an A-level member of the International Organization for Standardization's Technical Committee 176 that wrote the ISO 9000 Quality System Standards, and Technical Committee 207 that wrote the Environmental System Standards. In 1996, he released a series of video and CD ROM programs that covered ISO 9000 and QS-9000. He has written 8 books on performance improvement and hundreds of technical reports. The Harrington/Ishikawa Medal was named after him to recognize his support to developing nations in implementing Quality systems. China named him their Honorary Quality Advisor, and he was elected into the Singapore Productivity Hall of Fame. He has been elected honorary member of seven quality professional societies and he has received numerous awards and medals for his work in the quality field. In 1996, he received the Lancaster Award from ASQC in recognition of his work to further the Quality Movement internationally.

Dwayne D. Mathers is a member of Braxton Associates, the strategy consulting division of Deloitte & Touche Tohmatsu International. Before joining Braxton, he was the International Secretary of the committee that developed the ISO 9000 series of standards (ISO/TC176). Mr. Mathers has assessed the quality systems of numerous multinational firms, and serves as an award examiner for the Canadian Award for Excellence. He has an MBA from the University of Western Ontario and a BESc in electrical engineering, also from Western. He has co-authored two previous books; The ISO 9000 Essentials, and The ISO 9000 Essentials for Medical Devices.

Introduction:
The Quality Management
System

The basic management structure of all organizations consists of a set of systems that define the way the organization operates. These operational systems can be formally documented systems similar to those used in large corporations and stored in corporate operating manuals, or they can be informal, as in a one-person operation in which a few systems (other than financial) are normally documented.

A system is defined as the organizational structure, responsibilities, procedures, and resources needed to conduct a major function within an organization or to support a common business need. Systems are usually made up of many major processes that take an input, add value to it, and produce an output. These processes may or may not be interconnected, such as the new product development process or the order entry process.

The first consideration in designing a system or a process is to produce a specific desired result. In addition to the basic process that creates the output, the following four factors need to be designed into all systems and processes:

1. Ways to prevent errors
2. Ways to segregate good items from bad items
3. Ways to correct bad items
4. Ways to prevent errors from recurring

Keeping this in mind, it is easy to understand how this process control perspective is readily applicable across many of the functions within an organization, such as the design of products and services, human resources management, marketing, sales, and invoicing. Process control is often embedded within management systems (see Figure A). The notion that processes and their interfaces should be subject to analysis and continuous improvement is the key conceptual basis for the ISO 9000 family and is the fundamental building block for a Quality Management System (QMS).

DEFINITION | QUALITY MANAGEMENT SYSTEM: ORGANIZATIONAL STRUCTURE, PROCEDURES, PROCESSES, AND RESOURCES NEEDED TO IMPLEMENT QUALITY MANAGEMENT.

An organization's QMS impacts all areas of any business, because every system, process, activity, and task has the potential to create errors. Given the

	Quality Management System
Personnel System	
Safety System	
Environmental System	
Security System	
Production System	
Financial System	
Information System	
Development System	
Procurement System	

FIGURE A Typical Management Systems

size and complexity of the total QMS within most organizations, many of the QMS elements have been designed into the individual systems. For example, the QMS elements that support the financial system are designed into the financial system and include third-party audits. Universities have dedicated major parts of their accounting curriculum to this one small part of a total QMS. Major accounting firms like Ernst & Young LLP and Deloitte & Touche LLP provide third-party financial auditing services to organizations on a yearly basis. Although all areas of the business are involved in the QMS, this book simplifies its scope, limiting it to the activities that are involved in or affect the product and service cycle (see Figure B).

Limiting our scope to the QMS that supports the product and/or service cycle greatly simplifies our subject matter. It also allows us to focus on the parts of a total QMS that affect external customers the most—the products and services that the organization delivers to them.

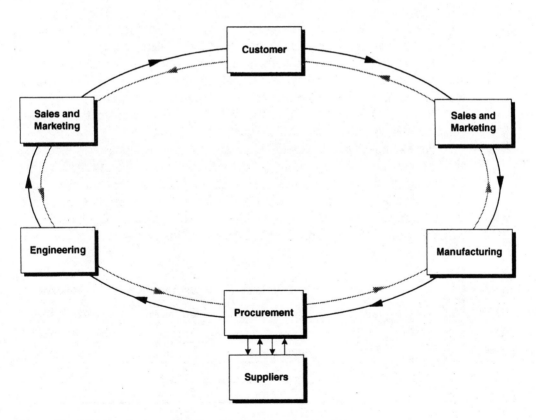

FIGURE B   The Product and/or Service Cycle

Limiting the discussion of the QMS in this manner also aligns this book with a number of national and international guidelines and procedures that are used to define the elements of a QMS that a supplier should have. Many such standards have been, and still are, widely used in North America, including MIL-Q-9858A (which dates back to 1959) and NATO military standards (AQAP 1, AQAP 4, AQAP 9), ASME Boiler and Pressure Vessel Codes (ASME NQA-1, NCA-3800), nuclear quality assurance standards (10 CFR 50 App. B, and the CSA N286 Series), as well as commercial quality assurance standards, such as CSA's CAN3-Z299-1985 series, Ford's Q-101 program, General Motors' Targets for Excellence Program, and Chrysler's SPEAR program. Today, the most well known standards are

- the ISO 9000 Series of International standards (updated in 1994) and
- the QS-9000 (Automotive Industry Supplier Standards for Chrysler, Ford, and General Motors, released in 1994).

Most of these quality management system standards began as procurement requirements to meet two-party contractual needs. As such, they have been written in a way that explains the type of quality management system a supplier should have, and they are typically imposed on a supplier of an organization that is not the end consumer of the product or service.

In the ISO 9000 series and the MIL-Q-9858A document, the supplier-customer relationship is defined as depicted in Figure C.

For example, QS-9000 applies to all of the first-tier suppliers to Ford, GM, and Chrysler, but it does not apply to the "Big Three" themselves. We truly believe that a good quality management system is a basic building block that every organization should have in place prior to delivering products or services to any customer or consumer. Keeping this in mind, we are going to talk about the supplier-customer relationship with much more proactive terms, as described in Figure D.

Standard	Year	Supplier	Organization	External Customer
ISO 9001, 9002, 9003	1994	Subcontractor	Supplier	Customer
ISO 9001, 9002, 9003	1987	Subcontractor	Supplier	Purchaser
ISO 9004	1994	Subcontractor	Organization	Customer
ISO 9004	1987	Supplier	Company	Customer
MIL-Q-9858A	1963	Subcontractor	Contractor	Procurer
ISO 9000-1	1994	Subcontractor	Supplier	Customer

FIGURE C Supplier Chain: Supplier-Customer Relationships by Standard

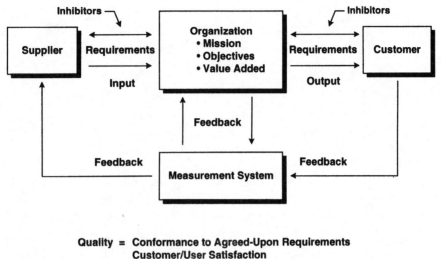

FIGURE D Supplier-Customer Relationship

Throughout this book, except when direct quotations are made relating to the ISO standards, we will refer to the organization that is implementing the quality management system as *the organization* or *your organization,* rather than using terms such as *the supplier* or *the contractor.* Also, we much prefer the term *supplier* to identify an organization that provides key inputs (products, services, or both) that form a part, and ultimately influence the quality, of your organization's final product. Although this may initially seem inconsistent with the ISO 9000 standards' use of the term *subcontractor,* we have taken this approach because we believe all organizations can benefit from having a formal QMS in place, not just those organizations that are involved in contracting. Keeping the terms *supplier, your organization,* and *customer* in context is particularly useful for the more nontraditional users of the ISO 9000 series. For example, many not-for-profit organizations, volunteers, organizations that donate equipment, and even municipalities that provide infrastructure services may be key *suppliers* in delivering the product or service.

H. James Harrington
International Quality Advisor, Ernst & Young LLP

Dwayne D. Mathers
Braxton Associates,
Deloitte & Touche Tohmatsu International

1 | Total Quality Management System

ISO 9000—What Is It?

The ISO 9000 quality management system standards have been proclaimed as everything from the savior of the quality movement to a complete waste of time and money. For example, at one end of the spectrum, Tat Y. Lee from the University of Hong Kong reported on September 27, 1994, at the Taipei International Quality Conference that the results of a survey conducted in Asia indicated that ISO 9000 has no short-term improvement benefit because it did not improve the efficiency or effectiveness of the organizations that were certified. On the other side of the world, Harold Bredrup of the Norwegian Institute of Technology reported that "A survey of mid-size engineering companies found no evidence of an improved competitive position. Instead, it appears that many companies are adopting ISO 9000 only as an alibi for quality." However, his analysis of the survey concluded that "Companies which have implemented ISO standards believe the quality assurance system is an effective tool for improving quality."

The subject of ISO 9000 reaches to the heart of every person in every organization. ISO 9000 represents the documented, controlled, understood, standardized approach to managing quality, in contrast to the freewheeling, unstructured, customized approach that most people feel comfortable with. In truth, much of the most recent quality movement has been directed at removing the rules and regulations in favor of guidelines and empowerment. The authors of a groundbreaking study conducted by AT&T reported, "In a world divided into two halves, one representing life, growth, and breakthrough, and the other representing rigidity, conformity, and status quo, quality seems to be lodged in the latter camp. Some control is viewed negatively (it suggests inflexibility and an absence of opportunity); it's no wonder that 'quality control' has failed to inspire Americans to great heights." Certainly in the eyes of most people, ISO 9000 is viewed as rigid conformance to preestablished standards, which gives it a negative connotation. Rigid conformance is exactly what can happen if the implementing organization does not understand the true purpose for each requirement and just forges ahead, writing and flowcharting existing procedures solely to get a certificate that it can hang on the wall and use as a marketing tool.

ISO 9000 is not an end unto itself. It is a starting point that gets an organization into the competitive race. Many organizations have found that in today's business environment, success comes with focusing on doing things right the first time, on time, every time, and always to the customer's satisfaction (both external and internal customers). Achieving this focus while building a lasting foundation for improving business operating systems is easier said than done. More and more organizations are finding that implementing the ISO 9000 series of International Standards provides the stimulus for reaching some important milestones along the improvement path.

The ISO 9000 series addresses those areas of quality management that are essential to winning (and keeping) customers' confidence in an organization's capability to consistently provide quality products and services. Since its introduction in 1987 the ISO 9000 series has become a major element of supplier management strategy for many multinational corporations and is fast becoming the central regulatory approach for many jurisdictions. Whether "customer" motivated, or "management" motivated, meeting or exceeding the requirements of ISO 9000 is becoming an essential competitive strategy for all businesses.

In H. J. Harrington's 1995 book *Total Improvement Management* (McGraw-Hill), the author points out that quality management systems are one of the key building blocks that make up the foundation of a Total Improvement Process (see Figure 1.1).

A QMS is on a par with

- Top Management Leadership
- Business Plans
- Environmental Change Plans
- External Customer Partnerships

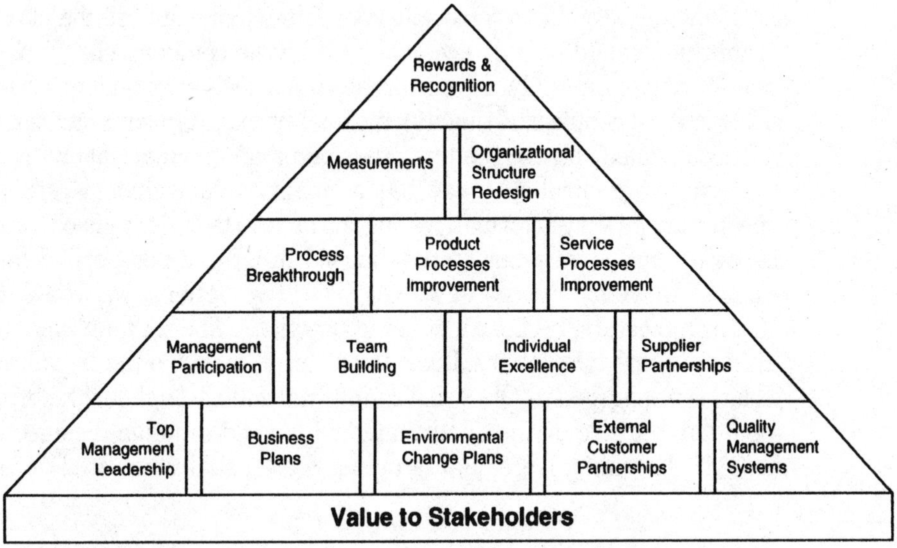
Rewards & Recognition
Measurements
Organizational Structure Redesign
Process Breakthrough
Product Processes Improvement
Service Processes Improvement
Management Participation
Team Building
Individual Excellence
Supplier Partnerships
Top Management Leadership
Business Plans
Environmental Change Plans
External Customer Partnerships
Quality Management Systems
Value to Stakeholders

FIGURE 1.1 The Total Improvement Management Pyramid

And ahead of:

- Management Participation
- Team Building
- Individual Excellence
- Supplier Partnerships
- Process Breakthrough
- Product Processes Improvement
- Service Processes Improvement
- Measurements
- Organizational Structure Redesign
- Rewards and Recognition

Many of the gains that the TQM efforts realized were lost because the QMS was not put in place to ensure that the gains made by the TQM process were long lasting.

To compete today, every organization needs to have a QMS that sets performance standards and establishes the relevant operating procedures. Just as the financial community has accounting standards (rules) that are well known and rigidly followed, the way we manage quality needs to be equally defined. No organization, regardless of its size (3 people to 300,000 people), would consider not following very strict financial procedures. Just think of the chaos that an organization would be in if everyone could write company checks at his or her own discretion. Certainly if your organization feels that quality is first among equals (cost, schedule, and quality), the quality management practices need to be well documented and even better understood than the financial practices.

Every organization today has a quality management system of some type. It may be very informal, resting in the hearts and minds of your employees, or it may be very structured, housed in a large book called the "quality manual." If we had to choose one of these two options, we would choose the informal structure, because it is being practiced. The right answer, however, is neither of these two options. It is a third option in which the organization has a documented, agreed-to QMS that is internalized throughout the organization. Too often, the size of the quality manual is used to judge the effectiveness of the QMS. In reality, large quality manuals are usually not used or understood

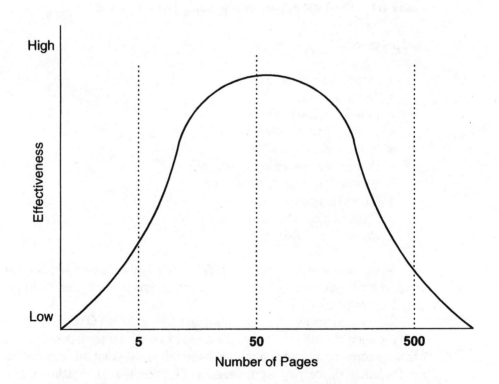

Figure 1.2 Size of the Quality Manual Versus Its Effectiveness

and as a result are not effective (see Figure 1.2). An effective QMS has the following four elements:

1. Documented procedures that establish the minimum required controls necessary to meet the needs of the stakeholders
2. Well-trained people who understand the procedures and why they exist
3. Measurements that verify how effectively the system is being utilized
4. A means to control and improve the present system

Quality Management System History

It is really hard to understand why the ISO 9000 standards are creating such a flurry of activity. Quality management systems are not a new concept. The basic quality management system strategy was created in the 1940s. I (H. James Harrington) can remember an assignment I had in the 1950s to ensure that IBM's quality manual reflected the requirements in MIL-Q-9858A. About two years ago while cleaning out my basement, I ran across this 35-year-old document and I compared it with the requirements in the latest release of ISO 9001. I was not surprised to discover that it met most of the present ISO 9001 requirements and contained some additional elements that are required to have an outstanding QMS but not required in ISO 9001. Quality management system requirements were well defined when Dr. Armand V. Feigenbaum created the term "Total Quality Control" back in the early 1950s and were well documented in his book entitled *Total Quality Control,* released and copyrighted in 1951.

When we look back in time, we can find documented quality management systems in the Hammurabi housing construction code item 229 in 2150 B.C. It stated: "If a builder built a house for a man, and his work was not strong, and the house fell in and killed the householder, that builder shall be slain." The Phoenicians cut off the right hand of anyone who produced unsatisfactory products or services. One of the oldest documented feedback systems was found in the tomb of Rekh-Mi-Re at Thebes, Egypt. It was a drawing of an Egyptian checking a stone's measurements with a string. The drawing was dated 1450 B.C. Imposing quality requirements on a supplier is a well-established practice.

So What's New?

Quality manuals and quality management system requirements have been imposed on most suppliers to the government and major industries for the past

50 years. So what's new? In the past, each customer (usually meaning large contractor, or procurement organization) imposed different QMS requirements on its suppliers (usually meaning subcontractors). Suppliers (like your organization) were caught in the middle with each of their customers wanting their QMS to meet different requirements. We have had personal experience with suppliers that had different quality manuals prepared for different preferred customers. Does that mean that the supplier was functioning differently when it was processing parts for the different customers? The answer is a resounding *No!* It just means that the documents highlighted the particular issues that were important to particular customers. Even the same industry didn't agree on what a quality management system should look like. For example, Ford's Q-101 (Q-1) program, General Motors' Targets for Excellence Program, and Chrysler's Supplier Quality Assurance Manual requirements and audit procedures were all uniquely different. The same was true of IBM, Apple Computer, and Hewlett-Packard (HP). To make it even worse, different locations within the same corporation had different QMS requirements for the same subcontractor.

Now the best minds from around the world have come together and agreed on the key elements that should be included in every QMS. The QMS elements in the ISO 9000 series outline the "what should be done," without prescribing the "how it should be done." This is usually the point where confusion between "quality principles," "quality management system elements," and "best practices" sets in. Understanding the distinction between, and interrelationships of, *what you should manage,* that is,

- the need for leadership and involvement of management in the QMS;
- the need to apply the principles of process management and control;
- the need to provide some supporting-system infrastructure; and
- the need for ongoing process and system improvement

and *how you should manage,* using TQM concepts such as

- primary focus on customers;
- leadership through involvement and by example;
- involvement of people;
- factual approach to decision making; and
- a focus on mutually beneficial supplier partnering

is the key to understanding how ISO 9000 can be used as a foundation in search of *best practices* such as

- policy deployment;
- electronic document management;
- total productive maintenance;
- ship-to-stock; and so on.

Unfortunately, these underlying concepts, which are implied in the ISO 9000 series, are not clearly expressed in the everyday language of management. Also, in the rush to "comply with ISO 9001, ISO 9002, or ISO 9003 requirements," the basic notion of *what an organization should be trying to accomplish by improving its QMS* sometimes gets lost or overlooked. This misunderstanding results in statements like "Adhering to ISO 9000 can ensure that an organization makes excellent cement life jackets."

The ISO 9000 series is designed to ensure that procedures are in place and being used that will minimize variations and maximize the probability that future products of the same type will be equally as good. The organization's performance is not as much controlled by its procedures as by the way these procedures and their processes are executed. The QMS is designed to institutionalize a standard set of quality processes so that they can become a way of life within the organization.

Organizations have six options related to their quality management system.

Option 1   Have an informal QMS.

Option 2   Have their own documented QMS based on their past experience and their present needs.

Option 3   Have a QMS that reflects the requirements imposed on them by their customers.

Option 4   Have a QMS that meets the requirements defined in the ISO 9000 series.

Option 5   Have a QMS certified to the ISO 9000 specification.

Option 6   Have a complete QMS that meets the needs and expectations of all of the stakeholders and includes the minimum requirements defined in ISO 9000, allowing the organization to be certified to the ISO specification.

Each of these approaches has its own unique advantages and disadvantages that need to be weighed by the particular organization. We believe that option number 6 is the right option for most organizations.

The ISO standards for quality management systems are taking hold around the world. The U.S. Department of Defense (DOD) is dropping MIL-Q-9858A in favor of the ISO standards. Ford, General Motors, and Chrysler have gotten together and built upon the ISO 9000 standards to create an industry-specific standard called QS-9000 that will apply to all of their first-tier suppliers. Third-party certification organizations have sprung up from Monaco to Maine, from Buenos Aires to Belgium, from Nome, Alaska, to Rome. This new business is eliminating the need for customers to spend large amounts of resources personally verifying suppliers' quality management systems. It also has the potential of saving small suppliers a major portion of their quality budget that was previously used to host customers and/or potential customers who visited their organizations to verify their quality management systems. We have seen small companies that spend up to 20 percent of their management resources explaining their business and processes to visiting customers or potential customers. The third-party certification movement has the potential of greatly reducing the cost of evaluating and verifying quality management systems for the supplier and the customer. In addition, it allows organizations to consider many more suppliers as distance becomes less of a consideration.

Like a two-sided coin, ISO 9000 also has two sides. One is a generic model for ensuring process quality; the other, third-party registration for supplier-certification schemes. Throughout the world, the prevailing view has certification heads up on the table. We believe that the true value lies in the effective use of both sides of the coin. Currently, third-party registration to ISO 9000 has not had a major impact on reducing the number of customer reviews. Originally we thought that registration would eliminate or reduce the number of potential supplier visits, but it has not worked that way. The financial and the engineering people continue to make site visits to potential suppliers and the quality people come along, too, even if the supplier is registered to ISO 9000 by a third party. Part of the reason is that the quality professionals feel the need to develop a personal relationship with their counterparts at the supplier. They want to understand the people whom they will be working with. They want to talk to them. They want to develop personal relationships. They feel that if they are going to partner with a subcontractor, it cannot be through a third-party analysis of what the supplier is doing. Frequently today, certification is being used not to certify a supplier's QMS as being acceptable but to eliminate suppliers from potential consideration. If an organization has 12 potential suppliers for a particular part number and four of them are certified to ISO 9000, chances are the field would be narrowed to these four.

Although few organizations pass an ISO 9000 certification audit on the first try, any organization that cannot meet the ISO standard should worry. A QMS is a prerequisite for an effective improvement process. The systems described in ISO 9000 are so fundamental that any organization that cannot meet them probably will not survive in the 1990s. After all, the ISO 9000 series describes quality management systems pretty much as they were defined in the 1950s. The ISO 9000 standards are basic, and we are amazed that so many organizations have tried implementing TQM without having this basic building block in place. TQM efforts fail when organizations attempt to apply the TQM methodology to a faulty structure. Process improvement teams should go to work after the building blocks of a QMS are put in place. It is as simple as this: You really need control over things like nonconforming materials before you start figuring out how to stop making bad parts. Without proper controls, you can send an awful lot of bad materials to customers while teams are in meetings discussing the problem.

Quality Management System Standard MIL-Q-9858A Status

There is little doubt that after MIL-Q-9858A was released in 1959, it served as the leading quality standard until the latter part of the 1980s, when the ISO 9000 series was released. Since that time MIL-Q-9858A has slowly been slipping into the background, even in North America. Until recently, the U.S. Department of Defense had dogmatically been holding onto MIL-Q-9858A for contracts related to major procurement efforts. Since 1992 the DOD has been considering dropping MIL-Q-9858A in favor of ISO 9000 specifications. This change has had its ups and downs. But as the U.S. government pursued moving closer and closer to the "buy commercial" approach in late 1994, the die was cast. It was no longer a matter of *would* the DOD be dropping MIL-Q-9858A in favor of ISO 9000 but *when* and *how* it would be dropped. Although military officials stated that contractors would have the option of not using ISO 9000 in favor of other industrial standards, DOD's direction is very clear. DOD's primary quality standard will be ISO 9000 by 1997.

The first U.S. government agency to award contracts specifying ISO 9000 or its equivalent was the U.S. Postal Service. With the Postal Service's 60,000 subcontractors of goods and services, ISO 9000 is off to a good start in the U.S. government. But they are looking at a five-year rollout plan due to the cost and difficulties that ISO 9000 imposes on small suppliers.

Based on the future demise of MIL-Q-9858A as an important QMS standard, we will not focus on it during the remainder of this book.

Overview of the ISO 9000 Series

As a result of pressure from quality professionals, quality organizations, and businesses around the world for a common approach to evaluate suppliers' quality management systems, the International Organization for Standardization (ISO) founded Technical Committee (TC) 176, "Quality Management and Quality Assurance," in 1979. The secretariat of this technical committee was awarded to Canada and is held by the Canadian Standards Association, on behalf of the Standards Council of Canada. ISO/TC 176 is made up of 66 member bodies from countries as small as Sri Lanka and as large as the Russian Federation. (For a more detailed list of the makeup of ISO/TC 176, see Appendix I.)

ISO/TC 176 is made up of a cross section of practicing quality professionals, consultants, academicians, and standards professionals. This committee brought together some of the finest minds and practical experience in the quality field to define the basic ingredients of a QMS.

In 1987, after eight years of work and rework, the ISO 9000 series of standards was released. These standards consisted of five primary documents, as follows:

ISO 9000-1:	Quality Management and Quality Assurance Standards—Guidelines for Selection and Use
ISO 9001:	Quality Systems—Model for Quality Assurance in Design, Development, Production, Installation, and Servicing
ISO 9002:	Quality Systems—Model for Quality Assurance in Production, Installation, and Servicing
ISO 9003:	Quality Systems—Model for Quality Assurance in Final Inspection and Test
ISO 9004-1:	Quality Management and Quality System Elements—Guidelines

The ISO 9000 series is supported by a set of definitions published in ISO 8402: 1994—"Quality Management and Quality Assurance-Vocabulary." The structure of the ISO series can be seen in Figure 1.3. Figure 1.4 provides a more comprehensive list of the related ISO Quality Management and Quality Assurance standards set of documents.

Since these standards were released in 1987 more than 100 countries have approved them as their national standard. These standards have been translated into each country's official language and are usually re-released using a country-specific control number. For example, they have been released in the United States as the ANSI/ASQC Q9000 series, and in Canada as the CAN/CSA ISO 9000 series. (See Appendix II for a more complete list.)

The following is a list of the currently released standards and ones that are being developed, divided into two groups—"Requirements" standards and

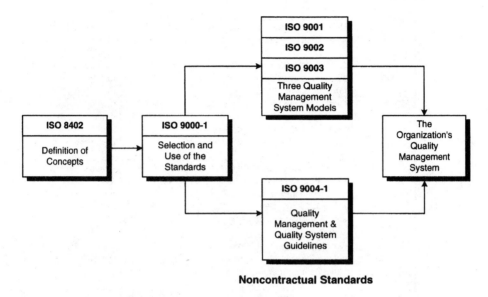

FIGURE 1.3   ISO 9000 Standards Structure

"Guideline" standards. This list will help you understand which standards can be imposed on an organization and which standards were written to help in developing an organization's QMS and audit activities.

Requirements Standards for Quality Management Systems
- Models for quality assurance
  - ISO 9001:   In design, development, installation, and customer service
  - ISO 9002:   In production, installation, and customer service
  - ISO 9003:   In final inspection and test
- Supporting tools and techniques
  - ISO 10012-1:   Metrological confirmation system for measuring equipment
  - ISO 10012-2:   Control of measurement processes

Guideline Standards
- Guidelines for applying and implementing quality assurance standards
  (9001/9002/9003)
  - ISO 9000-1:   Selection and application
  - ISO 9000-2:   Application of ISO 9001, ISO 9002, and ISO 9003

ISO 8402: 1994	Quality management and quality assurance—Vocabulary	ISO 9004-1: 1994	Quality management and quality system elements—Guidelines
ISO 9000-1: 1994	Quality management and quality assurance standards—Guidelines for selection and use	ISO 9004-2: 1991	Quality management and quality system elements—Part 2: Guidelines for services
ISO 9000-2: 1993	Quality management and quality assurance standards—Part 2: Generic guidelines for the application of ISO 9001, ISO 9002 and ISO 9003	ISO 9004-3: 1993	Quality management and quality system elements—Part 3: Guidelines for processed materials
ISO 9000-3: 1991	Quality management and quality assurance standards—Part 3: Guidelines for the application of ISO 9001 to the development, supply and maintenance of software	ISO 9004-4: 1993	Quality management and quality system elements—Part 4: Guidelines for quality improvement
ISO 9000-4: 1993/ IEC 300-1	Quality management and quality assurance standards—Part 4: Guide to dependability program management	ISO 10011-1: 1990	Guidelines for auditing quality systems—Part 1: Auditing
ISO 9001: 1994	Quality systems—Model for quality assurance in design, development, production, installation and servicing	ISO 10011-2: 1991	Guidelines for auditing quality systems—Part 2: Qualification criteria for quality systems auditors
ISO 9002: 1994	Quality systems—Model for quality assurance in production, installation and servicing	ISO 10011-3: 1991	Guidelines for auditing quality systems—Part 3: Management of audit programs
ISO 9003: 1994	Quality systems—Model for quality assurance in final inspection and test	ISO 10012-1: 1992	Quality assurance requirements for measuring equipment—Part 1: Metrological confirmation system for measuring equipment

FIGURE 1.4 ISO Quality Management and Quality Assurance Standards

ISO 9000-3: Application of ISO 9001 to development, supply, and maintenance of software
ISO 9000-4: Application of dependability (reliability) management
- Guidelines for quality management and elements of quality management systems
ISO 9004-1: General guidelines
ISO 9004-2: Guidelines for service
ISO 9004-3: Guidelines for processed materials

ISO 9004-4:   Guidelines for quality improvement

ISO 9004-8:   Quality principles applied to management practices

- Supporting tools and techniques

ISO 10005:   Guidelines for quality plans

ISO 10006:   Quality in project management

ISO 10007:   Guidelines for configuration management

ISO 10011-1:   Auditing

ISO 10011-2:   Qualification criteria for quality systems auditors

ISO 10011-3:   Management of audit programs

ISO 10013:   Quality manuals

ISO 10014:   Economic effects of quality

ISO 10015:   Continuing education and training

ISO 10016:   Quality documentation

ISO 9000-1—Quality Management and Quality Assurance Standards— Part 1: Guidelines for Selection and Use

ISO 9000-1 provides an introduction to the ISO 9000 series and concepts. It provides the reader with direction on how to use the ISO series, with particular emphasis placed on principal concepts related to quality management systems, management's involvement and review, and treating work as a process that should be documented and controlled. It emphasizes that

- processes should be defined,
- procedures should be appropriately documented,
- the organization should be functioning as documented, and
- records should be kept to verify that the procedures are being followed.

Figure 1.5 is the table of contents for ISO 9000-1.

ISO 9001: Quality Systems—Model for Quality Assurance in Design, Development, Production, Installation, and Servicing

ISO 9001 is the most comprehensive of the three contractual quality assurance standards, ISO 9001, ISO 9002, and ISO 9003. These three standards are used for demonstrating an organization's capability to supply products that meet customers' expectations. ISO 9001 was intended primarily for organizations that develop unique designs for each customer's need. ISO 9001 applies to providers of both products and service, for example, consulting, architecture and engineering (see Figure 1.6 for ISO 9001 scope). ISO 9001 and ISO 9002 only differ in that ISO 9002 does not address product design. Organizations

1 Scope

2 Normative references

3 Definitions

4 Principal concepts

     4.1   Key objectives and responsibilities for quality

     4.2   Stakeholders and their expectations

     4.3   Distinguishing between quality system requirements

          and product requirements

     4.4   Generic product categories

     4.5   Facets of quality

     4.6   Concept of a process

     4.7   Network of processes in an organization

     4.8   Quality system in relation to the network

          of processes

     4.9   Evaluating quality systems

5 Roles of documentation

6 Quality system situations

7 Selection and use of international standards on quality

8 Selection and use of international standards for external quality assurance

Annexes

A Terms and definitions taken from ISO 8402

B Product and process factors

C Proliferation of standards

D Cross-reference list of clause numbers for corresponding topics

E Bibliography

FIGURE 1.5   Table of Contents for ISO 9000-1

that meet all the requirements of ISO 9001 will also be in full compliance to ISO 9002 and 9003. It covers 20 different key QMS elements. Figure 1.7 is the table of contents for ISO 9001.

    A detailed discussion on the 20 subclauses in Clause 4.0 of ISO 9001 and how to apply them will be covered in Chapter 2.

The scope of ISO 9001 states:

"This International Standard specifies quality system requirements for use where a supplier's capability to design and supply conforming product needs to be demonstrated.

"The requirements specified are aimed primarily at achieving customer satisfaction by preventing nonconformity at all stages from design through to servicing.

"This International Standard is applicable in situations when

a) design is required and the product requirements are stated principally in performance terms, or they need to be established, and

b) confidence in product conformance can be attained by adequate demonstration of a supplier's capabilities in design, development, production, installation, and servicing."

FIGURE 1.6   Scope of ISO 9001

ISO 9002: Quality Systems–Model for Quality Assurance in Production, Installation, and Servicing

ISO 9002, the second in the contractual quality assurance standards, is identical to ISO 9001, except that it does not include the QMS requirements for the design function (see Figure 1.8). It applies to an organization in which the customer provides the product design and/or specification. It includes 19 of the 20 elements defined in ISO 9001 (see Figure 1.9 for the scope of ISO 9002).

ISO 9003: Quality Systems–Model for Quality Assurance in Final Inspection and Test

ISO 9003 is the least stringent of the three ISO contractual standards. In general, it applies to organizations that supply less complex products whose quality can be evaluated based on inspection and test only. In the case of ISO 9003, six of the required elements are the same as they are in ISO 9001 and 9002. Ten of the required elements are less stringent than in ISO 9001 or 9002, and four of the ISO 9001 elements do not apply (see Figure 1.8). See Figure 1.10 for the scope of ISO 9003.

1   Scope

2   Normative reference

3   Definitions

4   Quality system requirements

    4.1   Management responsibility

    4.2   Quality system

    4.3   Contract review

    4.4   Design control

    4.5   Document and data control

    4.6   Purchasing

    4.7   Control of customer-supplied product

    4.8   Product identification and traceability

    4.9   Process control

    4.10 Inspection and testing

    4.11 Control of inspection, measuring, and test equipment

    4.12 Inspection and test status

    4.13 Control of nonconforming product

    4.14 Corrective and preventive action

    4.15 Handling, storage, packaging, preservation, and delivery

    4.16 Control of quality records

    4.17 Internal quality audits

    4.18 Training

    4.19 Servicing

    4.20 Statistical techniques

Annex

A   Bibliography

Figure 1.7   Table of Contents for ISO 9001

Cross-Reference of ISO 9000 Quality Assurance Requirements				
ISO 9000 Clause and Title		Quality Assurance Requirements		
		ISO 9001	ISO 9002	ISO 9003
4.1	Management responsibility	O	O	▶
4.2	Quality system	O	O	▶
4.3	Contract review	O	O	O
4.4	Design control	O	●	●
4.5	Document and data control	O	O	O
4.6	Purchasing	O	O	●
4.7	Control of customer-supplied product	O	O	O
4.8	Product identification and traceability	O	O	▶
4.9	Process control	O	O	●
4.10	Inspection and testing	O	O	▶
4.11	Control of inspection, measuring, and test equipment	O	O	O
4.12	Inspection and test status	O	O	O
4.13	Control of nonconforming product	O	O	▶
4.14	Corrective and preventive action	O	O	▶
4.15	Handling, storage, packaging, preservation, and delivery	O	O	O
4.16	Control of quality records	O	O	▶
4.17	Internal quality audits	O	O	▶
4.18	Training	O	O	▶
4.19	Servicing	O	O	●
4.20	Statistical techniques	O	O	▶

Key:

O	Required
▶	Less stringent requirement than ISO 9001 and 9002
●	Not Required

FIGURE 1.8 Comparative Table of Contents for ISO 9001, 9002, and 9003

ISO 9004-1: Quality Management and Quality System Elements—Guidelines

ISO 9004-1 provides a deeper view of most of the quality elements defined in ISO 9001. (See Figure 1.11 for the scope of ISO 9004-1.) It is designed to assist an organization in defining how each of the elements could be applied to its particular application. ISO 9004-1 goes beyond ISO 9001 elements, addressing other elements that should be part of a comprehensive QMS (e.g., product safety and liability). It is not a standard that can be contractually applied to an

"This International Standard specifies quality system requirements for use where a supplier's capability to supply conforming product to an established design needs to be demonstrated.

"The requirements specified are aimed primarily at achieving customer satisfaction by preventing nonconformity at all stages from production through to servicing.

"This International Standard is applicable in situations when

a) the specified requirements for product are stated in terms of an established design or specification, and

b) confidence in product conformance can be attained by adequate demonstration of a supplier's capabilities in production, installation, and servicing."

FIGURE 1.9 Scope of ISO 9002

organization, but it is one that your organization should fully consider when designing its QMS, because of the following reasons:

- It further elaborates on the requirements called out in ISO 9001, 9002, and 9003.
- It provides helpful direction needed to comply with the ISO 9000 series.
- It provides the organization with useful concepts that should be part of a complete quality management system.

The scope of ISO 9003 states:

"This International Standard specifies quality system requirements for use where a supplier's capability to detect and control the disposition of any product nonconformity during final inspection and test needs to be demonstrated."

"It is applicable in situations when the conformance of product to specified requirements can be shown with adequate confidence providing that certain suppliers' capabilities for inspection and tests conducted on finished product can be satisfactorily demonstrated."

FIGURE 1.10 Scope of ISO 9003

ISO 9004-1 provides guidance on quality management and quality system elements.

"The quality system elements are suitable for use in the development and implementation of a comprehensive and effective in-house quality system, with a view to ensuring customer satisfaction."

"ISO 9004-1 is not intended for contractual, regulatory, or certification use. Consequently, it is not a guideline for the implementing of ISO 9001, 9002, or 9003. ISO 9000-2 should be used for that purpose."

"The selection of appropriate elements contained in this part of ISO 9004-1 and the extent to which these elements are adopted and applied by an organization depends upon factors such as the market being served, nature of the product, production processes, and customer and consumer needs."

Figure 1.11   Scope of ISO 9004-1

- It helps to anticipate problems that can occur when applying for registration.

Figure 1.12 is a table of contents for ISO 9004-1.

Key Definitions

Before we proceed, we would like to provide you with key definitions that will be frequently referred to throughout this book. They are based, whenever possible, on the official ISO definitions.

>**Accreditation:** Procedure by which an authoritative body formally recognizes that a body or person is competent to carry out specific tasks. (ISO/IEC Guide 2)
>
>**Activities:** Things that go on within a process or subprocess. Activities that are connected together can be referred to as a process.
>
>**Assessment:** An estimate or determination of the significance, importance, or value of something. (ASQC Quality Auditing Technical Committee)
>
>**Assessment Body:** Third party that assesses products and registers the quality management systems of suppliers.

1   Scope
2   Normative references
3   Definitions
4   Management responsibility
5   Quality system elements
6   Financial considerations of quality systems
7   Quality in marketing
8   Quality in specification and design
9   Quality in purchasing
10   Quality in processes
11   Control of processes
12   Product verification
13   Control of inspection, measuring, and test equipment
14   Control of nonconforming product
15   Corrective action
16   Postproduction activities
17   Quality records
18   Personnel
19   Product safety
20   Use of statistical methods

Annex

A   Bibliography

FIGURE 1.12   Table of Contents for ISO 9004-1

Certification: Procedure by which a third party gives written assurance that a product, process, or service conforms to specified requirements. (ISO/IEC Guide 2)

Clause (*Article* is the French term): In ISO documents a clause is the basic component in the subdivision of the text of a standard. The clauses in each standard are numbered with arabic numerals, beginning with 1 for "Scope." A title is placed immediately after its number.

Company: Term used primarily to refer to a business first party, the purpose of which is to supply a product or service. (DIS 9004-3, Subclause 3.2)

Compliance: An affirmative indication or judgment that the supplier of a product or service has met the requirements of the relevant specifications, contract, or regulation; also the state of meeting the requirements. (ANSI/ASQC A3) (See also **conformance**)

Conformance: An affirmative indication or judgment that a product or service has met the requirements of the relevant specifications, contract, or regulation; also the state of meeting the requirements. (ANSI/ASQC A3) (See also **compliance**)

Customer: Ultimate consumer, user, client, beneficiary, or second party. (DIS 9004-3, Subclause 3.4)

Design Review: A formal, documented, comprehensive, and systematic examination of a design to evaluate the design requirements and the capability of the design to meet these requirements and to identify problems and propose solutions. (ISO 8402, Subclause 3.13)

Inspection: Activities such as measuring, examining, testing, and gauging one or more characteristics of a product or service and comparing these with specified requirements to determine conformity. (ISO 8402, Subclause 3.14)

Item: An item can be anything. It includes processes, products, services, equipment, and/or computer programs.

Organization: A company, corporation, firm, enterprise, or association, or part thereof, whether incorporated or not, public or private, that has its own functions and administration. (ISO 8402: 1994)

Organizational Structure: The responsibilities, authorities, and relationships, arranged in a pattern, through which an organization performs its functions. (ISO 8402: 1994)

Paragraph (*Alinéa* is the French term): In an ISO document, a paragraph is an unnumbered subdivision of a clause or subclause.

Part (*Partie* is the French term): A part in an ISO document is one of a series of documents published separately under the same International Standard number. The number of a part shall be indicated by an arabic numeral following the International Standard number and preceded by a hyphen; for example, 3333-1, 3333-2, 3333-4, and so on.

Procedure: A specified way to perform an activity. (ISO 8402: 1994)

Process: A set of interrelated resources and activities that transforms inputs into outputs. (ISO 8402: 1994)

Product: The result of activities or processes. (ISO 8402: 1994)

Purchaser: The customer in a contractual situation. (ISO 8402: 1994)

Quality: The totality of features and characteristics of an entity that bear on its ability to satisfy stated or implied needs. (ISO 8402: 1994) Subclause 4.5 of ISO 9000-1 looks at the following four facets of quality:

Quality due to definition of needs for the product
Quality due to product design
Quality due to conformance to product design
Quality due to product support

Quality Assurance: All the planned and systematic activities implemented within the QMS and demonstrated as needed, to provide adequate confidence that an entity will fulfill requirements for quality. (ISO 8402: 1994)

Quality Audit: A systematic and independent examination to determine whether quality activities and related results comply with planned arrangements and whether these arrangements are implemented effectively and are suitable to achieve objectives. (ISO 10011-1, 3.1)

Quality Control: The operational techniques and activities that are used to fulfill requirements for quality. (ISO 8402: 1994)

Quality Management: All activities of the overall management function that determine the quality policy, objectives, and responsibilities and implement them by means such as quality planning, quality control, quality assurance, and quality improvement within the QMS. (ISO 8402: 1994)

Quality Manual: A document stating the quality policy and describing the QMS of an organization. (ISO 8402: 1994)

Quality Plan: A document setting out the specific quality practices, resources, and sequence of activities relevant to a particular product, project, or contract. (ISO 8402: 1994)

Quality Policy: The overall quality intentions and direction of an organization with regard to quality, as formally expressed by top management. (ISO 8402: 1994)

Quality System: The organizational structure, procedures, processes, and resources needed to implement quality management. (ISO 8402: 1994)

Registered: A procedure by which a body indicates the relevant characteristics of a product, process, or service, or the particulars of a body or person, in a published list. ISO 9000 registration is the evaluation of a company's QMS against the requirements of ISO 9001, 9002, or 9003.

Registration: Procedure by which a body indicates relevant characteristics of a product, process, or service, or particulars of a body or person, and then includes or registers the product, process, or service in an appropriate publicly available list. (ISO/IEC Guide 2)

Specification: The document that prescribes the requirements with which the product or service must conform. (ANSI/ASQC A3)

Subclause (*Paragraphe* is the French term): In ISO documents a subclause is a numbered subdivision of a clause. A primary subclause may be further subdivided into numbered secondary subclauses, and this process of further subdivision may be continued as far as is necessary.

Subcontractor: An organization that provides a product to the supplier. (ISO 8402: 1994)

Subcontractor: An organization that provides a product to the organization that is upgrading its QMS. (This definition is used throughout the book.)

Supplier: An organization that provides a product to the customer. (ISO 8402: 1994)

Tasks: Individual elements and/or subsets of an activity. Normally, tasks relate to how an item performs a specific assignment.

Testing: A means of determining an item's capability to meet specified requirements by subjecting them to a set of physical, chemical, environmental, or operating actions and conditions. (ANSI/ASQC A3)

Total Quality Management: A management approach of an organization, centered on quality, based on the participation of all its members and aiming at long-term success through customer satisfaction and benefits to the members of the organization and to society. (ISO 8204: 1994)

Traceability: The ability to trace the history, application, or location of an entity, by means of recorded identifications. (ISO 8402: 1994)

Verification: The act of reviewing, inspecting, testing, checking, auditing, or otherwise establishing and documenting whether items, processes, services, or documents conform to specified requirements. (ANSI/ASQC A3)

Registration

One of the primary advantages of the ISO 9000 series is the third-party registration process that has evolved in support of the ISO 9000 activities. Despite the obvious advantage of third-party registration, this is one area that has raised some concern with many organizations.

Basic Third-Party Registration Concept

The basic concept behind ISO 9000 registration by a third party is to eliminate the need for each customer to perform initial assessments and periodic assessments of a supplier's QMS. Through the effective use of third-party registration, the cost of QMS evaluation to both the customer and the supplier can be greatly reduced. An additional advantage of third-party assessment in lieu of each customer performing an individual assessment is that the length and depth of the assessment can be increased, giving the customer more confidence in the supplier's QMS while reducing the overall cost to both parties. It also provides the supplier with an independent evaluation of its QMS that defines weaknesses so they can be corrected. Typically, the cost of registration is borne by the supplier. Appendix III is a list of typical ISO 9000 registrars.

The United Kingdom is leading the rest of the world when it comes to registration to the ISO 9000 standards. As of March 1995, there were 95,475 organizations registered worldwide. The ten countries with the largest number of registered organizations are:

- UK   44,107
- North America   7,256
- Germany   5,875
- France   4,277
- Netherlands   4,198
- Italy   3,146
- Switzerland   1,520
- Ireland   1,410
- Belgium   1,226
- Denmark   1,183

(Source: Fourth Mobil Survey of ISO 9000 Certificates Awarded Worldwide—1996)

Why Pursue Registration?

Organizations become registered for many reasons. Some of them are to

- Meet government regulations.
- Meet customer requirements.
- Gain a competitive advantage.
- Improve their quality management system.
- Reduce the cost related to customer and potential customer visits.

Registration is not a required part of the ISO 9000 series, but it is one of the decided advantages. More and more organizations around the world are using ISO 9000 registration as a means of identifying suppliers that have acceptable quality management systems. As a result, it is now frequently included as a requirement in the request-for-quotation packages.

Registrar Controls

ISO and International Electrotechnical Commission (IEC) have developed a series of documents that serve as the guidelines that define the requirements for groups and individuals that are accredited to register an organization. These documents are as follows:

- ISO/IEC Guide 40: General Requirements for the Acceptance of Certification Bodies
- ISO/IEC Guide 48: Guidelines for Third-Party Assessment and Registration of a Supplier's Quality System
- ISO 10011: Guidelines for Auditing Quality Systems
- EN 45011: General Criteria for Certification Bodies Operating Product Certification. This includes the criteria required for national or European recognition of a product certification body.
- EN 45012: General Criteria for Certification Bodies Operating Quality System Certification. It focuses on the issue of QMS certification (registration) and parallels the criteria defined in EN 45011.
- EN 45013: General Criteria for Certification Bodies Operating Certification of Personnel. This applies to the certification of personnel who have a major effect on product quality.

(*Note:* EN stands for European Norm; it is the specification identification used by the European Union [EU].)

Accreditation of Registrars

The procedures for accreditation of registrars have not been formalized on a worldwide basis. In Europe, a number of governmental and quasi-governmental agencies have been established to regulate third-party registrars. For example:

- France: Association Française pour l'Assurance de la Qualité (AFAQ)
- Italy: Ente Nazionale Italiano de Unificazione (UNICEI)
- Netherlands: Raad voor de Certificatie (RvC)
- Spain: Asociación Española de Normalización y Certificación (AENOR)
- United Kingdom: National Accreditation Council for Certification Bodies (NACCB) formed in 1984

In North America, these controls are handled by:

- Canada: Registration Accreditation Subcommittee (RASC) of the Standards Council of Canada. The subcommittee was established in late 1991.
- United States: Registrar Accreditation Board (RAB). This board was established by the American Society of Quality Control in 1989.

In the United States, the Registrar Accreditation Board not only accreditates QMS registrars but also certifies programs for auditors of quality management systems. This same activity is also performed by many other national accreditation bodies. As the accreditation system develops, it should look something like this:

- A high-level recognition body **RECOGNIZES** accreditation bodies.
- The accreditation bodies **ACCREDITATE** registrars.
- Registrars **REGISTER** individual organizations.

Cost to Be Registered

The cost of registration per location varies based on the organization's size, the number of sites that will be evaluated, and the status of the QMS. Typical costs are as follows:

Organization Size	Initial Document Review	Follow-up Reviews
Small	$ 6,000	$2,500
Medium	$10,000	$5,000
Large	$18,000	$7,000

Source: 1995 Survey by Duscharme

Once the organization is registered, there is an ISO 9000 requirement for the registrar to perform a short review of the organization's QMS every six months to ensure it has not degraded. Every three years a complete assessment must be performed. Successful compliance to these assessments is required to maintain the organization's registration. The cost provided above does not include the cost required to upgrade the organization's QMS to meet the ISO requirements.

ISO 9000 Applied to the Service Industry

At first glance, it may seem that the ISO 9000 series was developed for the hardware industries only, but nothing could be further from the truth. All organizations need to have well-developed quality management systems. It makes no difference if the organization's output is bonds or bottles, whether it processes bills or produces dolls, whether it entertains or builds airplanes. All these industries need an effective quality system, and ISO 9000 is applicable. ISO 9000 has been effectively applied to small freight-forwarding operations like OMNI North American (12 people, located in Hackettstown, NJ), and to big consulting firms like Ernst & Young LLP. There is nothing radical about the ISO 9000 quality system standards that excludes them from the service industry. Basically, ISO 9000 requires an organization to be sure that it is doing the correct things, document what it is doing, and then do what it documented. We think that that is just good business.

Typically, service industry categories that can or have had the ISO 9000 series applied to them are as follows:

- Travel
- Health Care
- Consulting
- Financial
- Restaurant
- Retailing
- Entertainment
- Utilities
- Government
- Education
- Scientific
- Trading (wholesaling, retailing, etc.)

ISO/TC 176 was quick to recognize the importance of quality management systems in the service industry and as a result has prepared a number of documents to help service organizations implement the ISO quality system standards. Typical examples of these documents are

- ISO 9000-3: Quality Management and Quality Assurance Standards—Part 3: Guidelines for the Application of ISO 9001 to the Development, Supply, and Maintenance of Software.
- ISO 9004-2: Quality Management and Quality System Elements—Part 2: Guidelines for Services.

In the United States, ISO 9000 is being applied to the education system. As a result, the guideline ANSI/ASQC Z1.11, entitled "Quality Management and Quality Assurance Standards—Guideline for the Application of ANSI/ASQC Q91 (ISO 9001) or Q92 (ISO 9002) for Education and Training Institutes," has already been published.

To date, hardware/materials industries have been leading the charge to ISO registration within North America. Of the organizations registered to ISO 9000 in the United States, 18 percent are electronics manufacturers, 17 percent are chemical manufacturers, and 15 percent are industrial and commercial machinery manufacturers. The service industries lag far behind, but this is not unusual because the service sector has historically lagged behind the hardware and materials manufacturers when it comes to implementing quality programs. But a service organization will reap many benefits from having a QMS that meets the requirements defined in the ISO 9000 series. Not the least of them is improved customer satisfaction. Dennis Fahen, branch manager at Butler Design, points out that installing an ISO 9000–type system within the organization resulted in a 30 percent reduction in in-house reports. Donna Vniski, quality assurance manager for OMNI North American, states, "Maybe 20% to 30% of our customers have stayed with us because they knew we were pursuing certification" (*Export Today,* March 1995).

The Future Direction of ISO 9000

ISO 9000 is a living, changing document. The international standards procedures require that it be periodically updated and approved when appropriate. A new revision, referred to as Vision 2000 (which reflects the type of QMS that needs to be in place to compete in the twenty-first century), was scheduled for release in 1996.

Vision 2000 was developed by ISO/TC 176 in 1990 and was designed to be a two-phase approach to improving the then-released ISO 9000 series of standards. Vision 2000's stated purpose was to produce

- "a *single* quality management standard, an updated 'ISO 9004' (including new topics, as appropriate), and
- an external quality assurance requirements standard, an updated 'ISO 9001,'
- tied together by a road map standard 'ISO 9000'."

As work progressed on Vision 2000 it became obvious that a key objective had to be to promote a better understanding of the interrelationships and differences between quality management and quality assurance.

ISO/TC 176 views quality assurance as activities

- Whose objective is to satisfy all external customers.
- That impact on the results of the process and/or product.
- Designed to ensure quality results are achieved.
- Driven by external customers.
- Designed to provide confidence in product quality.

ISO/TC 176's view of quality management is much broader. It views quality management as activities

- Whose objective is to satisfy all stakeholders (external customers, suppliers, management, investors, employees, and humankind).
- That drive total business performance.
- Where quality impacts final results.
- Driven by internal stakeholders (management and investors).
- That impact overall performance.

It is easy to see that quality management as defined by ISO/TC 176 goes far beyond the originally released ISO 9000 series. With the completion of Vision 2000, the ISO 9000 series should include the following:

- Quality management principles and guides to their application
- Quality management practices
- Implementation guidance
- Quantitative measuring systems that measure the maturity of the QMS
- Quality management process models including all main process elements

It is obvious that the many national quality award programs implemented around the world are now influencing ISO/TC 176 as well as the realization that quality processes that do not produce favorable tangible business results will not sustain themselves.

Phase I of Vision 2000 was completed in 1994. Its focus was on upgrading quality assurance requirements in ISO 9001, 9002, and 9003 and was an incremental improvement. The next revision (which will probably be out in 2001) will not add a lot of new requirements but will concentrate on a better understanding of how quality management and quality assurance can coexist. It will also focus on better harmonizing and integration of the ISO 9000 family of standards. From our perspective, it looks like Vision 2000 objectives will not be fully met during the twentieth century.

We believe that the proliferation of quality standards documents will be turned around, and fewer documents will be involved in the ISO 9000 series. For example, we believe that ISO 9001, 9002, and 9003 will be combined into a single quality assurance standard that will probably be numbered ISO 9001. ISO 9000-1, 9000-2, 9000-3, and 9000-4 will probably be greatly restructured, with information on quality concepts and definitions moved into a single document. Other parts of the documents may even be published under the IEC 300-1 series. The ISO 9004 group of documents will also merge, making ISO 9004 a single document that provides guidance and reflects the quality award programs' criteria. The object of these changes will be to

- Make the series more intelligible and user-friendly by using plain language.
- Reduce the number of guidance standards.
- Make the standards applicable to all sizes of organizations.

At the same time, much work will be directed at ensuring that the standards community does not confuse the general public by issuing other standards that compete with the total business results orientation of quality management as defined by ISO/TC 176 (e.g., ISO/TC 207—environmental management, and ISO/TC 210—medical devices, activities).

European Union (EU)

The initial driving force that set the ISO 9000 quality system requirements into orbit came from the need to unite the European Union (then called the European Common Market) into a homogeneous market and trading partnership. As the EU pushed toward unification in 1986, a single market known as EC 92 became effective at midnight on December 31, 1992. Part of this plan was called the "conformity assessment system." This system was to have a standard way of assessing all processes, products, quality management systems, and laboratories throughout the EU. Two categories of products were defined in Europe, as follows:

- Regulated products—products that have important health, safety, or environmental implications. Their requirements are specified in official EU legislation, and all members of the EU must comply with them.
- Nonregulated products—products that do not meet the requirements defined above.

As part of the conformity assessment system, the ISO 9000 series was recommended as the standard to define acceptable quality management systems. As a result, organizations around the world began to believe that they would be required to have ISO 9000 registration by 1992 if they were going to sell products to countries within the EU. With a potential market of 500 to 800 million people at stake, organizations around the world began to embrace the ISO 9000 series. However, ISO 9000 requirements have never become a legal part of the EU. As 1992 came and went, the so-called deadline for ISO 9000 compliance was slipped to 1994. Now with the passing of 1994, there is no future plan to make ISO 9000 registration an official requirement to do business in the EU, although today the ISO standards have become a de facto requirement for many organizations within the EU.

In 1995 the EU was aggressively pursuing a European quality program that is more in line with the Malcolm Baldrige award than with the ISO 9000 approach. Although the ISO 9000 methodology will be included in the plan, certification may be abolished or, at a minimum, played down in importance. In the May 1995 issue of *Quality Digest,* Jacques McMillan, chief of Senior Standards Policy Group for Directorate-General III for Industry stated, "A lot of people thought we are trying to kill ISO 9000. Now people are understanding the message. We are not trying to kill it, we are trying to save it. One problem industry faces is that they shouldn't do things that don't give added value. They shouldn't pay for things that don't give added value. I got into fights with certifiers and consultants who have found a good market (in ISO 9000). But if industry pays for services that provide no value added, then that's not a good market." He goes on to point out that many European companies have complained that ISO 9000 hasn't lived up to its advertised hype as a quality tool.

North America

In North America, the ISO 9000 fever has hit most organizations. Every day the number of organizations applying for registration is increasing. We recently attended the American Society for Quality Control's Annual Quality Congress and were amazed to see that at least two out of three booths in the exhibit hall advertised ISO 9000 products and services, in contrast to two years ago, when TQM reigned supreme. Throughout North America, a huge new industry has been created around ISO 9000 specifications that rivals the industry developed to audit the financial statements of organizations.

The automotive industry has struck out on its own with the Big Three automakers—Ford, GM, and Chrysler—coming together to create a new industry-specific version of ISO 9000 called QS-9000. QS-9000 builds on the basic ISO 9001 specification, adding additional requirements that cover the auto industry and specific Big Three requirements. The first QS-9000 document was released in September 1994 and has been undergoing numerous modifications since then. Currently, North American suppliers are required to be in compliance by December 31, 1997.

The electronics industry has taken just the opposite approach. Led by Motorola and HP, a group of 37 major electronics companies worldwide are pushing for the streamlining of ISO 9000 registration processes. This group, which includes companies like AT&T, Digital Equipment Corp., Microsoft Corp., Phillips Electronics, Bausch & Lomb, Xerox, and others, is pushing for what they call a "supplier's declaration of conformity." The purpose of this would be to greatly reduce the amount of work ISO registrars perform in major corporations, with much greater dependency on the internal audit process.

Asia

The Chinese government has embraced ISO 9000 and has been applying it to specific industries on a prioritization basis. The first industry that was legally required to have ISO 9000 certification to export goods was the toy industry.

In Japan, progress has been a little slower, although the Japanese are moving toward ISO 9000 registration. For example, Japan plans to make ISO registration a requirement for all software manufacturers doing business in Japan.

Summary of Worldview

Although many initiatives are under way to improve the present ISO 9000 standards and processes, the future is very clear. The ISO 9000 series will become more and more important to international trade, and by the twenty-first century, it will be fully embraced by both service and hardware industries.

ISO 9000's Biggest Problem

Although major organizations are quick to impose ISO 9000 standards on their suppliers, they are not willing to live up to these same standards and become registered themselves. As a result, the general public is not receiving the same benefits from these standards that major organizations are receiving. We wonder whether governments around the world should require organizations like Hewlett-Packard, Ford, General Motors, and Chrysler—in fact, any organization that delivers products and services to the general public—to be ISO 9000 registered. It would be interesting to see how fast the world would implement the ISO 9000 series if the standard required that the purchasing organization (excluding the general public) be registered before it could impose the requirement on its suppliers.

The Auto Industry Improves on ISO 9000

The North American Big Three auto companies (Ford, Chrysler, and General Motors) were not satisfied with having suppliers that met minimum requirements for a quality system. As a result, they built upon the ISO 9000 structure to create a new QMS standard called QS-9000. We believe that QS-9000 represents good business practices for quality management systems and is an improvement over the present ISO 9000 standards. Also embracing QS-9000 are several heavy truck manufacturers (Freightliner Corp., Kenworth Trucks, Mack Trucks, Navistart International, Peterbilt Trucks, and Volvo GM Heavy Trucks). We believe that many of the automotive original equipment manufacturers (OEMs) will be adopting QS-9000 soon.

QS-9000 is divided into three major sections:

- Section I: ISO 9000-Based Requirements
- Section II: Sector-Specific Requirements
- Section III: Customer-Specific Requirements

Section I: ISO 9000–Based Requirements

Section I builds on the foundations established in ISO 9001. It includes the same 20 elements with the same titles as the ones used in Clause 4.0 of ISO

9001. Each of the 20 elements starts with an exact quote from the relevant element in ISO 9001 shown in italics. This is followed by new additional quality system requirements, as defined by the auto and truck industries. These additional requirements are printed in regular text format. For example, the QS-9000 element 4.1 "Management Responsibility" includes everything that is in ISO 9001 element 4.1, with the following new requirements:

- 4.1.2.3 During the concept development, prototype, and production phase of a new part, a system of management is to be in place to ensure the quality of the part. A second addition in this area is the requirement that a multidisciplinary approach to decision making is to be used, with information and data being communicated in customer-prescribed formats.
- 4.1.4 Business Plan—This element requires that a formal, documented, comprehensive business plan be developed by each supplier.
- 4.1.5 Analysis and Use of Company-Level Data—This requires that the organization maintain records on how the business is operating in the areas of quality, operational performance, and current quality levels for key product and service features. Data must be presented in a trend format.
- 4.1.6 Customer Satisfaction—The organization is required to document the process that it is using to determine customer satisfaction. The data are required to be shown in trend format, which documents continuous improvement efforts.

Section II: Sector-Specific Requirements

Section II specifies additional requirements that go beyond the scope of ISO 9001. It covers quality management systems like continuous improvement, manufacturing capabilities, and production parts approval process. For example:

- In element 2.1 "Continuous Improvement," the organization is required to have a continuous improvement philosophy fully developed and in place throughout the organization. Documented improvements must at a minimum include price, service, and quality. Action plans for continuous improvement must be identified for all areas that the customer believes to be important. The auto industry places major emphasis on the use of variable data wherever possible when evaluating continuous improvement programs.

Section III: Customer-Specific Requirements

This section includes quality system requirements that are unique to any one of the Big Three automakers. The heavy truck requirements are not included in this document but are handled individually by each manufacturer. For example, the Ford-specific requirements have extended the methodology beyond "shall" to include "must," "will," and "is required." Some of the key elements of the Ford-specific requirements are as follows:

- Control Item Parts
- Control Plans and FMEAs
- Shipping Container Label
- Equipment Standard Parts
- Critical Characteristics
- Setup Verification
- Control Item Fasteners
- Heat Treatment
- Process Changes and Design Changes for Supplier-Responsible Designs
- Supplier Modification of Control Item Requirements
- Engineering Specification Test Performance Requirements
- System Design Specification
- Ongoing Process Monitoring
  - Qualification of all Product Characteristics
  - Ongoing Process and Product Monitoring
- Prototype Part Quality Initiatives
- Quality Operating System
- Qualification and Acceptance Criteria for Materials
- Ford Bibliography

Third-Party Registration

QS-9000 has taken advantage of ISO 9000's third-party registration activities. Currently, training programs varying from two to five days in duration are being conducted for organizations already accredited to register organizations to ISO 9000 requirements. The names of the organizations that successfully complete these training sessions are being added to a list of approved registrars for QS-9000. An updated list of approved registrars can be obtained from

National ISO 9000 Support Group
9864 Cherry Valley, Suite C
Caledonia, MI 49316
Phone/Fax (616) 891-9114

QS-9000 Summary

Having Ford, Chrysler, and General Motors combine forces to advance the quality methodology is not new. For example, a Measurement Quality System Manual was developed jointly in 1990, and a Statistical Process Control Reference Manual was developed in 1991. Although these previous cooperative efforts were valuable, the release of "Quality System Requirements: QS-9000" is by far the most important joint venture undertaken to date. To implement QS-9000, General Motors is requiring that all its current suppliers be registered by a third party no later than December 31, 1997, and has already started to evaluate potential new suppliers to the QS-9000 standard. GM also required that by January 1, 1996, all new suppliers must be registered by a third party. Ford's expected cutoff date for QS-9000 implementation is December 31, 1996. Chrysler announced to its present suppliers on January 11, 1995, that, "As a valued Chrysler supplier, you are expected to update your existing quality management systems to meet the requirements of QS-9000. The success of QS-9000 will depend upon the commitment of key individuals such as yourself." Chrysler required that a self-assessment to QS-9000 be completed by each of its current suppliers before July 7, 1995, and all production and service part suppliers to Chrysler have third-party registration to QS-9000 by July 31, 1997.

Copies of QS-9000 are available through the Automotive Industry Action Group (AIAG) at a cost of $17 for nonmembers and $15 for AIAG members. We also suggest that you get a copy of "Quality System Assessment (QSA)," which includes a detailed checklist for QS-9000 compliance, at a cost of $12 for nonmembers and $10 for members. These books can be obtained from

AIAG
26200 Lahser Road, Suite 200
Southfield, MI 48034
Phone: (810) 358-3570
Fax: (810) 358-3253
Order Dept. Phone: (810) 358-3003

Until 1997 the primary emphasis will be placed on applying QS-9000 to Tier 1 suppliers. QS-9000 requires Tier 1 suppliers to have the Tier 2 suppliers comply with the same document, which will have a cascading effect throughout the supplier chain.

Many of the elements defined in QS-9000 are good business practice and should be considered by all organizations for inclusion in their quality management systems. It is important to note that many of the items defined in QS-9000 are already being looked at by ISO/TC 176 for inclusion in the next update of the ISO 9000 series. We are seeing a number of organizations around the world that are not in the automotive industry designing their QMS to meet the requirements of QS-9000 and becoming registered to it because they believe that they will end up with a much better QMS. We are also seeing customers who will prefer suppliers that are registered to QS-9000 over ones that are registered to ISO 9000. We recommend that every organization that is redesigning its QMS consider the additional requirements defined in QS-9000.

In a June 1996 survey of the biggest ISO auto industry first-tier suppliers conducted by Ernst & Young LLP, the suppliers documented their mixed feelings about the QS-9000 standard. For example:

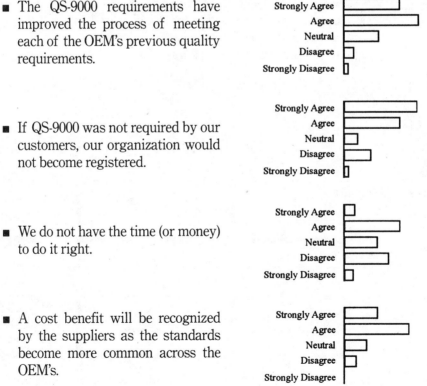

- The QS-9000 requirements have improved the process of meeting each of the OEM's previous quality requirements.

- If QS-9000 was not required by our customers, our organization would not become registered.

- We do not have the time (or money) to do it right.

- A cost benefit will be recognized by the suppliers as the standards become more common across the OEM's.

Upgrading and Maintaining a Quality Management System

As we have previously stated, all organizations already have a QMS of some kind in place, but today many individuals and/or organizations are considering or are in the process of upgrading their QMS. Obviously, you are one of these individuals, or you would not be reading this book. This flurry of activity has been driven by the release of the ISO 9000 series of standards, combined with the international concept of third-party registration.

We see the process of upgrading and maintaining a QMS as a six-phase process (see Figure 1.13). Chapters 3 to 9 of this book will address each of these six phases. Figure 1.14 is a simplified flowchart of the process for upgrading a typical QMS.

This book is designed to take you step by step through the QMS upgrade process.

- Phase I: Assessment—consists of 9 steps.
- Phase II: Planning—consists of 15 steps.
- Phase III: Upgrading—consists of 17 steps.
- Phase IV: Implementation—consists of 13 steps.
- Phase V: Auditing—consists of 6 steps.
- Phase VI: Continuous Improvement—consists of 8 steps.

Total steps equal 68.

The Quality Management System Cycle

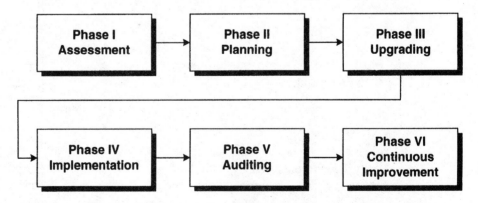

FIGURE 1.13 The Six Phases to Upgrading a Quality Management System

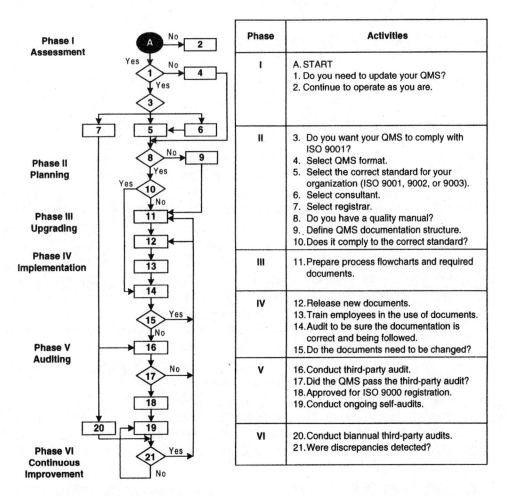

FIGURE 1.14 Flowchart of the Process for Upgrading an Organization's Quality Management System

Phase I: Assessment

Phase I, the assessment phase, consists of the following 9 steps:

1. Listen to the warning signs.
2. Discuss with the chief operating officer the possible need for improving the QMS.
3. Form an assessment team.

4. Train the assessment team.
5. Conduct the assessment.
6. Define preliminary action plan.
7. Estimate costs and benefits.
8. Obtain top management approval and support.
9. Appoint a project manager.

During Phase I, a small task team or an individual (called the assessment team) will evaluate the advantages and disadvantages of upgrading the present QMS. The advantages need to consider the positive impact that the upgraded QMS will have on the problems that are facing the organization today, as well as the future lost opportunities that will occur if the organization does not upgrade its QMS. Obviously, input from your present and future potential customers is a very important factor in defining these advantages.

The disadvantages are primarily the cost and effort required to define, document, implement, and maintain the upgraded QMS. The upgraded quality management system may also have a temporary negative impact on the organization's personality as it goes through the transitional period, but that negative impact will soon pass as management and the employees begin to feel comfortable with following the documented procedures.

To help define the resources that are required to implement the upgraded QMS, we suggest that the assessment team and/or an outside consultant do a very quick initial comparison of the present QMS to ISO 9001 or QS-9000, if the organization is doing business within the auto industry. (Appendix IV provides a typical list of some of the consulting firms that, in our opinion, are qualified to help an organization establish its QMS. This list is not intended to be a complete list but just a representative sample.) At this point in time, the analysis can be based on opinion, not verified fact, because it will be used to define the approximate magnitude of the resources required to upgrade the present QMS and to help define whether the new QMS should be designed to be in compliance with ISO 9001, 9002, or 9003.

When the cost-benefits analysis is complete, the assessment team should review the data to determine whether the resources should be expended to upgrade the present QMS. If the decision is to recommend to the executive committee that effort be expended to upgrade the QMS, the assessment team should prepare a rough time schedule for developing and implementing the appropriate procedures and supporting documentation. The results of the assessment team's work should be presented to the executive committee for approval. If the executive committee decides to fund the effort to upgrade the existing QMS, the project will progress into Phase II.

The executive team should now appoint an executive-level person to take charge of this project and to be held accountable and responsible for maintaining the QMS after it is implemented. In most organizations, the vice president or director of quality has the responsibility for maintaining the QMS, but this responsibility can be assigned to anyone at the executive level.

Phase II: Planning

Phase II, the planning phase, consists of the following 15 steps:

1. Form the Quality System Team (QST).
2. Train the QST.
3. Define the support system that the QST will use.
4. Define the documentation formats and structure.
5. Block-diagram the major quality processes.
6. Define process owners for each major quality process.
7. Develop a list of quality manual and procedural documents that need to be written or rewritten.
8. Identify subcommittees.
9. Prepare and implement a communication plan.
10. Develop training plans to support the QMS.
11. Prepare and implement an Organizational Change Management (OCM) plan.
12. Establish a project file and tracking system.
13. Identify who will do the internal audits.
14. Select a registrar.
15. Update the project plan and review it with top management.

The individual to whom the executive team has assigned the responsibility for coordinating the design and implementation of the upgraded quality management system should form a Quality System Team (QST) made up of individuals who represent each function within the organization whose output impacts the organization's quality. Typical functions that would be represented on this team are procurement, sales, product engineering, manufacturing, after-sales service, manufacturing engineering, and quality assurance.

The QST will be trained to understand the concepts contained within the appropriate standard. The team will then do a detailed analysis that compares the present QMS with the requirements outlined in the standard. This analysis will be supported with estimates of the efforts required to upgrade each element of the QMS to the standards requirements. The QST shall not be limited to the items defined in the particular QMS standard that it is using. Additional processes that are of specific interest to the organization should be considered at this time. Remember, the ISO 9000 series sets only the minimum requirements. In using the ISO 9000 document, use both 9004 and 9001 to help define your QMS even if all the parts of 9004 are not required to be registered. We believe that most organizations are not satisfied at meeting minimum requirements but want to excel in their industry.

The QST will define the quality management system documentation structure and which documents will be included in the quality manual and the supporting operating procedures. Basically, the QMS documentation structure is divided into four levels:

- Strategic level—The Quality Manual
- Tactical level—Procedures
- Operational level—Work Instructions
- Historical level—Quality Data and Records

The following is a typical quality manual table of contents for an organization that is registered to ISO 9001.

Quality Manual Table of Contents

Sections
1.0 Introduction
- What is the quality manual and how should it be used?
- How does it support the organization's objectives, goals, and business plan?
- Scope and field of application
2.0 Management Responsibilities for Quality
- Quality Policy
- Quality Objectives
- Quality Management System
- Key Managers' Personal Quality Responsibilities and Authorities
- Organizational Structure
- Management Reviews
3.0 Quality System Management
- Structure of the Quality Management System
- Documentation of the Quality Management System
- Quality Planning

- Auditing the Quality Management System
4.0 Contract and Contract Amendment Review and Record Controls
5.0 New Product and Production Process Design
- Design Planning and Objectives
- New Product Qualification and Validation
- Design Reviews
- New Production Process Design Qualification and Validation
- Process Capability Analysis
- Product Safety and Liability
6.0 Document and Data Control
- Document Release
- Document Change Control
7.0 Control of Procured Parts, Materials, and Services
- Precontract Release Evaluation of Potential Subcontractors
- Subcontractor Qualification Planning
- Approved Subcontractor Evaluation
- Subcontractor Reporting and Corrective Action
- Receiving Inspection Planning and Controls
- Current Subcontractor Evaluation
- Handling of Customer-Supplied Materials and Equipment
8.0 Production Quality
- Planning for Controlled Production
- Materials, Parts and Assembly Control, Traceability, and Status
- Equipment Control and Maintenance
- Control of Nonconforming Materials
- Engineering Design Phase-In Controls
- Inspection and Testing Records Controls
- Control of Inspection, Measurement, and Test Equipment
9.0 Preventive and Corrective Action Systems
10.0 Postproduction Quality
- Handling, Storage, Identification, Packaging, Installation, and Delivery Controls
- After-Sales Servicing
- Customer-Related Reporting
11.0 Quality Management System Self-Audits
12.0 Control of Quality Records
13.0 Personnel
- Training Requirements
- Job Qualifications
- Rewards and Recognition

14.0 Environmental Controls
- Pollution Controls
- Safety Controls

15.0 Statistical Methods
- Applied to the Product Design
- Applied to the Production Process
- Applied to After-Sales Service
- Applied to the Support Areas

16.0 Quality in the Support Areas (Personnel, Finance, Industrial Engineering, Production Control, Project Office, etc.)
- Quality Measurement Systems
- Internal Customer Requirements

(Note: This table of contents goes beyond the basic requirements called out in ISO 9001.)

The QST should also develop a set of measurements that will be used to define the effect that the upgraded QMS has on the organization, and how this effect will be measured.

Within most organizations, changing the QMS has a significant impact on the emotions of most employees. As a result, an Organizational Change Management (OCM) plan should be prepared to help the organization internalize the changes to the QMS. The importance of an effective OCM plan in support of any major revision to the QMS cannot be overemphasized. It is important to note that part of the assessment effort that took place in Phase I was directed at identifying the level of resistance to a change that the QST would encounter. The OCM plan is designed to minimize this resistance and its impact. (See Appendix V for more information on Organizational Change Management.)

One of the ouputs from Phase I was a project file that includes the resources required to support the project, an OCM plan, a document development plan, an implementation plan, and a timeline for the entire project.

The complete project plan should be reviewed and approved by the executive committee before the QST progresses into Phase III.

Phase III: Upgrading (Redesigning) the Quality Management System

Phase III, the upgrade phase, consists of the following 17 steps:

1. Define the documentation structure and contents of the quality manual.
2. Form and train subcommittees.

3. Prepare individual sections of the quality manual.
4. Prepare flowcharts of the assigned processes.
5. Conduct process walk-throughs to verify the accuracy of the flow-charts.
6. Compare the present process to the ISO 9000 standards and identify discrepancies.
7. Change the process flowcharts to correct discrepancies and include suggested improvements.
8. Document the assigned processes.
9. Compare the draft procedures to the related documents in the quality manual to identify discrepancies and inadequacies. Then alter the documentation to correct any discrepancies and/or inadequacies.
10. Analyze each procedure and its supporting flowchart to identify activities that require documented instructions (Tier 4 documents).
11. Assign individuals or teams to generate the required instructions.
12. Prepare an interrelationship matrix and analyze it to identify missing documents.
13. Prepare missing documents.
14. Expand the Organizational Change Management activities.
15. Circulate the documents for comments and update them as required.
16. Send documents to the registrar for review and comments.
17. Release the preliminary documentation for pilot studies only.

During Phase III, the QST will form subcommittees that will be responsible for documenting the present processes and/or upgrading the present processes and their documentation so that they are in conformance with the requirements defined in the ISO 9000 standards and any additional requirements that the organization has placed on the QMS.

One of the chief advantages of upgrading the QMS is to challenge the present system and create a new system that is more in line with international best practices and provides more value to the organization. The newer QMS must exist in an environment that is continuously changing, thereby requiring the new system to be preventive-based rather than corrective action–based. Adding to the complexity of the organization that a QMS must operate in is a changing workforce driven by an information and technology-based environment that eliminates much of the management control and direction previously required. This new world of customer-focused, employee-empowered organizations has placed new requirements on the QMS, often making the ones that were outstanding in 1990 obsolete in 1996. This changing business environment has resulted in the need to make major changes to the present QMS as the organization reviews and upgrades it. Today our quality management systems need to be proactive preventive rather than reactive corrective as they were in the early 1990s. Take advantage of redesigning your QMS to create and reinvent new business processes. You have a call to arms every time you hear, "This is the way we have been doing it for years."

Each member of these subcommittees should be trained in all the requirements needed to be in compliance with the appropriate ISO 9000 standard and why these requirements are needed to help the organization function better. If the QMS upgrade is extensive and/or the organization is planning on being registered, all employees should receive introductory training related to the appropriate ISO 9000 standard and be provided with information defining why the upgrade is important to the organization. This training should occur during Phase III because many of the operational-level employees will become involved in preparing the new QMS by either documenting their activities or through interviews with the quality system subcommittee members. The outcome from Phase III will be a new quality manual, a set of supporting procedures, and a set of work instructions, all of which have been reviewed and approved by the appropriate functions.

Phase IV: Implementation

Phase IV, the implementation phase, consists of the following 13 steps:

1. Define the documentation distribution and control system.
2. Determine when sets of documents are ready to be implemented.
3. Expand the QMS and individual OCM activities.
4. Develop a document set implementation plan.
5. Define pilot area and prepare the pilot study plan.
6. Execute the pilot study plan.
7. Review the pilot results and alter the processes if necessary.
8. Circulate the revised documentation for formal release.
9. Implement the formally released document set.
10. Evaluate the new processes to identify weaknesses and correct them before they become problems.
11. Conduct internal audits.
12. Measure the performance level of the new processes.
13. Analyze the total QMS.

Why Implementation Is Critical

- An excellent plan, poorly implemented, produces poor results.
- A poor plan, superbly implemented, produces poor results.
- A poor plan, poorly implemented, is disastrous.

The only acceptable combination is to have a well-constructed, well-thought-out plan that is superbly implemented, giving careful consideration to the organization's culture. For a quality management system to function well, three factors must be considered:

- The organization's processes
- The organization's technology status
- The beliefs and behavior patterns of the people who make up the organization (organization's culture)

These three factors are important drivers that influence the planning process (Phase II), but they become critical factors and key considerations during the implementation phase. Many approaches are used to implement an upgraded QMS. Three of them are as follows:

1. Hold off starting the implementation until all documents are complete.
2. Prepare all the documents for the quality manual first and release these documents. Then prepare the supporting procedures and implement these procedures. Finally, prepare the supporting work instructions and data collection and reporting documents and implement them.
3. Release, install, and audit key stand-alone documents that are part of the quality manual (e.g., quality policy, management responsibilities and authority, etc.) first. Then release, install, and audit the documents that define how the job is being done today. Then as families of documents are completed, release, install, and audit these interrelated documents until the total system has been completely released.

We believe that the best way to implement an upgraded QMS is the third approach. Starting with the quality manual document, release and install all documents that set policy and impact the culture that do not require supporting procedures. Then release, install, and audit documents that reflect the current mode of operation within the organization. Then document, release, install, and audit all procedures that support the released quality manual documents, and, finally, release all work instructions that support each of the procedures. By starting your documentation process with activities that reflect the present mode of operation, there is minimum exposure to culture shock caused by the new QMS.

Certainly the simplest document to be implemented is one that is already written and in place, but even in these situations, audits should be conducted to ensure that it is being followed by all employees.

Implementing Changes to the Quality Management System

The organization needs to be very careful in the way it rolls out changes to the present QMS. Changes that are in line with the organization's culture will be accepted with some resistance. Ones that are not in line with the present culture are going to be strongly resisted. Organizations that have not been effective in implementing other initiatives (e.g., reengineering, TQM, activity-based costing) are going to face major problems in implementing the new quality management system. For these reasons, an effective OCM process was developed that is fully supportive of the new QMS.

The question is, how do you introduce the new documentation and procedures into the organization? The first step in implementing the new QMS is the release of procedures that define the documentation system and its hierarchy. The next priority is to document the release and change control procedure related to the QMS. The next step is to implement the documentation related to management responsibility because it sets the stage for all the rest of the procedures. Subcommittees should then implement the documentation that is directly in line with the way things are being done today. These procedures will require a minimum amount of training for the employees involved and will normally be in line with the organization's present culture, minimizing the disruptions within the organization. Even these current processes should be carefully audited to be sure they truly reflect the way everyone is performing the individual activities and tasks. In most cases there is a time of adjustment as everyone starts to follow the same process.

The processes that are being changed will be the last to be implemented because they require the most OCM effort, employee training, and detailed piloting. A word of caution: Do not wait until all the documentation is complete and implement it in one massive change, because it will completely disrupt the organization's performance. Roll out the new documented processes in groups of interrelated supporting documents, often called "families." For example, there would typically be a document in the quality manual that defines the new product development requirements. Included in these requirements might be the following:

- Customer inputs
- Design verification
- Reliability prediction
- Maintainability analysis
- Manufacturing process qualification
- Product qualification
- Design review

A typical family of documents would be the completion of the new product development part of the quality manual, the design review procedure, and all the work instructions related to the design review. When the subcommittee has completed a family of documents, it should select an area to pilot its new process on a limited basis to identify problems and potential improvements. The documents should then be updated and released. This is followed by training everyone involved in the process on their new roles. As the family of documents are integrated into the day-to-day operations, the new procedures should be closely audited until the subcommittee has a high degree of confidence that everyone understands his or her role in the process. Often during the implementation stage, shortcomings in the process are identified, requiring that the procedures and/or work instructions be modified and the employees retrained. Care must be taken to ensure change-level control is maintained throughout this process.

Phase V: Auditing

Phase V, the audit phase, consists of the following six steps:

1. Establish and maintain the employee self-assessment process.
2. Establish and maintain the management self-assessment process.
3. Establish and maintain the internal staff audit process.
4. Establish and maintain the executive audit process.
5. Host second-party audits.
6. Host third-party audits.

Systems left to operate on their own soon become self-serving, ineffective, and inefficient. It is for these reasons that an effective QMS audit process must be established to support and monitor a QMS after it is implemented. There are two basic types of QMS audits.

- *Internal (Self) audits*—These are audits that the organization imposes upon itself to measure compliance and to identify improvement opportunities.
- *External audits*—These audits are conducted by external organizations to measure compliance to their imposed QMS requirements or to the requirements called out in a specific quality standard (e.g., ISO 9001).

Internal (Self) Audits

There are four types of self-audits. They are as follows:

- Employee self-assessment
- Management self-assessment
- Internal staff audits
- Executive audits

Employee self-assessments—These are assessments that are conducted by the employees related to their own activities. Often they take the form of check sheets that are filled out as a requirement defined in the job instruction (e.g., design review check sheets, inspection check sheets, supplier evaluation check sheets).

Management self-assessments—These are audits of the quality management system and other management systems for which the manager is personally responsible. Usually these assessments are conducted once every three months using an audit plan developed by the individual manager and approved by his or her immediate supervisor. Immediate action plans are developed for each discrepancy. Assessment reports are documented by the manager and submitted to his or her immediate supervisor. These reports are summarized by the executives and reported to the executive committee.

Internal staff audits—These audits are conducted by a department within the organization that has been assigned the responsibility for auditing the organization's compliance to practices and procedures. These audits usually follow a set schedule over a number of months that allows the organization to be completely audited once every two years. The standard schedule is usually supplemented with special audits that focus on areas that are having problems and/or are implementing changes to the related management systems. Often the quality organization is assigned responsibilities for auditing the processes to ensure that they are following established quality, safety, environmental, personnel, and financial procedures. This new quality organization is often called "Systems Assurance." (See McGraw-Hill's 1987 book *The Improvement Process,* Chapter 10, by H. James Harrington.)

Executive audits (management reviews)—Executive audits should be conducted of the total quality management system, placing particular emphasis on customer-related quality data and processes. ISO 9000 calls these audits management reviews. We prefer the term *executive audits* because we believe that it is extremely important for the executives to obtain firsthand, personal knowledge of the QMS and not rely solely on audits conducted by internal employees or external organizations. At a very minimum the executive committee should include a complete review of all major internal audits and external audits of the QMS results in its schedule. Particular emphasis should be placed on the corrective actions proposed to eliminate discrepancies. Often the executive committee will focus its audit on personally evaluating the corrective action's effectiveness at eliminating this discrepancy. This provides an excellent way for the executive team to demonstrate its support of the QMS and, at the same time, ensures that discrepancies are handled expeditiously.

As a result of the executive audits, the following questions should have been answered:

- Is the present QMS providing the organization with a competitive advantage?
- Is the present QMS aligned with the organization's business plan?
- Are activities under way or planned for that will require the QMS to be modified?
- Is the organization achieving the goals defined in the quality policy and its supporting objectives?
- Is the present QMS working effectively?
- Is the QMS preventing errors from occurring?

External Audits

These audits are conducted by organizations that are not within the management structure of the organization being audited. They are usually conducted by customers, registrars, and/or government agencies. Two types of external audits exist:

- Second-party audits
- Third-party audits

Second-party audits—These are audits conducted by an organization of its subcontractor's or potential subcontractor's QMS to ensure that the subcontractor's QMS meets the minimum requirements defined by the purchasing organization. These audits are usually conducted prior to issuing a contract to a new subcontractor, and every 6 to 12 months for currently active subcontractors. Usually the semiannual audit of current active subcontractors goes beyond the QMS to include audits of the product and/or service processes.

Third-Party Audits—Typically, third-party audits can be classified into two subcategories. Legally required audits such as financial audits of a public organization's books or government audits usually focus on issues like safety, health, and product quality for the protection of the general public. The other type of third-party audits are ones conducted by registration bodies at the request of the organization to provide documented independent evidence of the organization's compliance to a specific standard. The third-party audit organization should be completely independent of the organization that is being audited so that no conflict of interest exists. The third-party organization provides a written report that defines how well the organization that is being evaluated complies to a specific standard. These documents published by the third-party auditor are used to ensure interested parties that the organization is in compliance with a specific standard, policy, and/or legal requirements (e.g., yearly audits of the financial records for a publicly owned organization; Underwriters Laboratory safety approval or registration of the organization to one of the ISO 9000 documents). ISO 9000 registrars must be completely independent and not also provide consulting services either directly or indirectly on quality-related activities. It is not ethical for a registrar to be financially connected to an organization that provides training on TQM subjects or helps to establish quality management systems.

Phase VI: Continuous Improvement of the Quality Management System

Phase VI, the continuous improvement phase, consists of the following eight steps:

1. Assess today's organization's personality.
2. Establish environmental vision statements.
3. Set performance improvement goals.
4. Define desired behavior and habit patterns.

5. Develop individual three-year improvement plans.
6. Develop a combined three-year plan.
7. Develop a rolling 90-day implementation plan.
8. Implement the improvement plan.

Designing, documenting, and implementing a quality management system requires a great deal of concentrated effort. Often organizations have a tendency to sit back and relax once the QMS is in place, which is a serious mistake. As soon as the QMS is implemented, it starts to become obsolete. The audit processes are an effective way of maintaining the status quo, but in today's rapidly changing environment, no organization can afford not to continuously be changing. Activities like TQM programs, reengineering, and organizational restructuring are continuously affecting the organization's structure and are operations that in turn often have a major influence on the QMS. It is very important to keep the quality management system's documentation in tune with the changes that are going on throughout the organization.

Employees should be instructed to always follow the documentation and if conflicting directions are given, stop the activity until the document is changed or the employee is told to continue following the documentation. Another condition that frequently occurs is that the employee discovers a perceived better way of performing the activity. In no case should the employee deviate from the documented process, even if the employee has identified what he or she believes to be a better way of performing the activity. In these cases the employee should not use the new method until it has been evaluated and the documentation changed, because frequently the employee is not able to assess the effect of the change on the total process. In both of the aforementioned conditions, there is a need to quickly identify a discrepancy or improvement opportunity, evaluate its impact, and quickly change the documentation or explain to the employee why the documentation will not be changed. As a result, an effective change-evaluation and/or problem-solving process must be in place to support the QMS.

The second major problem that faces the organization during the continuous improvement phase (sometimes called the maintenance phase) is controlling the change level of the QMS documents. Often, old documents are not removed when new ones are released, causing confusion and errors. In addition, frequently when documents are changed the employees are not retrained to follow the new documentation. Great care should be exercised during the continuous improvement phase to be sure that the employees know what the latest release level is for each document that they use and that they have the required training needed to perform at that level.

The third major problem occurs when one document is changed and the supporting documents or interrelated documents are not changed. For example, a procedure could be changed but the supporting work instructions are not updated to reflect the change in the parent document. If the organization used the family of documents approach to implementing its upgraded QMS, it has already set up a matrix of supporting documents that can be used as a checklist to ensure that all supporting documents have been modified, if needed, when a change to an interrelated document is implemented.

The job is not done when the QMS is documented, released, and installed. This is just the starting point. The QMS is a living, operating, complex series of processes that are continuously changing. The key to making your QMS a competitive advantage to your organization, rather than a millstone around its neck, is the way the QMS is maintained during the continuous improvement phase.

Continuous improvement efforts have failed time after time because they were not well designed, nor did they consider all the 420-plus improvement tools that are available today. In Phase VI, the organization will develop a set of vision statements that will define how the management and employee team would like to see the environment within the organization change over a five-year period. Once the future-state visions have been established, a three-year improvement plan should be designed to bring about the desired behavioral patterns in management and the employees. This three-year plan will be used to drive the continuous improvement activities. A well-designed improvement process should at least break even the first year and then improve the organization's total performance between 10 and 20 percent each year, year after year.

The Advantages of a Good Quality Management System

Having an effective quality management system that meets and/or exceeds the requirements defined in the ISO 9000 series has many advantages. Some of these advantages include:

- Management's expectations are clearly communicated to the employees.
- The organization performs much more predictably.
- There is international acceptance of the organization's QMS.
- It provides a base for all the organization's improvement activities.
- It minimizes the number of errors that occur because work instructions are not documented.
- It reduces the time required to train a reassigned employee.

- It is required by many organizations as part of their contract with their suppliers and/or subcontractors.
- It saves time because key procedures are documented, eliminating the need to reinvent the wheel each time.
- Third-party registration reduces the number of second-party audits.
- It provides a base that ensures that improvement gains are captured and internalized.

We like to think of a good quality management system as the stable base that other improvement efforts should be built upon. Improvements that are made in a poorly defined system are a lot like pushing a big round boulder up a steep incline. The moment you relax and turn your back on the boulder, it rolls right back down the hill, often crushing the people who have worked so hard to push it up the incline. This is what has happened to many organizations when they tried to implement process reengineering, quality circles, TQM, or activity-based costing. A good QMS provides the block under the boulder that keeps it from rolling back down the hill (see Figure 1.15).

ISO 9000
Prevents Losing Ground

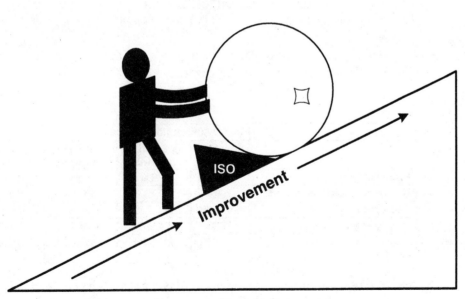

FIGURE 1.15   Quality Management System Internalizes Improvements

Quality World magazine, in its October 1995 issue, reported that ISO 9000–registered organizations perform better than ones that were not registered. Surrey University compared the performance of more than 200 organizations that were registered to ISO 9000 with the general market indexes. Researchers divided up the data by small (£10–£20 mil.), medium (£20–£50 mil.) and large (more than £50 mil. in sales). In all cases the ISO 9000–registered organizations outperformed the organizations that were not registered (see Figure 1.16).

Be careful about using these numbers because no data are available that prove that installing the new QMS improved the organizations' performance. The study did not include data related to the organizations' performance before they were registered to ISO 9000.

A Word of Caution

Don't undertake the upgrading of your QMS to meet the ISO 9000 series requirements lightly. It will require a major commitment of the executive team's personal time and the organization's resources. In a freewheeling, entrepreneurial-type organization, defining, documenting, and implementing procedures that define how the processes operate often directly oppose the current culture and force the organization to change in ways that decrease creativity. Before you decide to upgrade your QMS ask yourself the following questions:

- Why should the organization upgrade its QMS?
- What benefits will the organization receive from a better QMS?

	ISO 9000-Certified Companies			
	Industry average	Small companies	Medium companies	Large companies
Profit margin	1.9%	6.8%	4.9%	4.4%
Return on capital employed	7.7%	17.5%	16.2%	16.6%
Sales per employee	£47,700	£53,700	£62,200	£93,500
Profit per employee	£900	£4,200	£2,900	£3,600
Capital employed per employee	£11,000	£18,900	£23,900	£21,200

FIGURE 1.16 Performance Comparison of ISO 9000–Certified Companies in the Mechanical Engineering Manufacturing Sector with the Industry Average

- How will we measure these benefits?
- How much will it cost the organization?
- What will be the organization's return on investment?

Data on Quality Management System Upgrading

Quality Management Systems Update/Deloitte & Touche conducted a joint survey in 1993 of 620 organizations in the United States and Canada that were registered to ISO 9000. The survey's authors reported that the average total cost to develop the new quality management system and become registered was $245,200 and the average annual savings was $179,000 per year. When asked what the internal benefits from registration were, the surveyed organizations reported:

Better documentation	32.4%
Greater quality awareness	25.6%
Positive "cultural" change	15.0%
Increased operational efficiency/productivity	9.0%
Enhanced intercompany communications	7.3%
Reduced scrap and rework expenses	6.6%

When the survey asked what the external benefits of registration were, the response was:

Higher perceived quality	33.5%
Improved customer satisfaction	26.6%
Competitive edge	21.5%
Reduced customer quality audits	8.5%
Increased market share	4.5%

Summary

There is no doubt about it. Quality management systems are here to stay, and registration to the ISO 9000 series standards is gaining momentum in every part of the world. Soon it will be a major consideration in the selection of new subcontractors. Already many requests for bid documents require that only organizations registered to ISO 9000 are allowed to quote on the proposal. Two prime reasons are driving the ISO 9000 landslide. The first and primary reason is that customers are demanding and expecting their suppliers and subcontractors to be registered. The second reason for implementing formal quality management systems is the quality benefits that the organization receives as a result of formalizing its QMS. After carefully examining the pros and cons of a formal documented QMS, we strongly support the concept and encourage all organizations to place a high priority on this activity within their organization's business plan. We find it hard to understand how a modern organization can operate without a formally documented QMS and are surprised that this issue was not highlighted and addressed back in the 1970s when the quality improvement effort first became an executive issue. Can you imagine trying to reduce cost on your product without having a formal financial system?

Don't stop when your organization is registered. It is just the starting point. A 1996 survey of 641 manufacturers in Finland, Germany, the Netherlands, and the UK reported: "Companies with certification such as ISO 9000 reported significantly higher quality than those without" (*European Quality Magazine* 3, no. 1, p. 28). It went on to report that organizations that were certified and had a TQM process in place outperformed the organizations that did not. For example:

Return on assets	+3.8%
Market share	+4.1%
Productivity	+4.2%
Customer satisfaction	+3.7%
Cash flow	+4.5%
External quality	+3.9%

Appendix VI is a list of reference books and audio/video programs related to the ISO 9000 series.

2

ISO 9001 in Detail

Introduction

This chapter provides a broad overview of the 20 ISO 9001 elements listed in Clause 4.0. In addition, explanatory guidance is provided to help the reader understand each individual clause, to explain the requirement and the commonly understood principles of TQM. Note: All users of this book should read this chapter, even if the organization is planning to implement ISO 9002 or ISO 9003. This is necessary because we believe that once an individual or organization understands ISO 9001 it will be easy for them to select the parts of ISO 9001 that apply to ISO 9002 or ISO 9003, as guided by Figure 1.7 in Chapter 1. As a result, we will only present a detailed view of ISO 9001.

(Note: The macrolevel requirement is known in the industry as an "element." There are actually well over 100 requirements.)

ISO 9001 is the most comprehensive standard of the three contractible standards (ISO 9001, 9002, and 9003). It is used when the contract requires your organization to develop a unique design to fulfill a customer's need. Organizations that meet all of the requirements of ISO 9001 will also be in full compliance to ISO 9002 and 9003. ISO 9001 applies to both providers of products and service (e.g., consulting, architecture, engineering). Clause 4.0 (Figure 1.7) defines the 20 fundamental quality elements in ISO 9001.

The scope of the ANSI/ASQC version of ISO 9001 states:

This American National Standard specifies quality-system requirements for use where a supplier's capability to design and supply conforming product needs to be demonstrated.

The requirements specified are aimed primarily at achieving customer satisfaction by preventing nonconformity at all stages from design through servicing.

This American National Standard is applicable in situations when
a) design is required and the product requirements are stated principally in performance terms, or they need to be established, and
b) confidence in product conformance can be attained by adequate demonstration of a supplier's capabilities in design, development, production, installation, and servicing.

The 20 Elements of ISO 9001

To provide the reader with some of the key concepts that make up ISO 9001, the following highlights important points included in each of the 20 elements.

4.1 Management Responsibility

The single most important part of any quality system is management's active involvement. Subclause 4.1 of ISO 9001 addresses management's responsibilities related to

- 4.1.1 Developing and communicating a quality policy
- 4.1.1.2.1 Defining the responsibilities, authority, and interrelationship between management and/or employees whose work affects quality
- 4.1.2.2 Assigning the proper level of resources to activities that impact quality
- 4.1.2.3 Identifying an executive who is responsible for ensuring that a quality system is established, implemented, and maintained
- 4.1.3 Assigning an executive-level individual the responsibilities for reviewing the quality system at defined intervals to be sure that it conforms to ISO 9001

4.2 Quality System

Although all organizations have some type of quality system, the ISO series focuses heavily on establishing, documenting, and maintaining quality systems as a means of ensuring that product conforms to requirements. It requires that the organization prepare a four-tier formal process, its highest level being the quality manual supported by procedures that are implemented through the use of instruction. The fourth level in the documentation hierarchy is the information recorded to verify that the assigned tasks were performed so that the product meets its requirements.

4.2.3 New products, projects, or contracts

The organization needs to develop a quality plan that will define and document how the requirements for quality will be met. This plan should ensure the compatibility of the design, production process, installation, servicing, inspection, and test procedures. Appropriate documentation level controls and traceability are also required.

4.3 Contract Review

A contract review process must be established and implemented that covers each order, contract, or tender to ensure the product requirements are defined and documented. The procedure must also ensure that the organization has the capability of meeting these requirements.

4.4 Design Control

The effective transference of the customer's requirements into a design specification is crucial to the quality of the end product. Even the very best manufacturing process cannot offset the inadequacies that are built into a poor engineering design. Due to the importance of the design process on the end product quality, ISO 9001 requires the organization to establish and maintain documented procedures to control and verify the design of the product to ensure that all specified requirements are met. This includes the following activities:

- 4.4.2 Design and development planning
- 4.4.3 Organization and technical interfaces
- 4.4.4 Design input

- 4.4.5 Design output
- 4.4.6 Design reviews
- 4.4.7 Design verification
- 4.4.8 Design validation
- 4.4.9 Design changes

4.5 Document and Data Control

Control of data, documents, and information can overwhelm any organization. It is imperative that document controls be applied to any document and data systems that can affect quality. In Subclause 4.5 of ISO 9001, the necessary mechanisms to control the release and follow-up change to documents and data are defined.

- 4.5.3 The document and data approval release and change cycle should be defined, documented, and followed. It should ensure that obsolete documents are removed from all areas. If for legal and/or knowledge preservation purposes obsolete documents are maintained, they must be identified as obsolete.

4.6 Purchasing

Almost all organizations depend on suppliers in one way or another. If our employees are our most valuable product, our suppliers run a very close second. Without excellent input, your organization has little possibility of providing excellent output. Subclause 4.6 of ISO 9001 requires the organization to do the following:

- 4.6.2 Evaluate subcontractors (suppliers) and ensure that they have a quality system in place and have the capability of meeting product requirements. To ensure that this is accomplished in an effective manner, documented procedures should be developed and followed.
- 4.6.3 Ensure that the documents provided to the subcontractor (supplier) clearly describe the product ordered and include the supporting documentation (e.g., specification drawings, process requirements, inspection instructions, etc.).
- 4.6.4 Establish a process that allows the subcontractor's (supplier's) items' quality to be evaluated either at the subcontractor's premises, or at the organization's premises (receiving inspection).

4.7 Control of Customer-Supplied Product

ISO 9001 requires that the organization establish and maintain documented procedures for the control, verification, storage, and maintenance of customer-supplied products provided for incorporation into final products.

4.8 Product Identification and Traceability

Whenever applicable, the organization shall establish and maintain documented procedures for identifying the product by suitable means throughout the production and installation cycle (receipt, production, delivery, and installation). Depending upon the size, nature, and complexity of the individual item, identification can be at the individual product or batch levels.

4.9 Process Control

Process control applies to processes that are involved in production, installation, and servicing that have a direct effect on the quality of the item that is provided to the end customer. Subclause 4.9 of ISO 9001 defines controlled conditions as including:

- Documenting procedures where their absence could adversely affect quality.
- Monitoring and controlling suitable process parameters and product characteristics.
- Suitably maintaining equipment for continuing process capability.
- Continuous monitoring and control of the process parameters by qualified personnel where the results of the process cannot be fully verified by subsequent inspection and test of product, and where process deficiencies may become apparent only after the product is in use.
- Maintaining records for qualified processes, equipment, and personnel as appropriate.

4.10 Inspection and Testing

As part of the quality plan, a detailed inspection and testing plan should be defined. Records should be maintained for all inspection and test operations. Subclause 4.10 of ISO 9001 specifies that inspection and test plans should be developed and executed for the following areas:

- Receiving inspection and tests
- In-process inspection and tests
- Final inspection and tests

4.11 Control of Inspection, Measuring, and Test Equipment

Without having measuring, inspection, and test equipment that is controlled, maintained, and calibrated, it is impossible for an organization to be sure that it is shipping products to customers that meet their requirements. Subclause 4.11 of ISO 9001 states that an organization shall establish and maintain documented procedures to control, calibrate, and maintain inspection, measuring, and test equipment (which includes software) used by the organization to determine conformance of product to customer requirements. It further requires that inspection, measuring, and test equipment shall be used in a manner that ensures that the uncertainty of the measurement is known and is consistent with the required measurement capabilities. To accomplish this, the following control procedures should be included:

- Appropriate selection of equipment to ensure its accuracy and precision is in keeping with the product's requirements and specifications
- A document control program to maintain calibration for all the related equipment
- Calibration records and a system to show calibration status

4.12 Inspection and Test Status

It is important that only products that have completed the inspection and testing activities as defined in the quality plan be dispatched, used, or installed.

4.13 Control of Nonconforming Product

One of the basic requirements of any quality system is to minimize or eliminate the potential of delivering nonconforming products to customers. As a result, whenever a component, assembly, or product is identified as not conforming to its documented requirements either through visual inspection or tests, it should be identified and segregated from the good parts. Subclause 4.13 of ISO 9001 requires that controls shall be provided for identification, documentation, evaluation, segregation, and disposition of nonconforming products and for notification to the functions concerned. To accomplish this,

- Responsibilities related to review and authority for disposition of nonconforming products should be documented.
- Repaired and/or reworked products should be reinspected in accordance with the quality plan and/or documented procedures.
- Procedures must be in place to segregate rejected and/or reworked products from acceptable products.

4.14 Corrective and Preventive Action

If an organization had a perfect preventive QMS, the corrective action section of ISO 9001 would not be needed. Unfortunately, that perfect system does not exist and, as a result, errors do occur. When errors occur, the organization should aggressively pursue correcting these problems and preventing them from recurring. Subclause 4.14 of ISO 9001 requires that documented procedures should be established for

- Taking corrective action relating to customer complaints, reports of nonconformity detected during process audits, and in-process fallout. These procedures should be implemented and monitored to ensure that the corrective action is effective and that it eliminates the detected problem.
- Analyzing and eliminating potential causes of nonconformity through the use of appropriate source information, and implementing action that deals with the potential problems before errors occur. These preventive processes should be documented, implemented, and monitored to ensure they are effective.

4.15 Handling, Storage, Packaging, Preservation, and Delivery

The quality level of good products can be seriously jeopardized through poor handling, storage, packaging, preservation, and delivery. It is thereby absolutely essential that all organizations evaluate how the product is handled, stored, and moved throughout the production, delivery, and installation activities. Subclause 4.15 of ISO 9001 points out the importance of proper analysis and evaluation of handling, storage, packaging, preservation, and delivery processes. The subclause emphasizes not only the importance of proper controls to ensure the product is not damaged but also proper marking to ensure the product is identifiable.

4.16 Control of Quality Records

A good quality record system is essential to any organization just as a financial record system is key to the organization's performance. The quality record system provides an audit trail through the production, delivery, and installation processes that verifies compliance to requirements. These records take many forms and use many different types of media, such as hard copy or electronic media. Subclause 4.16 of ISO 9001 states, "The supplier (your organization) shall establish and maintain documented procedures for identification, collection, indexing, access, filing, storage, maintenance, and disposition of quality records."

4.17 Internal Quality Audits

"What gets measured gets done" is one of the basic rules in management. It is therefore very important that the QMS is regularly audited to ensure its viability and applicability. Subclause 4.17 of ISO 9001 requires that the organization establish documented procedures for conducting internal quality audits that are carried out by personnel independent of those individuals directly responsible for the activity. The results of these quality audits should be documented and be part of a management review process.

4.18 Training

Thomas J. Watson, Sr., first president of IBM, stated "There is no saturation point to education." (Source: *Excellence the IBM Way* by H. J. Harrington, published by Quality Press, 1988). As true as this was in the 1930s, it may be even more true in the 1990s. Our learning organization is a key element required to successfully compete in today's competitive environment. Subclause 4.18 of ISO 9001 requires that documented procedures be established that identify training needs and provide for the training of all personnel whose performance affects the quality of the product or service. It requires that appropriate records of all training shall be maintained.

4.19 Servicing

In today's competitive environment, an organization's reputation is based not only on the hardware that it delivers but also on the services that it provides.

Maintaining excellent after-sales service is extremely important in ensuring customer loyalty. Subclause 4.19 of ISO 9001 states, "Where servicing is a specified requirement (your organization) shall establish and maintain documented procedures for performing, verifying, and reporting that the service meets the specific requirements."

4.20 Statistical Techniques

Since the 1920s statistical techniques have played an important role in the QMS. And they have become even more important in recent years with the focus on minimizing the degree of variation within products and services. Techniques like statistical process control and lot sampling play a key role in minimizing the error potential and reducing poor-quality cost. Subclause 4.20 of ISO 9001 requires an organization to establish and maintain documented procedures to implement and control the application of statistical techniques when they are applicable. This does not mean that statistical techniques should be applied in all cases. It is important to determine where statistical techniques will aid your organization in establishing, controlling, and verifying process capabilities and product characteristics.

Summary

We believe that your organization should use the ISO 9000 series to ensure that customer expectations and requirements are consistently met. Often, in seeing the 20 clauses of ISO 9001 sequentially, the key elements of the standard are unclear. What will be abundantly clear is the need for documentation. This should be viewed in a balanced context, where the underlying notion is that the way work is performed in all parts of the business should be carefully planned, documented, and supported by training.

The key to having a viable and dynamic QMS is founded upon

1. the ongoing involvement of senior management,
2. ensuring process management control,
3. supporting the basic infrastructure, and
4. pursuing process and system improvement.

Phase I: Assessment

Introduction

For more than 50 years, one of the major responsibilities of the quality function has been to maintain the quality manual. No quality functional manager's job description would be complete unless it includes maintaining the quality manual as a primary responsibility. When a potential supplier is being considered, the questions that are asked are

- Can you provide what we need?
- Can you do it on schedule?
- How much will it cost?
- Can we review your quality manual?

Armand V. Feigenbaum, in his landmark book entitled *Total Quality Control* (first published in 1951), states the following about quality manuals: "Far from being merely a thick book of details, however, such thorough documentation provides a 'quality' road map, marking the short cuts, detours and alternate routes as well as the usually traveled expressway. It provides instant and graphic direction for every member of the firm when choosing his or her most expeditious route to genuine quality assurance." J. M. Juran, in his book *Quality Control Handbook* (published by McGraw-Hill, first copyrighted in 1951), in the section related to quality planning, states: "The moving force for the first quality manual is usually the quality control manager." Consequently, the first manual also tends to be mainly departmental in nature and to emphasize procedures for improving the effectiveness of the quality control department rather than for optimizing company performance. However, as evolution proceeds, the manual tends to expand into all activities that affect fitness for use.

A quality manual is as much a part of a basic business structure as a personnel manual or financial procedures. Organizations that don't have a quality manual are organizations that are ill prepared to be in business today. The sole exception to this is a one-person business, where documentation of organizational matters rests clearly in the mind of a single individual. Organizations of up to 20 people in size can squeak by with relatively few documented procedures. So if your organization has more than 20 employees and you don't have a quality manual, you may proceed directly to Step 2 in this discussion. If you do have a quality manual but it needs improvement, the following nine steps should be used to define what action should be taken by the organization.

1. Listen to the warning signs.
2. Discuss with the chief operating officer the possible need for improving the QMS.
3. Form an assessment team.
4. Train the assessment team.
5. Conduct the assessment.
6. Define preliminary action plan.
7. Estimate costs and benefits.
8. Obtain top management approval and support.
9. Appoint a project manager.

Step 1—Listen to the Warning Signs

The need to upgrade your QMS can come from many places. Some of the warning signs that your QMS may need to be improved are as follows:

- When the role of quality is not, or has not typically been, clearly within the strategic direction of the organization
- When the organization has not seen the value of documenting its QMS
- When customers are reluctant to enter into long-term partnership arrangements
- Out-of-control processes
- Many quality problems in the manufacturing process
- Customers who are unhappy with your procedures

- Many or increasing customer product complaints
- Potential customers who will not accept your present QMS
- Customers who are imposing new QMS requirements
- Improvement processes that do not retain the gain that they make over a number of years
- Present QMS does not meet good business practices and/or accepted standards
- Failure of internal or external audits
- New management who are not content with the present QMS
- Employees who make quality errors because they do not understand what to do
- Performance improvement activities are progressing at a slow rate
- Decreasing market share
- Poor customer-retention rates
- High poor-quality costs (greater than 5%)
- Increasing product-return rates

In good organizations, the perceived need to upgrade the QMS comes from a number of warning signals, each of which by itself is not a high priority but when analyzed together define the need to improve. All too often, the need to improve the QMS is triggered by an individual customer saying that he or she will not do business with your organization if your QMS does not meet his or her minimum standards. Whatever the conditions are that create the perceived need to improve your QMS, the individual who perceives the need should discuss the situation with the person responsible for maintaining the QMS. Usually the quality functional manager has this responsibility, but if no one else has been assigned to maintain the QMS, the chief operating officer (COO) has the responsibility until he or she delegates it to someone else. With this basic premise, every organization has someone who is responsible for the QMS. The result of this discussion should be a decision to review the adequacy of the QMS. In the context of ISO 9001, this is covered in Secondary Subclause 4.1.3 and, not surprisingly, is called "Management Review."

The individual who defines the need should not be reluctant to escalate it to the COO if the person responsible for the QMS does not adequately satisfy his or her concerns. Frequently, this is necessary because the person who has been put in charge of the QMS does not have the background to perform the original task. One of the major problems that faces the world today is the lack of experienced quality professionals. For every competent, trained vice president or director of quality, there are ten who are reading the book to try to determine what their role should be.

Unfortunately, most organizations do not view quality assurance (quality engineering) as a profession and often assign someone from marketing, product engineering, or manufacturing engineering the role of quality functional manager. Assigning inexperienced individuals to take over a leadership role has resulted in a degradation of the key quality processes in flavor-of-the-month programs like "reengineering, empowerment, quality function deployment, problem solving, just-in-time," and so on. This has left most organizations in a situation where they have built their improvement processes based on a faulty foundation, causing them to fail.

To our way of thinking, the quality functional manager needs as much quality technology background as the chief financial officer has in the financial areas. (You will note that the state of California registers quality engineers, just as it does certified public accountants.) At a minimum, the quality functional manager should have a BS or an MS degree in quality, or a minimum of five years of experience working as a quality engineer, and be certified as a quality engineer by the American Society for Quality Control. Without this type of background, the quality functional manager has little chance of establishing a sound quality process within his or her organization.

If the decision is made to take a serious look at upgrading the QMS, the person in charge of the QMS should prepare a plan to assess the extent of the improvements that are needed and to define the benefits that would be realized. This plan should provide a quick overview of the magnitude of the required changes. It is not designed to provide a detailed analysis. We suggest that this plan be based on comparing the current QMS to the world standards set forth in ISO 9001, plus any other unique requirements imposed by your specific organization and/or its customers. Typically, these assessments take less than two weeks to perform and will be conducted by a team of people representing the major functions within the organization (marketing, product engineering, quality assurance, production control, manufacturing, purchasing, after-sales service, etc.). It may be worthwhile to have an experienced ISO 9000 consultant assigned to help with the assessment. This will provide the team with an independent view of the quality management system. When this plan is complete, you are now ready to proceed to Step 2.

Step 2—Discuss with the Chief Operating Officer the Possible Need for Improving the Quality Management System

If a major upgrade to the QMS might be necessary, the person responsible for the system should set up a meeting with the COO to discuss the situation and make him or her aware of what action will be taken to define the need and to determine the possible benefits that would result from upgrading the QMS. Also, identify and communicate the potential costs to the organization of failing to take any corrective action. At this meeting, be sure to talk in the COO's language. What will be the return on investment? How much will an upgrade increase market share?

Additional resources are often required from other functions to conduct this assessment. At this meeting, these additional resources should be approved. We like to have the other functional managers who will need to provide resources to help with the assessment present at the meeting and participate in selecting the makeup of the assessment team. At least one person on the assessment team should have an excellent understanding of the 20 subclauses that make up Clause 4.0 of ISO 9001. If the organization does not have this type of individual, a consultant can fill this need and provide training for the other team members.

Step 3—Form an Assessment Team

Once the assessment team members have been identified and their managers have informed them about their roles on the assessment team, the assessment team leader should send a copy of the assessment plan, a copy of ISO 9001, a copy of ISO 9004-1, a copy of this book, and an agenda for the first meeting to each team member. Typical things that will be discussed at the first meeting are

- Why the team was formed.
- What the team's final output will be.
- What training is required.
- What each team member's role is.

In addition, at the first meeting, the following documents will be prepared:

- Assessment Team's Code of Conduct
- Team Mission Statement
- Team Project Plan and Schedule

The assessment team will meet regularly until the assessment is completed and the team's recommendations have been accepted by upper management.

Step 4—Train the Assessment Team

A four- to eight-hour training session on ISO 9000 should be sufficient to provide the assessment team with enough knowledge to perform the assessment, as long as one of the team members has a detailed understanding of ISO 9001. If the potential is high that there will be a major redesign to the QMS and the members of the assessment team will be responsible for orchestrating the redesign, a complete ISO 9000 training class should be given. Usually, it will take about 40 hours to provide the assessment team with the information required to redesign a QMS so that it is in compliance with ISO 9001. This training will be delivered in four key stages as the project unfolds.

Stage 1. A high-level two- to six-hour introduction to build enthusiasm, a degree of understanding, and commitment.
Stage 2. A one- to two-day overview of the detailed requirements, to build understanding at the team level.
Stage 3. A one- to two-day seminar on documenting the QMS.
Stage 4. A one- to two-day seminar on internal auditing.

Step 5—Conduct the Assessment

A number of approaches can be used to conduct the assessment. We will discuss only three of them:

Type 1. Process approach
Type 2. ISO 9001 Clause approach
Type 3. Designed Question approach

In the Type 1 assessment approach, the assessment team roughly sketches out the key processes in the product cycle, from concept development to servicing it in the external customer's location. The assessment should focus as much as possible on the direct product and/or service that is delivered to the external customer. Other external customer interface points such as order entry, invoicing, inquiry follow-up, and product support should be part of the analysis. The following questions should be asked about each of these key processes:

- Do you understand who the customer is for this process?
- Do you understand who the suppliers are that provide inputs to this process?

- Is the process documented?
- Is the documentation fully deployed?
- Are people following the procedures?
- Do the process measures indicate the need for further process control or improvement?

After discussing each process, the assessment team determines whether there is a need to improve the documentation related to that process or the process itself. After all processes have been reviewed, the results of these evaluations are summarized and a recommended action plan is prepared.

The Type 2 approach is a more systematic approach. The assessment team takes the 20 subclauses listed in Clause 4.0 of ISO 9001 and evaluates each of them individually. To perform this evaluation, the team should answer the following questions.

1. Are we doing it? Yes ___ No ___ Partly ___
2. Is it documented at the quality manual level? Yes ___ No ___ Partly ___
3. Is it documented at the procedural level? Yes ___ No ___ Partly ___
4. Is it documented at the work instruction level? Yes ___ No ___ Partly ___
5. Are there data to prove that it is being done? Yes ___ No ___ Partly ___
6. Is there a need to do this item better? Yes ___ No ___ Partly ___
7. Overall performance: On a scale of 1 to 10, with 1 being very bad and 10 being world class, how would you rate your quality management system's compliance to the specific clause in ISO 9001?

To perform this analysis, a form similar to the one in Figure 3.1 should be prepared for each of the 20 subclauses in Clause 4.0 of ISO 9001. Each member of the assessment team should separately fill out the set of forms and turn them in to the team chairperson. The team should select one of its members to compile the data to determine whether the team members have a common view of the QMS. Figure 3.2 is an example of a simple way to summarize a typical clause.

Now the team should repeat the exercise, discussing each question and coming to a common agreement on each answer. Highlights of these discussions should be recorded, because they can be used to define the degree of change that is required. If the team cannot agree on a common answer, hard data should be collected, allowing an informed decision to be made.

For questions 1 through 6, give your QMS 2 points for every "yes" answer (12 points maximum); for every "partly" answer, 1 point; and 0 points for a "no"

Subclause 4.1—Management Responsibility	Yes	No	Partly	Don't Know	N/A
1. Are we doing the above?					
2. Is it documented at the quality manual level?					
3. Is it documented at the procedural level?					
4. Is it documented at the work instruction level?					
5. Are there data to prove it is being done?					
6. Is there a need to do this item better?					
7. Overall Performance: On a scale of 1 to 10, with 1 being very bad and 10 being world class, how would you rate your quality management system's compliance to Subclause 4.1 of ISO 9001? Circle the appropriate number.	1 2 3 4 5 6 7 8 9 10				

FIGURE 3.1   Type 2 Status Assessment Form

answer. Using this system, the organization can get a maximum of 240 points (20 subclauses × 6 questions × 2 points for each "yes" answer = 240 points). The column labeled "Questions 1–6: Point scores" in Figure 3.3 is a typical summary analysis report.

An overall score of less than 200 points, or an individual score of less than 8 points for any one of the 20 subclauses indicates a problem. An overall score of less than 180 points indicates that a major redesign of the organization's QMS is required.

In evaluating the overall performance of the QMS (question 7), the organization could receive a maximum score of 200 points (20 subclauses × 10 points per subclause). A total point score of less than 150 points and an individual rating below 6 indicate problems (see the "Overall Performance" column

Subclause 4.1—Management Responsibility	Yes	No	Partly	Don't Know	N/A
1. Are we doing the above?	2	5	1	0	
2. Is it documented at the quality manual level?	2	0	0	6	
3. Is it documented at the procedural level?	1	0	4	3	
4. Is it documented at the work instruction level?	0	8	0	0	
5. Are there data to prove it is being done?	2	2	1	3	
6. Is there a need to do this item better?	8	0	0	0	

7. Overall Performance: On a scale of 1 to 10, with 1 being very bad and 10 being world class, how would you rate your quality management system's compliance to Subclause 4.1 of ISO 9001? Circle the appropriate number.	1	2	3	4	5	6	7	8	9	10	Avg
• Number of ratings			2	3	3						4.1

FIGURE 3.2 Type 2 Summary Assessment Form

in Figure 3.3). For both indicators, the guideline numbers need to be adjusted if sections of ISO 9001 are not applicable to the organization.

A Type 3 assessment is an alternative approach to doing an assessment. In the Type 3 approach, the assessment team rates each of the 130 questions in Appendix VIII. These are the same 130 questions that the CD-ROM program, "Harrington's ISO 9000 Step by Step," produced by SystemCorp, is based on. Typical questions that can be found in Appendix VIII are

1. Are your organization's policy, objectives, and commitments for quality defined and documented?
2. At all levels of the organization, do you ensure that the quality policy is communicated, implemented, and understood?

Sub-Clause No.	Name	Questions 1-6 Point Scores	Overall Performance
4.1	Management Responsibility	* 7	6
4.2	Quality System	9	7
4.3	Contract Review	* 2	* 3
4.4	Design Control	* 7	* 5
4.5	Document and Data Control	* 4	* 4
4.6	Purchasing	10	7
4.7	Control of Customer-Supplied Product	12	9
4.8	Product Identification and Traceability	* 6	* 4
4.9	Process Control	10	8
4.10	Inspection and Testing	11	10
4.11	Control of Inspection, Measuring, and Test Equipment	11	10
4.12	Inspection and Test Status	12	9
4.13	Control of Nonconforming Product	12	9
4.14	Corrective and Preventive Action	* 5	6
4.15	Handling, Storage, Packaging, Preservation, and Delivery	10	7
4.16	Control of Quality Records	* 7	* 5
4.17	Internal Quality Audits	* 2	* 2
4.18	Training	10	8
4.19	Servicing	* 6	* 4
4.20	Statistical Techniques	12	8
	Total	165	131

FIGURE 3.3   Summary Analysis of a Total Type 2 Status Assessment

The assessment team should evaluate each question on a scale of 1 to 10, with 1 being no compliance and 10 being complete compliance. In this case, the maximum score would be 1,300 points (130 questions × 10 points). Total scores of less than 1,000 points indicate that the QMS needs to be improved. Scores of less than 800 indicate that a major redesign to the organization's QMS is required. Individual sections whose score is less than 75 percent of the maximum possible score for that section are also considered to be in need of improvement.

To start this evaluation cycle, each member of the assessment team should fill out a form individually, where all 130 questions are evaluated. Figure 3.4 is a typical form layout.

These forms should be collected and analyzed. The average and range for each question should be plotted. Figure 3.5 is an example of how 20 of the 130

Degree of Compliance

No.	Question	1	2	3	4	5	6	7	8	9	10	N/A	Not Known
1.	Are your organization's policy, objectives, and commitments for quality defined and documented?												
2.	At all levels of the organization, do you ensure that the quality policy is communicated, implemented, and understood?												
3.	Etc.												

FIGURE 3.4 Type 3 Status Assessment Form

questions could be plotted. All 130 questions should be plotted in the same manner.

With this information in hand, the total assessment team should review each question, and explore the questions where there is a range of more than three numbers (see Figure 3.5) to define why the team has different views of the same subject.

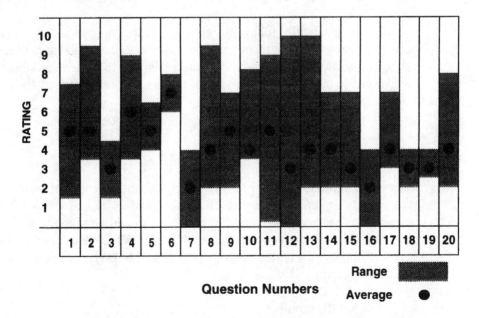

FIGURE 3.5 Plot of the Team's Evaluation for 20 of the 130 Questions

We suggest that before the assessment team rates each of the 130 questions, the members discuss the following four questions:

1. Are we doing it?
2. How do we know we are doing it?
3. Where can we find the documentation?
4. Is there any proof that we are doing it, and if there is, where is that proof located?

It is good practice to audit the opinions of the assessment team by having the team members pull samples of the documentation and the supporting performance data to ensure that there is not a gap between the assessment team's belief and actual in-process practices. In many organizations there are significant differences in what the management team believes is going on within the quality process and what actually is happening, making this verification activity mandatory.

Although we have provided you with a set of go/no-go rules, in truth they are only used as guidelines. The QMS is a living, changing group of processes that are critical to the organization's function. The final decision on the need to improve the QMS has to rest on the knowledge and understanding that the assessment team has about the organization, its objectives, its operations, and its customers.

By systematically following one of the three approaches defined in its activities, the assessment team will discuss the key issues related to the present QMS, define its weaknesses, and be in a position to determine whether the QMS needs to be updated and to define the general magnitude of the required improvement.

Step 6—Define Preliminary Action Plan

Once the magnitude of the problem is defined, the assessment team can prepare an action plan to correct it. This plan could go all the way from recommending to the executive team that no action should be taken to improve the present QMS, to recommending that a total new QMS be developed. If the decision is to improve the QMS, an action plan should be prepared. This action plan should include the following items:

1. What the problem is
2. What areas in the QMS need to be addressed

3. How the change will impact the culture of the organization
4. An estimate of the total Organizational Change Management effort that will be required to support the proposed changes
5. Whether third-party registration should be part of the action plan
6. The type of training that will be required to support redesigning the QMS and implementing the new system
7. The advantages and disadvantages of using an outside consultant and how the consultant should be used
8. The person who will be in charge of upgrading the QMS and the members of the project team who will support the team leader
9. A timeline for completing the project

It is important to realize that this action plan is a preliminary plan, because the assessment team was only chartered to evaluate whether there was a need to upgrade the QMS and to define the magnitude of that upgrade. If there is a need to upgrade the present QMS, then a project team will be assigned to prepare the final action plan. The plan that is prepared by the assessment team should be used by the project team as a guideline in preparing its final plan. It is very important that the team that will be designing the new QMS owns and is committed to the final action plan. It is for these reasons that the action plan and the cost-benefits estimate prepared by the assessment team can be based less on fact, and more on good judgment and past experience. Usually, resources and schedule estimates that are plus or minus 20 percent are sufficient for this phase of the improvement activities.

In the list of nine items that should be included in the action plan, Item 1 (What the problem is) and Item 2 (What areas in the QMS need to be addressed) should have been well defined during Step 5 in this phase. The analysis defined in Step 2 was specifically designed to provide this type of information and is the basis for moving forward with the project.

Item 3—How the Change Will Impact the Culture of the Organization

If your organization is already very systematic and disciplined in its operating approach, then the ISO 9000 series will be in line with your culture and will be fairly well accepted. If your organization is a freewheeling, creative organization that thinks procedures are guidelines, or doesn't prepare written procedures, applying ISO 9000 can be a dramatic shock to the organization's culture. This is a very important consideration, since the degree of implementation and internalization effort required to support the new QMS is greater (by a factor of ten) in the freewheeling type of organization, and implementation takes much longer.

Item 4—An Estimate of the Total Organizational Change Management Effort That Will Be Required

Once the magnitude of the QMS change is defined and its impact on the organization's culture is understood, the assessment team can estimate the amount of OCM effort that is required to support implementation.

Organizational Change Management effort will be required for any significant change to the QMS, but if the change is not in line with the organization's culture, the amount of OCM effort will be much greater, and a lot of effort will need to be expended before the QMS changes are ready for implementation. Another factor that needs to be considered when defining the OCM plan is how successful the organization has been in the past at implementing changes in budgets and schedules. If the organization has had a tendency to overrun change budgets and not meet change schedules, more OCM effort needs to be expended to overcome the attitudes developed in the past. For more information on OCM, see Appendix V.

Item 5—Whether Third-Party Registration Should Be Part of the Action Plan

One of the major advantages of the ISO 9000 series is its effective use of third-party registration. Although registration fees alone average about $18,000 per location and an ongoing cost every six months of about $7,000, registration has many advantages that have already been discussed. Many organizations' primary reason for redesigning their QMS is to become registered to ISO 9000, thereby providing their QMS with an internationally accepted degree of credibility. In most cases, if your QMS conforms to the ISO 9000 standards, it is a good investment to have it registered by a third party. As well as providing your QMS with a degree of credibility, the audit by a third-party assessor often highlights improvement opportunities that otherwise would have gone unnoticed. We believe that most organizations should be registered.

Item 6—The Type of Training That Will Be Required

Normally, two major types of training will be required to install a QMS that is in compliance with the ISO 9000 series. They are

1. Generic QMS (ISO 9000) training.
2. Operational/job-related training.

The extent of the generic training will vary based on the magnitude of the QMS redesign effort and/or whether the organization is planning on being registered by a third party. For a moderate QMS change that would include third-party registration, the following generic training is recommended.

Executive Team
- Eight-hour overview of the ISO 9000 series and the role of the executive team in supporting the QMS
- Eight-hour OCM training

Project Team
- Forty hours on QMS structure and implementation
- Sixteen hours on OCM
- Eight hours on auditing and sampling

General Management
- Eight-hour overview of ISO 9000 and general management's role in implementing and maintaining a QMS
- Four to eight hours on OCM, depending on the extent of the change involved, as determined during the assessment

Anyone Preparing Procedures or Job Instructions
- Eight-hour QMS overview
- Four hours on OCM
- Four hours on document writing and evaluation
- Four hours on preparing adult training methods and how to audit an activity

All Employees
- Two-hour overview of QMS and employee's role in supporting them

(*Note:* If the individual has already had OCM training, it will not have to be repeated.)

The following is a typical eight-hour class outline for general management.

QMS Workshop Content
- What is ISO 9000?
  — History
  — Scope
  — Relationship to TQM

- What's in it for the organization and me?
  - — Internal benefits: reduced variation and better controls
  - — Commercial benefits: international acceptance
- The Fundamentals and Terminology
  - — Quality control and quality assurance
  - — The QMS and the quality program
  - — The quality manual
  - — Registration bodies and the registration process
- The Quality Management System
  - — What the standards are
  - — How to interpret them
  - — Compliance and noncompliance
- The Quality Documentation System
  - — Why? What? Who? How?
  - — Control, review, and update
  - — Implementation
- Registration Process
  - — Getting commitment
  - — Preparation
  - — Assessment
  - — Registration
  - — Follow-up
- Compliance and Noncompliance
  - — Noncompliance categories
  - — Documentation
  - — Action plans

Organizational job-related training should be defined based on the individual document. We like to see included in every document the required prerequisite for a person to use that document and the training that should be provided before an individual is expected to comply with the document. In most organizations, the single biggest expenditure in implementing an upgraded QMS is the time and effort that are invested in training management and employees in how to effectively utilize the organization's QMS and the productivity lost during the early part of the learning curve after the new procedures are implemented.

Item 7—The Advantages and Disadvantages of Using an Outside Consultant

The assessment team should determine whether the organization has the required skills, available resources, and detailed understanding of the ISO 9000 requirements to redesign its QMS, or whether an outside specialist should be hired. Some organizations' resources are stretched so thin that they find it best to hire an experienced consultant to design and implement their new QMS. We feel that this should be a last resort. It is always best to have the QMS designed by the people who are going to use it and live with it. Obtaining organizational ownership of the redesigned QMS is a key part of the organization's change activities. Having an outside consultant do the total QMS redesign does not promote organizational ownership. The organization really has only three options:

1. Hire a consultant who will work with an internal team to redesign the QMS, and provide training and guidance on how to implement the new QMS.
2. Hire somebody from outside the organization who has had experience upgrading quality management systems, and make that person responsible for the QMS redesign.
3. Train internal people to understand the reasons behind the requirements and make them responsible for redesigning the QMS. This approach relies on third-party auditors to identify weaknesses in your QMS and usually takes the longest and will be the most expensive. The advantage is that it is a great learning experience for some of your employees.

For most organizations that do not already have the internal expertise, option 1 is the best answer. This option keeps the redesign process moving along at optimum speed and minimizes the number of rework cycles that the QMS undergoes. Be sure that you select your consultant very carefully. In the best case, the consulting firm will have quality engineers certified by the American Society for Quality Control, or quality engineers professionally licensed by a state governing body. The next level down would be consultants who have successfully completed the ISO 9000 registration course and have worked with a minimum of two other organizations installing successful ISO 9000–type quality management systems. They should also have a minimum of five years' experience working as a quality manager or quality engineer in an organization with an excellent QMS.

Be sure that the consultant has had experience managing the QMS after it has been implemented. This is necessary because there is a big difference between theory and practice. It is very easy to implement a QMS and get it registered, only to discover that the new QMS is very difficult and costly to maintain. Experience in living with a QMS is a very important prerequisite for a QMS consultant. Be very careful in selecting your consulting firm, because ISO

9000 consulting has been an exploding industry, with many organizations going in and out of business every day. Select an organization that has a proven reputation over a number of years and can be depended on to provide you with guidance after your QMS has been registered. Many organizations today are selecting consulting firms that have a depth of experience in fields other than quality (e.g., information technology, strategic planning, organizational restructuring) so the consulting firm can provide total business direction.

Item 8—The Quality Management System Upgrade Team

The assessment defined the parts of the QMS that needed to be redesigned. The people who make up the project team should be representatives from the organization who are most impacted by the redesign process. Typical areas that are represented on the Quality System Team (QST), often called the ISO 9000 team or project team, are product engineering, manufacturing engineering, manufacturing, procurement, sales, production control, quality engineering, and purchasing. The people assigned to the QST should have an excellent understanding of how the function that they represent operates, what is required from their (external and internal) suppliers, and what their (external and internal) customers require. They should also be people who have had team operation, project management, and problem-solving training. It is important that these individuals have a high degree of credibility with management and the employees, because their decisions will have a major impact on the way the organization will operate in the future. The assessment team should also recommend who will be the chairperson of the QST.

Item 9—A Timeline for Completing the Project

Upgrading an organization's QMS to meet the requirements of ISO 9001 can take anywhere from two months to two years, depending on the current status of the QMS, how effectively consultants are used, the technical support systems used, and whether the organization wishes to be registered by a third party. Figure 3.6 is a typical example of a preliminary timeline Gantt chart for a major upgrade to a QMS that includes third-party registration. In addition, a more detailed chart is often prepared that will define the major milestones in Phases I and II. This gets the QST off to a running start (see Figure 3.7).

We have seen this typical 18-month cycle reduced to 6 months or less with the use of trained consultants and/or effective on-line software packages (see Figure 3.8). To accomplish this reduced time schedule, priority has to be put on the record system so that adequate history records are available to the registrar.

Months

Activity	2	4	6	8	10	12	14	16	18
Phase II: Planning									
• Hold meetings of the QST									
• Select a consulting firm									
• Select a registrar									
• Prepare a detailed project plan									
Phase III: Upgrading the QMS									
• Prepare the quality manual									
• Prepare the procedures									
• Prepare the job instructions									
• Prepare support training									
• Implement the OCM plan									
Phase IV: Implementation									
• Pilot run									
• Refinement									
• Release document									
• Train affected personnel									
• Install new documents									
• Measure their effectiveness									
• Adjust documents as required									
• Release updated documents									
Phase V: Auditing the QMS									
• Conduct management self-audits									
• Conduct formal in-house audits									
• Conduct preregistration audits									
• Conduct formal registration audits									
• Conduct management reviews									
• Conduct third-party audits									
Phase VI: Continuous Improvement									

FIGURE 3.6 Overview of Quality Management System Upgrade Schedule

87

Weeks

Activity	2	4	6	8	10	12	14	16	18
Phase I: Assessment									
1. Present recommendation to top management									
2. Top management forms QST									
3. Review assessment report with QST chairperson									
4. Disband assessment team									
Phase II: Planning									
1. Hold QST meeting									
2. Select a consultant									
3. Select support system									
4. Define document structure									
5. Block-diagram major quality processes									
6. Select process owners and support subcommittees									
7. Prepare and implement a communication plan									
8. Provide ISO 9000-related training									
9. Prepare and implement OCM									
10. Establish a project tracking system									
11. Define required documents									
12. Identify internal auditors									
13. Select a registrar									
14. Finalize project plan and review with management									

FIGURE 3.7 Detailed Quality Management System Upgrade Schedule

88

Weeks

Activity	2	4	6	8	10	12	14	16	18

Phase II: Planning
- Hold meetings of the QST
- Select a consulting firm
- Select a registrar
- Prepare a detailed project plan

Phase III: Upgrading the QMS
- Prepare the quality manual
- Prepare the procedures
- Prepare the job instructions
- Prepare support training
- Implement the OCM plan

Phase IV: Implementation
- Pilot run
- Refinement
- Release document
- Train affected personnel
- Install new documents
- Measure their effectiveness
- Adjust documents as required
- Release updated documents

Phase V: Auditing the QMS
- Conduct management self-audits
- Conduct formal in-house audits
- Conduct preregistration audits
- Conduct formal registration audits
- Conduct management reviews
- Conduct third-party audits

Phase VI: Continuous Improvement

FIGURE 3.8 Overview of an Expedited Quality Management System Upgrade Schedule Using Consultants and On-Line Software

89

(Note that in Figure 3.8 the certification third-party audit is not on the graph. The certification audit will normally take place two to four months later, depending on the amount of history records that the organization has collected.)

Step 7—Estimate Costs and Benefits

With the completion of the action plan, the assessment team can estimate the resources that will be required to implement the plan. Do not forget to include the training, consulting, and registration costs in this estimate. Typically, consulting costs alone can range from $10,000 to $250,000. In addition, the assessment team should define the benefits the organization will receive from the upgraded, redesigned QMS when implemented. (See Chapter 1 for a list of benefits and typical costs.)

Step 8—Obtain Top Management Approval and Support

The assessment team should now prepare a preliminary assessment report that will be presented to top management. This report should include

- Procedures used to conduct the assessment.
- Results of the assessment, highlighting major exposure areas.
- Assessment team's recommendations.
- Proposed project schedule.
- Resources required to design and implement the suggested action.
- People who should be assigned to the project.
- The potential costs to the organization of failing to take any corrective action.
- Benefits that the organization will receive from the project.
- Estimated resources required to maintain the QMS once it is registered.

When the preliminary assessment report is completed, you are ready to start selling the project to top management. Without their personal support, as well as their allocation of the required resources, the project will fail. A top management commitment of "Sounds good to me. Go out and do it" is not adequate. This type of commitment is a "don't bother me" response, and "It's OK to do it as long as you get everything else done without an increase in costs." If you accept this type of go-head and get the job done without additional resources, you are telegraphing to top management that there is fat in your budget or that the job requires very little effort. The type of response from upper management that you need is, "We like the plan. Set up a budget to cover its cost and count us in to do our part to make the implementation of this project a success."

To get this type of response, the assessment team should assign one or two of its members to meet with each top manager who needs to approve the proposal, to review the preliminary report, and to answer any questions management may have related to it. A copy of the preliminary assessment report and an agenda should be in each top manager's hands at least two days before the meeting, for their personal review.

During these meetings, the ISO 9000 concepts should be reviewed and the preliminary report discussed. The objective should be to answer each top manager's questions and understand any concerns they may have. The top managers should also be asked for suggestions as to how the proposed project can be improved so that their suggestions can be incorporated into the final assessment report.

Following these meetings, the assessment team should meet to review the input they receive and to estimate the level of support each of the top management team members will give the project. The level of support (commitment) is estimated on a scale of 1 to 10. A rating of 1 means that the top manager is strongly against the project. A rating of 5 means that the top manager is neutral and will follow the rest of the top managers. A rating of 10 means that the top manager will be a champion for the project and will try to convince the other top managers to approve the project. If any top manager has a rating between 1 and 4, the assessment team should develop a plan to try to answer his or her concerns before a total management team meeting is held. This plan will often include having another top manager who is a strong advocate of the project talk to the top manager who views the project negatively. The potential problem to this approach is that the advocate could be convinced that he or she is wrong. Only call upon your advocates if the assessment team cannot convince the top manager that he or she should at least take a neutral position on the project (a rating of 5).

If the new QMS represents a significant change from the existing organizational culture and practices, its successful implementation will ultimately require attention to all elements of managing organizational change (see Appendix V).

Two of those elements that come into play, even at this early stage, are "Cost of the Status Quo" and "Vision Clarity." Both of these elements directly involve senior management and their commitment to the change process, their willingness to lead the organization from the status quo to a new future state.

In obtaining the commitment of top management to proceed, their understanding of the costs to the organization, frequently referred to as the "business imperative," of failing to implement the change must be obtained. Frequently, this is a matter of surfacing and communicating data that make the need to change readily apparent to all.

Vision clarity is highly correlated to people's willingness to embark on the journey and see it through to a successful conclusion. It also should start from the top of the organization but should be shared by all whose commitment is desired. Hopefully, an organization-wide vision already exists. Directly related to it should be a project-specific vision for the implementation of the QMS. The vision statement should describe in clear, exciting, achievable, understandable terms what the future state will look like upon successful implementation. It should address the people, process, and technology aspects of the desired future state. The statement should answer the natural questions people will have regarding the impact of QMS implementation. (How will my work change? What will the process be? What technology will be there to help us? What's in it for me? What will be required of me?) Top management participation in the development of a preliminary vision statement secures, in part at least, their "ownership" of the commitment to proceed. Input from them for the vision statement can be obtained in the one-on-one meetings and completed during the top management presentation.

The assessment report should be finalized based on input from the top managers. Then schedule a meeting to present the final report to top management and to gain their support for implementing the project. This meeting should not be held until at least 50 percent of the top managers are in support of the project. Be sure that the final report and the meeting agenda are set up well in advance. We strongly recommend that this meeting be held when your key top management advocates can personally attend the meeting. Be sure to point out in the meeting notice that the purpose of the meeting is to approve the resources required to upgrade your present QMS.

There will be little need to do a detailed review of the assessment process at the meeting because it has already been covered with the top managers individually. Concentrate the meeting presentation on defining what the project will entail, what resources will be required, the people who need to be assigned to the project, the project time schedule, and the role that the top managers will need to play in the project if it is to be successful. The purpose of this meeting is to

1. Get the project and project plan approved.
2. Obtain funding for the project.

3. Obtain commitment from the top management team to assign key individuals from their organization to work on the project.
4. Have a project manager named for the project.
5. Have top management identify the executive who will be responsible for the QMS.
6. Obtain top management agreement to be personally involved in redesigning and implementing the QMS.

Be sure to develop the agenda time schedule so there is adequate time for discussion and to get agreement on each of the previous six items.

Step 9—Appoint a Project Manager (QST Chairperson)

The project manager should be appointed during the top management meeting. The only thing left for the assessment team to do is to meet with the project manager and review in detail with him or her the final assessment report. When this is completed, the assessment team is disbanded. Many of the members of the assessment team are often assigned as members of the project team, which will be called the Quality System Team (QST) from this point on.

Summary

During Phase I, the assessment team was formed and completed the following:

- Compared the present QMS to Clause 4.0 of ISO 9001.
- Developed an overall rating for the organization's present QMS.
- Determined whether the QMS should be upgraded.
- Developed a plan to upgrade/redesign the present QMS.
- Prepared a cost-benefits analysis related to the redesigned QMS.
- Gained top management approval to assign a project team to upgrade/ redesign the QMS.
- Obtained a budget for the project team.
- Defined who would serve as chairperson and members of the Quality System Team.
- Turned the project over to the QST chairperson.

When these activities were completed, the assessment team was disbanded.

Phase II: Planning

Introduction

Now that the project is approved and a project chairperson has been assigned, a very detailed plan to redesign, implement, audit, and maintain the QMS must be developed. The Quality System Team (QST) must remember the "Five Ps."

"**P**roper **P**lanning **P**revents **P**oor **P**erformance"

The plan developed by the assessment team was a rough cut at what needed to be done and is not accurate or detailed enough to be used to manage a project of this magnitude. For the QMS upgrade project to be implemented on schedule and on budget, the QST must prepare a detailed plan that it has ownership for. It is absolutely imperative that the QST does not just rubber-stamp the budget and project plan that the assessment team prepared, or it will not have the degree of commitment to the project that is required to make it a success. The QST should not hesitate to change the plan and the schedule if it can be improved upon or is unrealistic. If the final project plan increases the total project cycle time or costs significantly (more than 10 percent is a good ground rule), the new project plan should be reviewed with the top management team and appropriate changes made to the budget. Remember that the assessment team has already notified top management that its estimate could be off by plus or minus 20 percent.

The following 15 steps will lead the organization through Phase II planning:

1. Form the QST.
2. Train the QST.
3. Define the support system that the QST will use.
4. Define the documentation formats and structure.
5. Block-diagram the major quality processes.
6. Define process owners for each major quality process.
7. Develop a list of quality manual and procedural documents that need to be written or rewritten.
8. Identify subcommittees.
9. Prepare and implement a communication plan.
10. Develop training plans to support the QMS.
11. Prepare and implement an Organizational Change Management (OCM) plan.
12. Establish a project file and tracking system.
13. Identify who will do the internal audits.
14. Select a registrar.
15. Update the project plan and review it with top management.

Step 1—Form the Quality System Team

The chairperson and QST members were appointed during Phase I, Step 8 by the top management team. It is now up to the QST chairperson to bring the team together and coordinate the team members' activities. To get this project started, the team chairperson should contact each of the top managers to verify that the individuals have been notified that they will be working on the QMS upgrade project. Soon after each team member has been notified about his or her new assignment, the chairperson should contact them by phone to discuss the new assignment and define when the first meeting of the QST will be held. Following these phone conversations, the chairperson should send a copy of the final report, an agenda for the first meeting, a copy of this book, and a copy of the related ISO 9000 documents to each QST member. A typical agenda for the first meeting would be as follows:

1. Introductions.
2. Review of the assessment report.
3. Develop a QST mission statement.

4. Survey the team to determine what team and problem-solving skills the individuals have been trained to use.
5. Develop a team code of conduct.
6. Develop a team member assignment description.
7. Define what training is required for the QST.
8. Discuss how a consultant can help with the project and decide whether one should be hired. (If a consultant will be used, a subcommittee will be assigned to make the selection. It is important to set a high priority in bringing the consultant on board as soon as possible, because the consultant can provide the QST training. The subcommittee should review the guidelines for selecting a consultant [see Phase I, Step 6] and use them to help select a consulting organization.)
9. Develop a schedule for future meetings and a detailed list of things that need to be done in the next 14 days, with individuals assigned to each task.

Step 2—Train the Quality System Team

The QST must have a very good understanding of what, how, and why a QMS works. In Chapter 2 of this book, each of the 20 subclauses in Clause 4.0 of ISO 9001 was discussed in detail. Chapter 2 provided the necessary information on the whats and hows behind a QMS. To add to this basic information, we suggest that all the members of the QST attend a formal class designed for ISO 9000 assessors. At a minimum, at least one member of the team should have this training. If the organization has selected a consultant to assist the team, the consultant will be able to provide the necessary QMS training for the QST, as well as the other required methodologies. The QMS training will take between 18 and 40 hours. It is best to provide this training in short two- to four-hour classes over a two- to three-week period. The next major training requirement for the QST is Organizational Change Management methodology training. Often, upgrading the QMS to meet the requirements defined in the ISO 9000 series results in changing the way many of the processes operate and the way people react to documentation. These major changes can have a significant impact on many people throughout the organization, and it is naive to think that these changes in operating philosophy will be embraced by the total organization without proper preparation.

The QST members must be very effective in the use of the OCM methodology. A typical OCM methodology class will take approximately 24 hours and include the following subjects:

- Pain management
- Cost to the status quo
- Developing vision statements
- The role of sponsors, change agents, and advocates
- Cultural and organization alignment
- Transition management
- Change mapping

Your consultant should be able to provide this training. If you are not using a consultant, there are a number of classes you can attend to gain the necessary expertise.

Step 3—Define the Support System
That the Quality System Team Will Use

There is no need for the QST to start from scratch. A lot of good books, computer programs, and educational classes are available that provide the QST with a jump start on this complex project. Appendix VI provides a list of available support tools. It is particularly important for the QST members to realize how today's modern technologies can simplify their assignment. Basically there are four technology helpers available to the QST:

1. Computer disk programs
2. CD-ROM programs
3. Audio-videotape programs
4. The Internet

Each of these has its own distinct advantages and disadvantages.

Computer Disk Programs

Many computer disk programs are available today. Typically they contain a complete set of procedures that can be easily modified to meet the needs of the specific organization. Some of them have interactive overviews of ISO 9000 concepts. They are relatively inexpensive and operate primarily on IBM-compatible PCs using Microsoft Windows™. Some of the programs can be used on a LAN so that people at different locations can work on the same document simultaneously. The disadvantages of most computer disk programs are that there is little automation and no sound. Most of the ISO 9000 programs are not designed to track the ISO 9000 implementation status and are not effective at communicating concepts to the total organization.

CD-ROM Programs

CD-ROMs are much more interesting to watch and operate than computer disk programs. There is a high degree of animation and sound to reinforce the QMS instructions. Most of the CD-ROM programs can be run on-line so that people at different locations can work on the same document. One of the two leading CD-ROM packages contains a feature that leads directly into the Internet so that the user can get specialized, customized advice from knowledgeable consultants. Typically, the CD-ROM programs are chock-full of good case studies and expert interpretation of what the ISO 9000 clauses truly mean and why they are important. This CD-ROM package also contains a complete quality manual that can be easily customized to an individual organization's needs. CD-ROM packages are more advanced than disk packages because most CD-ROM programs were prepared more recently than disk programs. In addition, the CD-ROM manufacturing cycle is more costly and the manufacturers have been very careful to provide a product that represents good value to their customers. In most cases, a CD-ROM package greatly reduces the QST's workload; however, because of the limited CD-ROM capabilities in most organizations, today's programs do not meet the need of providing a general awareness education for the rest of the organization. CD-ROM packages are also more expensive than disk or videotape packages—some run more than $5,000.

Audio-Videotape Programs

Audio-videotape programs are excellent for providing general awareness training and case study examples. The methodology is widely accepted as a way of disseminating information in most organizations. Audio and videotapes are extremely good at providing information to small groups. The disadvantage of audio-videotape programs is that they are not interactive and fall far short of helping the QST develop the organization's documentation and processes.

The Internet

The Internet is an excellent way of exchanging data among organizations. It is often used to contact other organizations that are implementing or have implemented ISO 9000. In addition, some consulting firms are using the Internet to provide on-the-spot help to their clients that are implementing ISO 9000. A great deal of information, data, and sample procedures is available to anyone who can effectively surf the Internet.

Is One Better Than the Others?

Figure 4.1 shows typical ways that each of the four technologies can help the QST improve its organization's QMS.

We personally recommend using a CD-ROM package complemented by videotapes to disseminate information throughout the organization. This combination is recommended because the CD-ROM program has the following features:

- Reduces cycle time and keeps the project on track by providing project management methodology and software. The planning function establishes the delegated tasks and milestones for the QMS upgrade project. The status function allows management to monitor the project's progress, preventing problems and delays.
- Reduces up to 70 percent of the documentation design activities associated with the creation of ISO 9000 policies and procedures. The system provides validated, electronic quality and procedures manuals and templates. These templates can quickly be modified to suit your business needs.
- Minimizes all implementation restarts and ensures that your managers do it right the first time. Actual certification checklists and real-life multimedia case studies prepare you for the audit by previewing test questions in advance.
- Eliminates many of your QST meetings by providing on-line training, document management, revisions, and validations electronically. The

Features	Disk	CD ROM	Videotape	Internet
1. Case studies	x	x	x	x
2. Standard forms/documents	x	x		x
3. Project management		x		
4. Training		x	x	
5. Best-practice examples	x	x		
6. Specialized consulting		x		x
7. Change control		x		

FIGURE 4.1 Comparison of Support System Technologies

system includes built-in security so that only those authorized can approve proposed changes to your electronic manual.

- Ensures maintenance of your ISO status through current on-line maintenance of your policies and procedures, thanks to the integrated on-line manual function.

- Cuts through the clutter surrounding the ISO 9000 standards and provides the organization with implementation tools that will enable it to be registered. Often, real-life case studies of other model organizations and their methods are provided, giving practical examples of how the QMS has been implemented by other organizations.

- Provides instant access to consulting expertise. You are one keystroke away from your quality consultant. Through the "expert" function, the application delivers valuable consultant field experience every step of the way.

- Provides Internet access to live consultant expertise. Through the use of the CD-ROM's Internet interface, users can communicate with the experts for their unique quality requirements, ask questions, and even download policies and procedures for validation.

- After the new QMS is implemented, the CD-ROM document control package provides automatic change control security and document change level control.

Step 4—Define the Documentation Formats and Structure

Subclauses 4.6 and 4.7 of ISO 9000-1 point out that all work is accomplished through processes. In fact, the total ISO 9000 series of documents focuses on a process view of the organization. The output from these processes can be tangible (products) or intangible (information). The QMS is made up of a network of related and interrelated processes.

Because your QMS should be built around and bring together many of the organization's processes, it is important that the QST has a common understanding of the process hierarchy (see Figure 4.2).

The different levels of the process hierarchy are defined as:

Macroprocesses   A group of major interrelated processes required to conduct a major business objective. These are sometimes called mega processes. There are around six to ten macroprocesses in an organization.

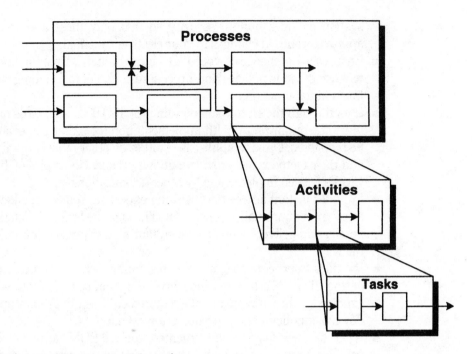

FIGURE 4.2   Process Hierarchy

Processes	A logical, related, sequential set of work flow (activities) that makes up a major part of the macroprocess. When a process is too complex to be flowcharted at the activity level, it is often divided into subprocesses. These subprocesses are shown as a single block in the process flowchart. Then the subprocesses are flowcharted down to the activity level. Processes are usually documented in operating procedures.
Activities	Things that take place within the process. They are usually performed by units of one (one person or one department). An activity is usually documented in an instruction. The instruction will document the tasks that make up the activity.
Tasks	Detailed steps taken to perform an activity.

Five tiers of documentation are used in most organizations (see Figure 4.3), although ISO 10013: "Guidelines for Developing Quality Manuals" refers to only three levels.

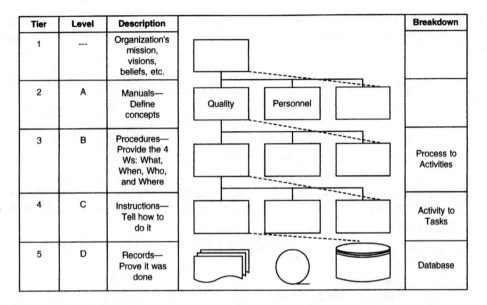

Tier	Level	Description		Breakdown
1	---	Organization's mission, visions, beliefs, etc.		
2	A	Manuals— Define concepts		
3	B	Procedures— Provide the 4 Ws: What, When, Who, and Where		Process to Activities
4	C	Instructions— Tell how to do it		Activity to Tasks
5	D	Records— Prove it was done		Database

Figure 4.3 Documentation Breakdown

Tier 1—Directive Documents

The Tier 1 documentation is the highest level of documents. Tier 1 documents consist of the organization's mission, values, long-range objectives, critical success factors, and visions. They are the documents that define and direct all the organization's activities and management systems. They are prepared by top management, because setting direction is top management's major role. Although the QST will not be involved in creating any of these documents, these documents guide the QST's activities. It is essential that the QMS be designed around the Tier 1 documents and support these documents. If any of these documents conflict with the principles set forth in the ISO 9000 series, the QST should bring it to top management's attention right away so that the top-level document can be changed. In no case should any lower-level document not be supportive of the top-level documents. The ISO 9000 standards do not address Tier 1 documentation.

Tier 2 (Level A)—Strategic Documents

These documents define what needs to be done and are conceptual in nature. The quality manual is one of the organization's Tier 2 document sets. These documents often define cross-functional strategies and responsibilities. It is best to keep these documents very simple and straightforward. They should explain what needs to be done and why it should be done, not how it is done. They provide direction on what the QMS is designed to accomplish. In the ISO 9000 series, Tier 2 (quality manual) documents describe the QMS in accordance with the stated quality policies and objectives in the applicable ISO 9000 series standards. To put it another way, the quality manual defines what is controlled and why. It describes the QMS structure; it defines the policies related to quality and links them to the procedures that implement the quality manual concepts. Using this approach, the documents that make up the quality manual will seldom be changed. The quality manual is the key document around which the QMS is built. ISO/DIS 10013 refers to Tier 2 documents as Level A documents. (See Figure 4.3.)

The format of a typical Tier 2 document would be as follows:

- Title
- Document number
- Responsible function
- Purpose
- Scope
- References
- Definitions
- Requirements (concept, policy, or quality element)
- Change level

Tier 3 (Level B)—Procedural Documents

The QMS is a network of processes that needs to be understood, documented, and controlled. Four key questions need to be asked in evaluating any QMS.

1. Are the processes that make up the QMS defined?
2. Are these processes documented?
3. Are the documented processes being followed?
4. Do the processes produce the desired results?

The organization's procedures (Tier 3 documents) are used to define the quality processes and, as such, play an important role in answering these four questions.

These documents are used to define the "Four Ws": What, When, Who, and Where. They focus on individual quality-related processes and show how the individual subprocesses and/or activities relate to each other. They do not go down to the task level. They are normally called procedures, since they provide direction on how these key business processes work throughout the organization. The procedures explain what different departments involved in each process do and how they work together to accomplish the business objectives. Procedures should define interfaces between people and organizations. They are not designed to define how individuals do their jobs, but they do provide a link to the job or work instructions (Tier 4). All of the quality-related procedures should support an individual or group of documents in the quality manual. A single quality manual–level document may have many procedures that define how the concept is implemented within the organization. For example, a document in the quality manual that defines a new product development cycle could have separate procedures written for new product release, manufacturing process qualification, new product reliability analysis, new product maintainability analysis, and so on. ISO/DIS 10013 refers to Tier 3 documents as Level B documents. The format for a typical procedure would be as follows:

- Title
- Document number
- Responsible department
- Involved departments
- Purpose
- Scope
- References
- Definitions
- Related quality manual document
- Change level
- Process block diagram
- Process description
  — Activity descriptions
  — Department responsible for each activity
  — Data flow
  — Required forms
- Prerequisites and training requirements
- Audit requirements

Because the procedures are very organization-specific, it is easy to see that the procedures will change frequently and that they must reflect organizational restructuring changes, data processing changes, and general continuous improvement changes.

Some organizations combine the quality manual documentation and the procedures into one document. We believe that this is poor practice because when concepts and processes are combined, the concepts can become a secondary consideration rather than the primary one. It also results in continuous disruption and frequent changes to the quality manual.

Most organizations will have a set of procedures that they call "quality procedures." We prefer not to separate the quality procedures from other procedures and as a result we call them "operating procedures."

Tier 4 (Level C)—Instructional Documents

These documents are used to define how the job is done. They have many different names, among them: work instructions, job instructions, setup instructions, job descriptions, activity instructions, and so on. These documents are written at the task level and provide detailed instructions on how the individual performs the job (activity). In a manufacturing machine-shop environment, a work instruction could be used to define, for a specific part number, how a machine is set up, the tools that are used, the speeds that the machine is set at, the self-inspection plan, and so on. In a clerical area, a work instruction could define the forms that need to be filled out, how to fill them out, and who to send them to.

Sometimes these documents are very focused, relating to a specific item or part number (e.g., setting up a sputtering unit to run part number 9376421, or how a manufacturing engineer will perform a design review). In other cases they are more general, defining what is involved in a specific assignment (e.g., a work instruction could be used to define what a quality engineer is responsible for, or how to run a sputtering machine). Because of the vast differences in the way instructions are used and the numerous areas they are applied to, their actual layouts frequently differ, even within an individual organization.

ISO/DIS 10013 refers to Tier 4 documents as Level C documents. The following is a typical list of the things that are included in a work or job instruction:

- Title
- Document number
- Department responsible for the documentation
- Purpose
- Scope
- Reference documents
- Definitions

- Activity block diagram
- Activity description
  — Task descriptions
  — Test descriptions
  — Data flow and related instructions
- Self-inspection plan or checklists
- Prerequisites and training requirements
- Audit requirements

Frequently, each assignment will have its own set of work instructions that together define the job and how it is performed. For example, most secretaries and administrative assistants have a set of work instructions that define their activities and how they should be performed. This serves four functions:

1. It allows a new person to fill in when an individual is sick or on vacation.
2. It provides individuals with a standard management-approved approach to the way they perform their assigned tasks.
3. It provides a baseline that is used by human resources to assess the individual job to determine whether the employee is receiving a fair day's pay for the work he or she is performing.
4. It provides an effective way to introduce and train personnel who have just been assigned to the job.

As you can readily see, the individual instruction set is unique to each job, and many of the documents can only be prepared by the person doing the job. This is particularly true in the nonmanufacturing areas and in the service industry.

Tier 5 (Level C)—Historical Documents

The fifth tier of the documentation system is the actual data recorded to show that a specific requirement has been met or an activity has been completed correctly. The format, who fills out the documents, how they are processed, and how they are stored are defined by the Tier 3 and 4 documents. ISO/DIS 10013 refers to Tier 5 documents as Level C documents, combining Tiers 4 and 5 together.

The QST should define the document format for at least the Tier 2 and Tier 3 documents, and preferably for the Tier 4 documents as well. The Tier 5 documents will be defined by the Tier 3 and Tier 4 documents. Appendix VII provides typical forms used in quality manuals, procedures, and supporting documentation. The documentation format should be the same as other Tier 2, 3, and 4 (operational document) formats, prepared by other parts of the organization whenever possible. The QST should obtain copies of each type of operational document and study these formats before the format of the QMS documents is defined. Usually operational documents are prepared by finance, human resources, purchasing, quality assurance, test engineering, and manufacturing engineering. If a wide variety of formats is already in use within your organization, this may be a good time to have the parties involved agree on a standard format for Tier 2, 3, and 4 documents.

Document Identification (Numbering) System

Once the documentation format is defined, a documentation numbering system needs to be developed. There are four common approaches to organizing the documentation numbering system.

1. *Independent.* In this case the numbering systems for Tiers 2, 3, 4, and 5 are unrelated. For example, the documents that make up the quality manual are assigned numbers in the order that they are originated. The same is true for the Tier 3 and 4 documents. To set the different levels of documentation apart, an alpha prefix is assigned. The following is a typical example:
   - Quality manual documents have a five-digit numbering system, starting with the alpha characters QM, followed by three numbers.
   - Procedures are numbered using a five-digit system, starting with the alpha character P, followed by four numbers.
   - The work or job instruction numbering system is a six-digit system, starting with the alpha character I, followed by five numbers.
2. *Interrelated.* The interrelated numbering system starts by assigning a set of numbers to the documents in the quality manual. Often this system reflects the 20 subclauses in Clause 4.0 of ISO 9001. For example, the quality manual document that relates to quality management responsibility would be numbered QM0100. As additional documents related to quality management responsibilities are added to the quality manual, they would be assigned a unique number by changing the last two digits (e.g., QM0101).

   The procedures that support the quality management responsibility would start with the alpha character P followed by the four related numbers in the quality manual document (e.g., P0100). This is followed by two numbers used to define the special procedure. For example, the document that defines the quality responsibilities for the Vice President of Engineering could be numbered P010002.

P   = Procedure
0100 = The document in the quality manual that the procedure supports
02   = The specific procedure identification number

3. *The organized independent document numbering system.* This system is a simplified version of option 2, which was just presented. The numbering system starts by assigning a set of numbers to the documents in the quality manual. Often this system reflects the 20 subclauses in Clause 4.0 of ISO 9001. For example, the quality manual document that relates to quality management responsibilities would be numbered QM0100. As additional documents are released related to quality management responsibilities, the numbers following the first two digits would be changed. This system allows for a maximum of 100 documents (numbered 0 to 99) for each of the 20 subclauses in Clause 4.0 of ISO 9001. The procedure numbering system is set up using the same 20 subclauses used in the quality manual. It is a five-digit system starting with the alpha letter P, followed by four digits (e.g., P0100).

P = Procedure
01 = Subclause 4.1 Management Responsibility in ISO 9001
00 = The specific procedure

As you can see, there is no relationship between the individual procedural document and the specific quality manual document, although the first two letters in each of the numbering systems are used to group the quality manual and supporting procedures into families of documents. In this case, the related quality manual document number should be referred to in the procedure text.

4. *Functional.* This numbering system starts with four alpha characters that define the type of document and the function that is responsible for maintaining the document; for example, QMMF would be a Quality Manual (QM) document that Manufacturing (MF) is responsible for updating, OPPE would be an Operating Procedure that Product Engineering is responsible for. This numbering system has the advantage that the document type and responsible function can be readily identified so that questions can be quickly directed to the right area. In addition, it allows each function to assign its own numbers to the documents it is responsible for. The biggest advantage of this numbering system is that it can be used for all of the organization's Tier 1, 2, 3,

and 4 documents. It works equally as well for the safety and personnel manuals as it does for the quality manual. The disadvantages to this numbering system are that it does not interlock tiers of documents and does not relate back to the ISO 9000 series of documents.

We recommend using the third approach, since it is a simple approach and still provides good grouping for the documentation. The fourth approach is the one that is most often used by large organizations that require extensive documentation.

Document Control

The QST should now define how the documents will be controlled and who will be responsible for controlling them. To accomplish this, the QST first has to decide who will be responsible for updating and distributing the documents. Many organizations make use of a document control center as a focal point for this activity. This is by far the best approach. Others rely on the function that has the assigned responsibility for the document to control the updating and distribution of its own documents. Still other organizations use a combination of these two approaches. The control center handles Tier 2 and 3 documents, and the responsible function handles Tier 4 and 5 documents.

At this point in the QMS project, the QST should define who will be responsible for the document control process and have them accept the responsibility. Document control will be discussed in more detail later in this book.

Step 5—Block-Diagram the Major Quality Processes

The QMS is made up of a number of processes that define how the organization functions. The major processes should be documented in the organization's procedures. To define the major quality processes, the QST should review each of the 20 subclauses in Clause 4.0 of ISO 9001 and define what concepts should be documented in the quality manual. In most cases, a minimum of one document is usually prepared for each of the 20 subclauses. In some quality manuals, common groups of subclauses are combined into one document and in some small organizations, we have seen all 20 subclauses included in one large document that makes up one section of the quality manual.

The QST should then define which major processes are used to implement each of the concepts defined in the quality manual documents. Once these major processes are defined, the QST should define the beginning and ending boundaries for each of the processes. It is important that the beginning boundary is a point that receives a definable input that starts the process into motion. The ending boundary should produce output to a defined customer, and the excellence of that output should be measurable. For example, the new product release process could begin with product engineering submitting the design folder to document control, and end with document control delivering the approved copies to the distribution list. To help you in defining these major processes, think of a process as a group of activities that takes an input from a supplier, adds value to it, and provides an output to a customer (see Figure 4.4). Note that all processes should have designed into them performance feedback activities. Typically when we discuss major processes, we are looking at processes that flow across organizations. These are the types of processes that are documented in the organization's operating procedures. Subprocesses or activities that are contained within a department would typically be documented in instructions.

The QST should then block-diagram each process to define which functions/departments are involved in the process (see Figure 4.5). It is not necessary to block-diagram to define what each department does at this point in the project. Figure 4.5 is a block diagram of a typical design review process.

The QMS operating procedures will vary depending on the organization and its products. The following is a list of QMS operating procedures Ernst & Young developed for one of its clients.

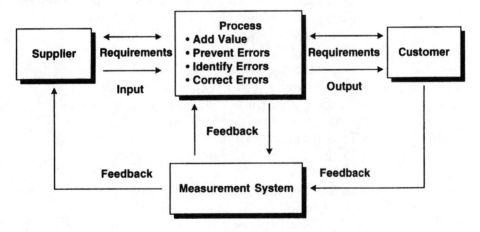

FIGURE 4.4 Process Interfaces

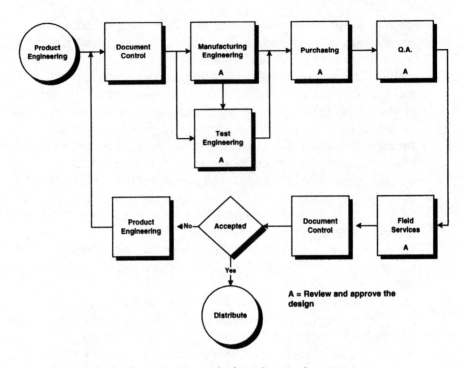

FIGURE 4.5   Block Diagram of a Typical Design Review Process

4.1 *Management Responsibility*
   1. Organization and Interrelationship Responsibilities and Authorities
   2. Management Review of Policies and Procedures
   3. Care and Maintenance of Quality Documents
   4. Integrating Quality into the Business Plan
   5. Continuous Improvement Planning
4.2 *Quality System*
   6. Quality Measurement and Reporting Systems
   7. Customer Satisfaction Measurement
   8. Product Quality Planning
   9. Product Failure Mode and Effect Analysis
4.3 *Contract Review*
   10. Compliance Contract Review Process
4.4 *Design Control*
   11. Feasibility Reviews

12. Product Design Reviews
13. Process Design Reviews
14. Product Design Verification
15. Product Design Validation
16. Design Change Analysis
17. Error-Proofing Requirements for the Production Processes
18. Production Part Approval Process (Process Qualification)
19. Production Process Change Controls

4.5 *Document and Data Control*

20. Document Control Procedures
21. Documentation Distribution and Removal
22. In-Process Performance Reporting

4.6 *Purchasing*

23. Supplier Evaluation
24. Supplier/Part Qualification
25. Supplier Performance Reporting
26. Request for Corrective Action
27. Scheduling Subcontractors
28. Purchase Order Review
29. Product Acceptance at the Supplier
30. Supplier Parts Identification and Traceability
31. Supplier Process Change Approval
32. Return of Defective Product

4.7 *Control of Customer-Supplied Product*

33. Control of Customer-Supplied Fixtures
34. Control of Customer-Supplied Component Parts and Assemblies
35. Loss-Damage Supplied Product Reporting

4.8 *Product Identification and Traceability*

36. Product Identification and Traceability Processes
37. First In–First Out Controls

4.9 *Process Control*

38. Process Capability Analysis
39. Preventive Maintenance Program and Controls
40. Statistical Process Controls
41. Standard Operating Procedures for Production
42. Off-Line Testing Requirements
43. Process Routings
44. Use of Special Characteristics for Control

45. Line Stoppage Procedure
46. Safety and Environmental Requirements

4.10 *Inspection and Testing*

47. Inspection and Test Procedure for Each Individual Part
48. Use of Accredited Laboratories
49. Calibration and Maintenance
50. Engineering Change Control Over Software Programs
51. Workmanship Standards

4.11 *Control of Inspection, Measuring, and Test Equipment*

52. Prepurchase Equipment Reviews
53. Equipment Capabilities and Drift Analysis
54. Equipment, Tools, and Fixture Calibration Process
55. Inspection and Test Status
56. Software Change Controls

4.12 *Inspection and Test Status*

57. Data Storage Retrieval and Termination
58. Status Identification Process

4.13 *Control of Nonconforming Product*

59. Product Identification and Controls
60. Materials Review Board
61. Rework Routings and Acceptance Procedure

4.14 *Corrective and Preventive Action*

62. Supplier Corrective Action Process
63. Reporting Corrective Action to the Customers
64. Engineering Change Request
65. Customer-Related Corrective Action
66. Returned-Product Test Analysis
67. Root Cause/Corrective Action Analysis
68. Request for Preventive Action

4.15 *Handling, Storage, Packaging, Preservation, and Delivery*

69. Handling, Storage, Packaging, Preservation, and Delivery Processes
70. Shelf-Life Controls
71. In-House Container and Packaging Evaluation
72. Delivery Supplier Performance Monitoring
73. Labeling According to Customer Requirements

4.16 *Control of Quality Records*

74. Records Collection and Report Handling
75. Records Retention

4.17 *Internal Quality Audits*
    76. Internal Management Self-Audits and Reporting
    77. Internal Quality Management System Audits (Includes House-keeping and Safety)
    78. Internal Product/Process Audits
4.18 *Training*
    79. Defining and Monitoring Training Requirements (Includes Annual Training Plan and Monitoring Compliance to the Plan)
    80. Job-Related Training and Operator Certification Planning and Controls
4.19 *Servicing*
    81. Spare Parts Planning and Provisioning
    82. Serviceability Analysis and Documentation
    83. Service Tooling and Equipment Identification
    84. Field Service Data Collection and Analysis
    85. Customer Interface Training Requirements
4.20 *Statistical Techniques*
    86. Statistical Techniques Training Requirements
    87. Design of Experiment Methodology

Step 6—Define Process Owners for Each Major Quality Process

By block-diagramming the process, the QST has defined which departments play key roles in each quality process. Now is the time to select an individual who will take ownership for coordinating and improving each of these major processes. Figure 4.6 shows the individual functions involved with the QMS. Each process needs to be assigned to a function and an individual within that function, who we will call the process owner. The process owner will be responsible for documenting and improving the process.

Because most of the major processes are cross-functional, no one at the middle management level has ownership of the total process. As a result, sub-optimization often occurs when processes are improved without thoroughly understanding how the change impacts the total process. The process owner is assigned by management to correct this problem and to improve the performance of each major process. The selection of a process owner should not be taken lightly because that individual plays a key role in designing the QMS, and an even more valuable role during the continuous improvement phase (VI).

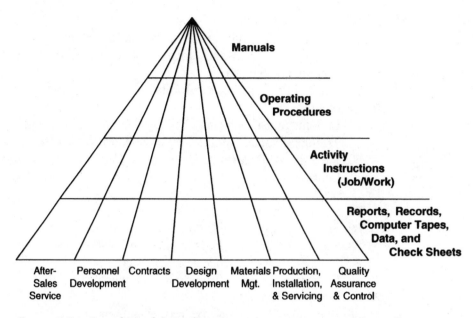

FIGURE 4.6 Overview of a Quality Management Documentation System

It is for this reason that we like to have the QST recommend the process owners and have top management make the actual assignment.

Select Process Owners

The process owner is responsible for ensuring that the total process is operating both effectively and efficiently. This is a key concept that must be understood to make the QMS work over a long period of time. Conventional functional management has worked well for a number of years and is probably the best type of organization, but it has its shortcomings. Functional competition, although healthy in some cases, can be self-defeating, since it puts all the functions in competition for limited resources. Frequently the organization that puts on the best show gets the most resources, but it may not have the biggest need. In other cases, resources are allocated to part of a critical process by one function, but interfacing functions have different priorities and, as a result, only minor improvements are made.

What needs to be done is to stop looking at the business as many large functions and start looking at it as many business processes. It is very evident that the process is the important element and that the process owner plays a critical role in making the total process mesh. The process-owner concept provides a means by which functional objectives can be met without losing sight of the larger business objective.

The process owner must be able to anticipate business changes and their impact on the process. The owner must be at a high enough level to understand what direction new business will be taking and how it will impact the process.

As Edward J. Kane, former Director of Quality for IBM Corporation, put it:

> In IBM's case, to accomplish these things, the process owner becomes the focal point of a new and permanent integrating structure. It introduces a type of matrix management (but is driven and controlled by line management) for the functions that operate within the process. The owner may require a "do" function (project office) which has representation from the functions/units in the process. These individuals would be assigned by owners of the critical subprocesses. They would provide functional expertise to the process owner and be the implementers of change and simplification within their subprocess. The owner is the voice of process capability to the business (up) and for process implementation of change (down) within the existing line management structure. Source: H. James Harrington, *Business Process Improvement* (McGraw-Hill, 1991), p. 45.

Perhaps we should briefly explain the choice of the word *owner.* Some organizations use the term *process manager* for the role. Although the term is basically correct, *manager* connotes responsibility for hiring, supervising, and signing paychecks. A *process owner* has no such supervisory responsibility. Another common term is *process leader.* Although not inappropriate, the word *leader* has so many connotations that we prefer to use it with great care. Ford uses the term *process sponsors.* Ultimately, your top management team should select a term appropriate to the organization's culture and the organization's accepted use of job titles.

Criteria for Selecting Process Owners

Ownership

Business processes seldom improve, because there isn't anyone who really feels that he or she owns them. Therefore, the first criterion must be ownership. One way to decide who feels (or should feel) the most ownership of a particular process is to answer the following questions. Who is the person with the most

- resources (people, systems)?
- work (time)?
- pain (critiques, complaints, firefighting)?
- actual (or potential) credit?
- to gain when everything works well?
- ability to effect change?

The answer to these questions should give a fairly good idea of who is the most concerned, and the most involved, with the process. Under some situations, the end customer of the process may be the best owner because he or she has the most to gain from its improvement.

Power to Act on the Process

A second issue to consider in process owner selection is that the major processes identified may come from varied organizational levels (corporate, divisional, regional, etc.). The owner should have sufficient power to act on the selected process. Because most major business processes are interfunctional or even international, most of them do not have someone in the organization's structure who is responsible for the total process. Consequently, the process owner must have the authority and responsibility for the total process.

The business process owner should be an individual who operates at a level high enough in the organization to

- Identify the impact of new business directions on the process.
- Influence changes in policies and procedures affecting the process.
- Commit to a plan and implement changes.
- Monitor the effectiveness and efficiency of the process.

Leadership Ability

A third criterion for process owner selection concerns the person's ability to lead a team. He or she should be

- Perceived as highly credible.
- Able to keep a group on schedule.
- Able to lead and direct a group.
- Able to support and encourage employees in their improvement efforts.
- A skilled negotiator.

- Willing to embrace change.
- Able to deal with higher-level management.
- Able to see the big picture.
- Unafraid to take risks.
- Able to live up to commitments.
- Able to handle poor performers.

Process Knowledge

The final criterion is that the process owner should have a good understanding of the process. If the process owner understands the total process, it is much easier for him or her to do the job, and there will be very few restarts. This is a desirable characteristic but is not mandatory.

Step 7—Develop a List of Quality Manual and Procedural Documents That Need to Be Written or Rewritten

Now that the QST has defined the content of the quality manual and the key quality processes, it should prepare a list of documents that will make up the Tier 2 and 3 documents. In many cases, some of these documents have already been generated and only need to be reviewed and updated if they do not reflect the current processes. In other cases, new documents need to be generated.

Two approaches can be used to progress from here. The QST could collect all of the related documentation and review it to determine what documents need to be written or rewritten. The other approach is to assign each document to a subcommittee or the process owner and have him or her conduct the review and determine whether a new document needs to be created or the old one is adequate. We prefer the second approach because it aligns accountability with responsibility.

Step 8—Identify Subcommittees

The QST will assign subcommittees and subcommittee chairpersons to develop the concept documents that make up the quality manual. These subcommittees are usually groups of two to five people who prepare the documentation and submit it to the QST for review and approval.

The Tier 3 documents (procedures) document the interrelationships between the activities that make up major quality processes. The block diagrams prepared in Phase II, Step 5, have identified the organizations that are involved in each of the major quality processes. The process owners should now meet with the managers in each of the departments involved in their assigned process to determine the amount of resources that the department has involved in the process and to understand the problems the department is having with the process today. Organizations that have a lot of resources devoted to the process or that feel they need to sign off on the completed documentation before it is implemented should assign a representative to work on the related subcommittees. These subcommittees are responsible for the following:

- Developing a project plan
- Flowcharting the present process
- Improving the present process if it does not meet the ISO requirements or if it presently does not meet the organization's needs
- Documenting the process in procedural format
- Defining the training requirements
- Piloting the new documented process
- Defining Tier 4 documentation requirements (instructions) and coordinating their preparation
- Developing and coordinating the Organizational Change Management plan that relates to the assigned document
- Defining how the redesigned process will be implemented
- Coordinating the redesigned process implementation with other subcommittees that are redesigning other processes
- Coordinating the implementation into the affected functions
- Measuring the effectiveness of the redesigned process

Each of these subcommittees typically will have a chairperson assigned to coordinate the committee's activities and a scribe (writer) who will be responsible for preparing draft documentation and keeping minutes of the subcommittee's meetings. For very important or difficult processes, a team facilitator is usually assigned.

Figure 4.7 is a list of typical quality-related procedures and the makeup of their subcommittees. The "R"s in Figure 4.7 serve as the subcommittee chairpersons and the "A"s are the subcommittee members.

Step 9—Prepare and Implement a Communication Plan

An updated, documented QMS can significantly alter the way the organization functions. This drastic change requires clear and direct top management

Procedure	Title	President/VP	Management Rep.	Quality Assurance	Marketing	Product Engineering	Material Control	Purchasing	Accounting	Production	Personnel	Warehouse	Quality Engineering
P-1	Quality System Management Review	A	R										
P-2	Contract Review			A	R	A	A	A		A			
P-3	Product Planning Development				A	R		A		A			A
P-4	Document Control		A	R		A				A			
P-5	External Customer Reporting		A	A	R	A				A			
P-6	Purchasing					A	A	R		A			A
P-7	Engineering Change Notice					R	A		A	A			A
P-8	Product Identification and Traceability					A	A	R			A		
P-9	Process Control			A			A	A		R			
P-10	Receiving Inspection/Test			R			A			A		A	A
P-11	In-process Inspection					A				R			A
P-12	Final Inspection				A	A				R			A
P-13	Inspection, Measuring, and Test Equipment			R		A							A
P-14	Inspection and Test Status						R			A			A
P-15	Control of Nonconforming Product			R		A	A	A		A			A
P-16	Corrective Action		A		A	A	A			A			R
P-17	Customer Complaints	A		A	R	A				A			A
P-18	Handling, Storage, Packaging, and Preservation					A				A		R	A
P-19	Quality Records		A	R		A				A			
P-20	Internal Quality Audits	A	R	A		A	A		A	A	A	A	
P-21	Training		A	A						A	R		
P-22	Statistical Techniques		A			A				A			R
P-23	Lot Setup Procedure - Cu & Br Pipe Fabrication						A	A		R			A
P-24	Quotation/Contract Review			A	R	A				A			
P-25	Supplier Approval Process					A		R		A			A
P-26	Return Goods Authorization			A	R	A				A			
P-27	Engineering Release				A	R		A	A	A			A
P-28	Production Process Qualification					A				A			R
P-29	Continuous Improvement	A		A		A			A	A			R
P-30	In-process Reporting			R	A	A	A			A			
P-31	Process Capability Analysis					A				A			R
P-32	Equipment Calibration			R		A				A			A
P-33	Layout and Functional Testing			A		A				R			
P-34	Lead Time						A	R		A			
P-35	Supplier Delivery Performance			A		A		R		A			
P-36	Production Scheduling and Inventory Management						R	A		A		A	
P-37	Shipment Notification and Labeling			A	A							R	
P-38	Release for Production	A				R		A	A	A			A
KEY:	R = Responsible												
	A = Approved												

FIGURE 4.7 Typical List of QMS Procedures and the Organizations That Make Up the Related Subcommittees

communication to all employees, explaining why the organization is focusing on the QMS. People in all areas of the organization need to understand their role in refining, documenting, implementing, and complying to this new system. One of the best ways to accomplish this is to have the COO or CEO issue a message that clearly states management's commitment to upgrading the QMS and outlines the role each person will play in this important undertaking. The following is part of a typical message:

> Your and my financial and professional security are dependent upon having customers that are delighted with our products and services. We have been diligently working on improving the quality that we deliver to our internal and external customers for more than eight years. Our improved quality performance is a testimonial to the fine job you are doing.
>
> We are now taking our quality improvement process a step further by upgrading our QMS so that it conforms to international standards as defined by the International Organization for Standardization (ISO) based in Geneva, Switzerland. Successfully implementing this upgrade to our QMS is crucial for our organization to stay competitive. More and more, our customers are requiring that we comply to these international quality standards. Our competitors have already started to upgrade their quality management systems.
>
> Each employee in our organization will be involved with this quality management system upgrade. Some of you will be called on to document and/or improve present quality processes. All of you will receive training on the quality processes that affect you and it is mandatory that you strictly adhere to these processes at all times.
>
> To provide the proper focus and sense of urgency on this project, I have assigned Irving M. Wright to be responsible for the project. Irving will report directly to me and will have no other assignment until the upgrade is complete. Ms. Mary I. Good will be taking over Irving's old assignment.
>
> Over the coming months I will personally be devoting a great deal of my time to this project. I hope I can count on each of you to make this project a success.
>
> *Walter L. Hurd, Jr.*
> *President and Chief Operating Officer*

The QST should develop a communication plan that prepares the total workforce for the changes that will be driven by the new QMS. Remember, once the project is approved, everyone will be apprehensive about what it is and how it is going to affect them. It's like hearing one shoe drop and standing there breathlessly waiting for the second one to fall. Without an effective communication system, resistance to the redesigned QMS will develop and productivity throughout the organization will drop off. It is absolutely essential that this communication start during Phase II and is reinforced through Phases III, IV, and V. The following are typical ways that this message can be communicated:

- Presidential letters
- Articles in the organization's newsletter
- Presentations at department meetings
- Classroom training
- Posted notices on bulletin boards
- Town meetings
- Open conferences where case studies are presented
- Audio/video presentations
- In-house TV network
- Screen-saver programs for computers
- Regularly scheduled status reports communicated through the management chain
- Recognition lunches

There is no one most effective approach to communications, so use a number of different approaches to be sure that everyone gets the word. The point is that top management must set the direction, provide the necessary resources, and communicate the message to the people who will be impacted by the redesigned QMS.

Remember, everyone absorbs information in different ways. Some like to read; others like to watch TV. The QST's communication plan must meet each person's need, and the plan must be repeated until everyone understands their role, and then it needs to be repeated again. You cannot overcommunicate on this subject.

Step 10—Develop Training Plans to Support the QMS

By now the QST should have a good understanding of the ISO 9000 series requirements. As a result, the QST can now design the training package that will be used for the rest of the organization. Basically, it can be looked at in three categories:

- The total organization
- The subcommittees and people who generate the documents
- Top management

The typical training requirements for each of these areas have already been presented in Phase I, Step 6, and will not be repeated here.

The most effective ISO 9000 overview training can be accomplished using a customized videotape that starts with the president of your organization introducing the subject and explaining its importance to the organization. This is followed by a professional videotape that explains what ISO 9000 is all about and includes one to four good case studies. With small to medium-sized organizations, this introduction is often handled at an all-employee meeting, where the president addresses a large group of employees. We have seen these employee meetings held with as many as 3,000 employees at the same time. An alternative to this is a series of smaller meetings held by middle management where they explain why the organization is upgrading its QMS, followed by a professional videotape and a question-and-answer session. Many organizations prefer this approach because it gets middle management involved.

For the QST, subcommittees, and individuals who are preparing documents, there are a number of subjects other than the ISO 9000–related subjects that they must master. Two of the most important are

- Writing skills.
- Organizational Change Management.

"You should write not just so that you'll be understood, but so that you cannot be misunderstood."

Ralph Waldo Emerson

It is absolutely imperative that the individuals who prepare the documentation have a good understanding of flowcharting techniques and have good writing skills. Typically, highly educated people prepare the documentation because we naively believe that people with less education may find it hard to express themselves. As a result, many people prepare procedures to impress their colleagues with their knowledge rather than to communicate to the people who must use them. The more-advanced organizations are taking a different approach and improving the capabilities of their employees so that they can effectively document what they are doing. Often these organizations provide the operating employees with simple tools like small tape recorders to encourage them to step forth and take on the responsibilities for preparing their own job instructions. The clerical support people who transcribe these tapes can take care of punctuation and grammatical errors if necessary.

Most of the procedures in use today cannot be read or understood easily. After a cursory glance, they are usually routed to the nearest file cabinet or trash can. Although today's fast-paced world makes receiving accurate and timely information more important than ever, the quality of most business writing lingers in the Dark Ages. It is pompous, wordy, indirect, vague, and complex. One critic noted: "Too often, business reports are wanting in everything but size" (see Figure 4.8). The QST needs to evaluate each of the quality documents to ensure that they are written for the user.

Here are some key factors that will help you simplify communications:

- Determine the reading and comprehension level of your audience. The document should be written so that all readers can easily comprehend the message. If one reader has an eighth-grade comprehension level, prepare the document for seventh grade. Because your audience all graduated from high school, don't assume that they can read and comprehend at the twelfth-grade level. Many college graduates' reading and comprehension levels are below the tenth grade; when English is a second language, the reading and comprehension level often is much lower than the general education level. When writing for people whose second language is English, write at a level three grades below their general education level, and use the dictionary's first preference meaning only.
- How familiar is the audience with the terms and abbreviations? Unless it is critical to the work assignment, don't use new terms and jargon. If it is necessary to use these words, be sure to clearly define them.
- All procedures more than four pages long should start with a flow-chart containing annotations that lead the reader to the detailed paragraph within the procedure.
- Use acronyms with care. It is better to repeat the phrase and take a little more space than to use a shortened version (e.g., total quality management—TQM, or business process improvement—BPI). Don't force

Document	Number of Words
Lord's Prayer	57
Ten Commandments	71
Gettysburg Address	266
Declaration of Independence	3000
U.S. Government Contractor Management System Evaluation Program	38,000

FIGURE 4.8 Examples of Good and Poor Documents

the reader to learn a new acronym unless it will be used frequently throughout the document. Never use an abbreviation unless it is defined in the document.

Data indicate that an individual with a university degree can read a document written at the tenth-grade level in 32 percent of the time and have a 34 percent better retention level than if it were written at the undergraduate level. It doesn't have to be long to be good. For example, when Boeing focused on simplifying its operating manual, the company was able to cut its six manuals down to one that was smaller than any one of the set.

Generally, we do not give enough thought to forms when we are developing them. Much needless effort is expended, and many errors are created, because forms are poorly designed. Good form design requires a lot of thought. The form should be self-explanatory. Information should be recorded only once. All abbreviations must be defined on the form.

Does a good form make a difference? When British government agencies focused their attention on form design, errors plummeted and productivity soared. For example:

- The British Department of Defense redesigned its travel expense form. The new form cut errors by 50 percent, the time required to fill it out by 10 percent, and processing time by 15 percent.
- By redesigning the application form for legal aid, the British Department of Social Security saved more than 2 million hours per year in processing time.

A number of computer programs will calculate the reading grade level for a document. It can also be done by hand. Robert Gunning, a communications expert who conducted clear-writing clinics for hundreds of American corporations, referred to this unnecessary complexity as "The Fog." Recognizing that the two most important factors affecting readability are sentence length and word familiarity, Gunning developed a scientific method for measuring the clarity of a written piece. His premise was simple. Long sentences and big words, particularly when combined, can bore, confuse, or, worst of all, alienate the reader.

Consider a typical business letter presented in Robert Gunning's and Douglas Mueller's booklet, *How to Take the Fog Out of Writing.*

In accordance with suggestions embodied in your memorandum of June 5, issuance of a supplement to the April report was undertaken. Two (2) copies of said supplement are enclosed herewith for your information and records. We beg to thank you gratefully for this thoughtful suggestion and hope that you give forthcoming reports the same sort of careful consideration.

Deciphering the meaning of such foggy writing requires time and energy, reduces efficiency and profits, and leads to misunderstandings and mistakes. Unfamiliar words and an unwieldy sentence structure distract the reader from the essential element of a business communication—the ideas.

In the previous example, the same ideas could be expressed more effectively by writing:

> On June 5, you suggested we issue a supplement to the April report. Here are two copies of it for you. Thanks for your thoughtful suggestions. Keep them coming.

Businesspeople often mistakenly assume their writing style must be ponderous to be authoritative. Consequently, their writing sounds impersonal, unclear, and occasionally even menacing. Far from sounding impressive, they succeed only in making their correspondence harder than necessary to read and understand.

Anyone can learn to write better by using a two-step process. First, measure the complexity of your prose using Gunning's Fog Index; then, follow the basic guidelines of good writing discussed later in this book.

To Calculate the Fog Index

Select a writing sample—The sample should be at least 100 words. The larger the sample, the more reliable the results. To analyze the readability of a long manuscript, select a number of samples at random throughout the piece.

Calculate the average sentence length—Determine the average number of words per sentence by counting the number of words in the sample, then dividing it by the total number of sentences. Treat independent clauses as separate sentences.

Determine the percentage of multisyllabic words—Count the number of words containing three or more syllables, excluding

- Capitalized words
- Combinations of short, easy words (e.g., bookkeeper, stockbroker, businessman)
- Verb forms made into three syllables by adding suffixes such as "-ed" or "-es" (e.g., created, trespasses, repeated). Do include those ending in "-ing" or "-ly" (e.g., increasingly).

Graph the results on the readability index (sometimes called the Fog Index)—To ease the arithmetic, *The American People's Encyclopedia* (pages 16–38) published a graph to visually measure the complexity of a piece of writing (see Figure 4.9). Simply place an X on the right column, indicating the average number of words per sentence in your sample. Then place another X on the left column, indicating the percentage of multisyllabic words. Draw a line connecting the X's. The point where this line crosses the center column of the graph is the readability index.

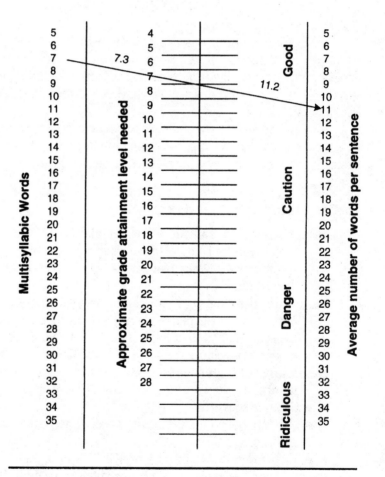

Figure 4.9 Readability Index

In Figure 4.9, the average number of words per sentence is 11.2, the percentage of multisyllabic words is 7.3, and the readability index is 7.7. Use the following as a guideline:

	College Graduates	**High School Graduates**
Good	10 or less	8 or less
Caution	10.1 to 16	8.1 to 12
Danger	16.1 to 22	12 to 14
Ridiculous	above 22	above 14

The index numbers roughly **correspond** to the reading **comprehension** levels of children and adults in **various** grades. The lower the index, the **easier** the piece is to **comprehend.** For instance, an 8 **indicates** that to read your sample with ease, the person should have at least an eighth-grade level of **ability.** A 15 requires **achievement** at the college level, and so on.

Do not confuse reading level with **intelligence** level. You do not have to write at the college level to challenge your readers. In fact, anything above a 10 rating would challenge the **average** college student. Most best-selling novels rate between 8 and 10. *Reader's Digest* rates a 10. *Time* rates an 11. *The Atlantic* rates a 12. Most business memos, letters, and reports are more **difficult** to read.

A high rating alone does not mean that your writing cannot be understood. It suggests that your readers will have to work harder to make sense of what you are saying. Sustained reading of complex **material** is very tiring. Why not make it **easier** for them?

Let's go back and analyze the last three paragraphs to see at what level they were written.

1. There are 179 words in three paragraphs.
2. The average number of words per sentence is 11.2 words (179 words divided by 16 sentences).
3. There are 13 words with three or more syllables that do not comply with the exclusion rules. To aid you in understanding this step, each multisyllabic word that did not meet the exclusion rule is highlighted in bold type in all three paragraphs.
4. By dividing 13 (multisyllabic words) by 179 (the total number of words in the three paragraphs), we find that 7.3 percent of the words are multisyllabic.
5. Go to Figure 4.9 (Readability Index) and draw a line from 7.3 percent on the left-hand scale (labeled Multisyllabic Words) to 11.2 on the right-hand scale (labeled Average Number of Words per Sentence). You will

note that this line intersects the center line (labeled Approximate Grade-Attainment Level Needed) between 7 and 8. Based on these calculations, the three paragraphs being evaluated were written for people who have an eighth-grade level of ability.

Unfortunately, this method does not measure the logical progression of ideas, nor can it determine if you used the right words. A low readability rating is no guarantee of good writing, but a high score indicates bad writing.

Good business writing, like any other skill, requires practice. To improve, try to spend 20 minutes each week analyzing and revising your memos, letters, and reports. Above all, try to write the same way you speak.

Consider These Tips from Gunning and Mueller

- Strive for simplicity and brevity. Don't rely on long words when short ones may be just as effective. For example, replace *endeavor* with *try, objective* with *aim, commence* with *begin,* and *aggregate* with *total.*
- Don't rely on passive verbs. Use the active voice. Write "we discussed" instead of "we had a discussion about."
- Avoid pomposity. Rather than write

The number of persons to attend any one of the various functions planned for June 10 cannot, of course, be reliably estimated until shortly before that date. It is therefore desirable that the detailed planning be based, and that tentative but noncommitting preparatory measures be initiated, on the assumption that there will be capacity attendance at all functions and that there may be overflows at some.

simply say

We have no way of telling until shortly before June 10 how many will attend that day's functions. We should plan, therefore, for capacity or even overflow crowds.

- Delete unnecessary words. Words and phrases like *herewith, this is to inform you that, the necessity of,* and *in our effort to* add bulk, not understanding.
- Keep sentences short and simple. Don't overburden them with several thoughts at once. Punctuate them appropriately to clarify the meaning, and divide the material into digestible bites.
- Be precise. Don't burden the reader with unnecessary information, or leave out important facts. Include relevant names, dates, and details.

- Avoid hedging. Words like *seems, perhaps, possible,* and *might* sound weak and uncertain. The fewer qualifiers you use, the more confident you sound.

Work hard at making the QMS documents easy to read. Develop an easy-to-follow hierarchical numbering system. Design the document format so that there is a lot of white space. Use 12-point letters for the body of the text and 14-point bold for headings. Make your line spacing 1.5 or 2. Use bullets followed with a short statement starting with a verb. Use these bullet points to help the reader understand what action needs to be taken. In short, impress your readers with the value and intelligence of your ideas, not with the sound of your words or the convolutions of your sentences. You may be surprised at their positive response.

Organizational Change Management Training

Organizational Change Management skills become a very critical requirement for all of the individuals involved in implementing the new upgraded QMS. At a minimum, 16 hours of OCM training should be provided to everyone involved in implementing Tier 2 or Tier 3 documents. (See Appendix V for more information on OCM.)

Step 11—Prepare and Implement an Organizational Change Management (OCM) Plan

An OCM plan should ultimately be prepared at two levels:

1. For the total QMS
2. For each individual Tier 2 and Tier 3 document

The total QMS OCM plan can be prepared during this activity, provided that any additional assessment required for its development is completed. Typically, the individual plans for Tier 2 and Tier 3 documents should be developed only after the redesign has been accomplished in Phase III. The reason for this distinction is that project-specific change plans must be predicated on an assessment of the risk factors implicit in the specific change. Understanding of the principles of managing change tends to be theoretical at best, until a very concrete and specific change is undertaken. It is at that time that the specific risks cease being "theoretical" and become readily apparent.

For both the total QMS level, and for individual tier plans, an assessment of the risk factors associated with the change should be made. Experience tells us that the most common implementation risks are as follows:

Cost of the Status Quo

- Is the cost of change perceived to be greater than the cost of the status quo? What price is the organization currently paying for past implementation failures?

Vision Clarity

- How clear is the definition of the future state at a strategic and tactical level? Are people, process, and technology requirements of the future state defined?

Sponsor Commitment

- How strong is the commitment of those individuals with the power to legitimize the change?

Change Agent and Advocacy Skills

- How skilled are the change agents in developing transition management plans? Are they knowledgeable and experienced enough to address the human aspects of change management?

Target Response

- How resistant to the change are those individuals who must change the way they work?

Culture/Organizational Alignment

- How consistent or inconsistent is the change with the existing culture?
- How consistent or inconsistent are the current reward, recognition, performance management, compensation, employment, and communication mechanisms with the objectives of the change?

Internal/External Organizational Events

- How prepared is the organization to deal with economic turns, market shifts, regulatory changes, changes in leadership, merger/acquisitions, downsizing that are/will occur in their industry? What events may occur in the near term and how might they affect the implementation of the change?

Implementation Architecture

- How comprehensive are the plans and support structures to manage the people, process, and technological objectives?

The central purposes of these activities are to (1) gain an in-depth understanding of the potential enablers and barriers to the successful business change implementation, (2) incorporate this knowledge into a participative implementation planning process, and (3) involve people at all levels of the organization in the assessment and planning process, to build the necessary level of commitment. Without an adequate understanding of likely enablers and barriers (whether people, process, or technology-related), transition plans will be less realistic and usable. In addition, people will be less willing to move to the future state. Effective transition management plans are developed with participation from all groups affected by the change and reduce implementation risk considerably.

The key to change assessment and planning activities is to involve as many people affected by the change as possible in the process of identifying and planning for potential enablers and barriers to the change. The results of this activity are then folded into a comprehensive transition management plan, which guides the change process as it unfolds.

The assessment and planning activities continue the work of technically assessing the readiness of the organization for the change and to identify the specific enablers and barriers that should be incorporated into the OCM plan to minimize the risk related to the project. One of the major tasks of this component is to design and implement a data-gathering process to identify reactions to the upcoming change. These reactions, from targets affected by the change, are then analyzed into enablers and barriers to the change.

As a result of change assessment and planning activities, the organization should have an ability to anticipate and manage implementation risks and to validate and generate the appropriate level of commitment needed to ensure business results. The transition management plan should provide strategies and tactics for managing the implementation risk.

One of the key decisions of the team at this juncture is the level of detail (and therefore the investment to be made) appropriate in assessing the answers to the preceding questions. Possibilities range from a minimal assessment (e.g., having the team members themselves provide subjective answers to the questions) to extensive interviewing, use of focus groups, evaluation of strength and weaknesses of past implementations, and the like. The extent of change to be undertaken, that is, the amount of disruption of expectations and status quo, should guide the decision regarding the investment to be made in assessment prior to the development of a total QMS plan. Competent consultants should have access to, and experience with, the variety of instruments available to conduct thorough assessments. The two basic types of OCM assessments are:

Change Readiness Assessment—This executive perspective of the organization's "fitness" for the change is created by looking at the organization's history of implementing change; projecting the impact of the change; looking at resistance, culture, synergy, sponsors, change inventory, and priority assessment of the organization.

Organizational Alignment Assessment—This assessment details the current state in light of the future-state context in the areas of organizational structure, compensation, benefits and rewards, performance management, leadership, management development, communications, human resource utilization, and education and training.

The QST should prepare the OCM plan that supports the total redesign of the QMS. The plan should respond to the information obtained in the assessment and, at a minimum, include:

Change Role Maps—The change role map identifies, and depicts the relationships between, the major constituency groups (sponsors, advocates, agents, targets) affected by the change. The change role map also identifies supporting and nonsupporting managers at all levels, and the individuals to fill the following key roles:

- Initiating sponsor
- Sustaining sponsor
- Change agent
- Change targets
- Change advocates

In any change process, there are five different types of roles that individuals involved in the change play:

1. *Initiating sponsor* is the individual or group with the power to initiate or legitimize the change for all the affected people in the organization.
2. *Sustaining sponsor* is the individual or group with the political, logistic, and economic proximity to the people who actually have to change. We often talk about initiating sponsors as senior management and sustaining sponsors as middle management, but that's not necessarily the case. Often sponsors can be people in the organization who have no real line power but have significant influence as a result of relationships with the people affected by the change, past successes of the individual, knowledge, or power.
3. *Change agent* is the individual or group with responsibility for implementing the change. They are given this responsibility by a sponsor. Although agents may not have the power to legitimize change, or to

motivate the members of the organization to change, they certainly have the responsibility for making it happen.

4. *Change target* is the individual or group who must actually change. There really is nothing derogative associated with the word *target*. In fact, it's really more of an indication of where the resources that are allocated to any specific project must be focused to achieve successful change.

5. *Change advocate* is an individual or group who wants to have an item changed but lacks sponsorship. Change advocates' role is to advise, influence, and lobby in support of the change.

People involved in the change process often fill more than one role, and their role often changes during different phases of the change process. For example, a middle manager may be a change target until he or she embraces the portion of the QMS that relates to his or her organization. Once middle management understands and agrees with the need to implement the change, they could become sustaining sponsors. That same middle manager could, at the same time, become a change advocate for another middle manager in another function.

The subcommittee needs to identify the role of every individual who is impacted with the part of the QMS that is being implemented. The formal organizational structure can be used to help develop a change role map (see Figure 4.10).

In Figure 4.10, Ms. A approves and funds the project. Essentially, she legitimizes the process. Ms. A is known as the initiating sponsor. As the initiating sponsor, she is responsible for converting Ms. B, Mr. C, and Mr. D from change targets to sustaining sponsors and for ensuring that the three sustaining sponsors do not become black holes. Black holes are individuals who take information in but do not effectively react or disseminate the information. We have all seen managers who act as black holes. They receive a lot of information but do not make effective use of it to ensure the project is completed within budget, on schedule, and embraced by the change targets. To keep this from happening, Ms. A must convince Mr. D to serve as a change advocate to Mr. C. In this role, Mr. D encourages Mr. C to continuously support the change and to prepare Targets 4, 5, and 6 to accept and embrace the change. Mr. X provides the same services to Ms. B. You will note that Ms. E, who is the change agent, has no organizational power that can impact the change targets and, as a result, is very ineffective in getting the targets to accept the change. Without Ms. B and Mr. C legitimizing Ms. E's activities, the change will probably fail. The change role map provides a picture of the organization that defines weaknesses in the change process. It also defines the change training and the performance required for each member of the organization. As you can see, Figure

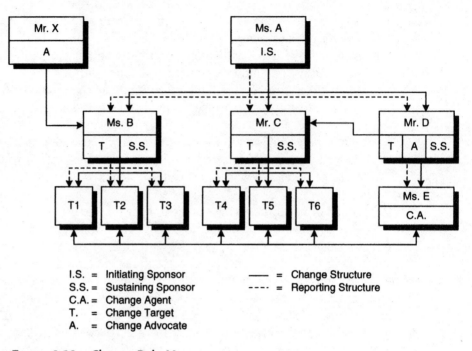

I.S. = Initiating Sponsor
S.S. = Sustaining Sponsor
C.A. = Change Agent
T. = Change Target
A. = Change Advocate

—— = Change Structure
---- = Reporting Structure

FIGURE 4.10   Change Role Map

4.10 presents a very simple change structure. In most QMS processes, much more complex change role mapping is required.

When the change role map is completed, it should be reviewed with all the individuals who perform roles as initiating or sustaining sponsors, change advocates, or change agents, to obtain their agreement. Appropriate training should also be provided to each of these individuals so they clearly understand their roles. (Note: This approach is based upon Organizational Development Resources' and Ernst & Young LLP's change processes.)

Enablers and Barriers Analysis Report—The deliverable is a document that presents the results of each of the assessment and feedback sessions and highlights the enablers and barriers identified.

Change Announcement Plan—This combines communication message and channel evaluations and recommendations into a single, integrated document that describes what should be communicated to whom, when it should be communicated, and how it should be communicated to successfully announce the change.

Communications Analysis—This should combine communication effectiveness evaluations and recommendations into a single, integrated document that describes what should be communicated to whom, when it should be communicated, and how (i.e., what channels, by whom . . .) it should be communicated. Smaller, more focused reports can be developed for particularly challenging or complex communications efforts as they arise.

Change Communication Plan—This should provide a comprehensive communication plan for managing change-specific communications throughout the change process, from the communications announcement through the celebration of successful attainment of the change project objectives.

The total OCM plan should be developed and start to be applied during Phase II because it will help offset some of the concerns that both management and the employees have. Figure 4.11 is a typical OCM timeline chart that

Typical Organizational Change Management Activities
Keyed to QMS Phases

Change Management Activities	Phase I Assess	Phase II Plan	Phase III Upgrade	Phase IV Implement	Phase V Audit	Phase VI Improve
Identify, Document, & Communicate Cost of Status Quo (Business Imperative)	■	■	■	■		
Create & Communicate a Future-State Vision (People, Process, & Technology)	■					
Clarify/Change & Obtain Initiating Sponsor Understanding & Commitment	■					
Create Infrastructure and Implementation Architecture	■	■				
Conduct High Level QMS-wide Change Risk Assessment (8 Risk Factors)		■	■			
Conduct High Level Organizational Change Plan		■	■			
Create Role Maps to Identify all Key Roles in the Change Process		■	■	■		
Conduct Tier Level Change Risk Assessments (8 Factors)		■	■			
Change Readiness Assessment		■	■			
Organizational Alignment Assessment (Structure, Compensation, Rewards, etc.)		■	■			
Assess Enablers and Barriers		■	■			
Develop Tier Level Transition Management Plans		■	■			
Develop a Communication Plan		■	■			
Cascade Sponsorship (Training and Performance Management Techniques)			■	■	■	
Implement the Communication Plan			■	■	■	■
Provide Change Management Training for Sponsors, Change Agents, and Others			■	■		
Form Change Agent, Sponsor, and Advocate Teams			■	■		
Provide Training for Targets (those affected by the change)				■	■	■
Implement Organizational Alignment Enablers				■	■	■
Analyze Effectiveness of Communications and Training Strategies				■	■	■
Monitor Commitment Levels of Sponsors, Change Agents, Advocates, & Targets				■	■	■
Monitor and Measure Implementation Effectiveness and Schedule Adherence					■	■
Modify Transition Management Plans as Needed					■	■
Track and Report Planned Versus Actual Activities and Results					■	■
Identify Opportunities for Continuous Improvement to the Change Process						■

It is evident from the above chart that a number of change management activities are iterative in nature and are not confined to one QMS phase.

FIGURE 4.11 Typical OCM Timeline Chart

highlights the OCM activities that take place during each of the six phases in the QMS upgrade process.

The chairperson assigned to each document or process, working with his or her team, should prepare an individual OCM plan that supports *that* team's activities at whatever time the nature and extent of the planned changes are sufficiently clear to allow thoughtful assessment of risks and the planning necessary to mitigate them.

The subject of OCM is a complex one, but it is a process and like any other process, once it is understood, it can be managed. When the team realizes that change truly is a process, the change activity takes on a set of new dimensions. The team begins to manage the change, rather than the change managing the team.

Step 12—Establish a Project File and Tracking System

The QST should set up a project file that will be used to collect the relevant data. Many good books have been written on project management, and to do a detailed thesis on the subject would not be appropriate at this time. At the end of this chapter, we have listed a few of the books that we like on the subject.

It is appropriate to point out that ISO/CD 10006, "Guideline to Quality and Project Management," has been prepared by ISO/TC 176 as part of the ISO 9000 family. This draft informational standard provides an excellent reference on what should be considered in a project plan to ensure its quality. This document gives guidance on the application of quality concepts and practices to the management of the process and activities in the project. It introduces techniques for monitoring and assessing quality in addition to the status of the project. In ISO/CD 10006, a **project** is defined as:

DEFINITION | A UNIQUE PROCESS CONSISTING OF A SET OF COORDINATED AND CONTROLLED ACTIVITIES, WITH START AND FINISH DATES, UNDERTAKEN TO ACHIEVE AN OBJECTIVE CONFORMING TO SPECIFIC REQUIREMENTS, INCLUDING THE CONSTRAINT OF TIME, COST AND RESOURCES.

Note 1: The organization is temporary and established for the lifetime of the project.

Note 2: In many cases a project forms part of a larger project structure.

Note 3: The project objectives and product characteristics may be defined and achieved progressively during the course of the project.

Note 4: The result of a project may be the creation of one or several units of a product.

Note 5: The interrelation between project activities may be complex.

ISO/CD 10006 defines a **project plan** as:

DEFINITION | A DOCUMENT SETTING OUT THE SPECIFIC PRACTICES, RESOURCES, AND SEQUENCES OF ACTIVITIES REQUIRED TO MEET THE PROJECT OBJECTIVES.

Certainly, upgrading your QMS meets the definitions of a project, and, as such, a detailed project plan and a project file should be established. The project plan provides a detailed path that defines how the project will be accomplished. The project file is an organized approach to collecting, storing, and retrieving information related to the project plan. There are 12 major processes that make up a project plan:

1. Strategic Project Management Processes
2. Scope-Related Processes
3. Time-Related Processes
4. Cost-Related Processes
5. Resource Management Processes
6. Personnel Management Processes
7. Communication-Related Processes
8. Risk-Related Processes
9. Procurement-Related Processes
10. Product Quality–Related Processes
11. Creation-Related Processes
12. Organizational Change Management–Related Processes

(Note: The first ten processes are defined in ISO/CD 10006.)

The project plan should consider each of these 12 elements and be structured to cover them in Phases II, III, IV, and V. The process of maintaining the project file is greatly simplified if it is designed so that each of the subcommittees can manage its specific portion of the project file and the related tracking system. Figure 4.12 is a timeline chart for the overall upgrading of a QMS. It was provided by Bill McClane of Integrated Systems Solutions Corp., Inc.

The project plan can be very complex. For example, to start the QMS upgrade, the quality manager of Symbol Technologies wrote a plan that had 267 activities, and that was just to create the quality manual.

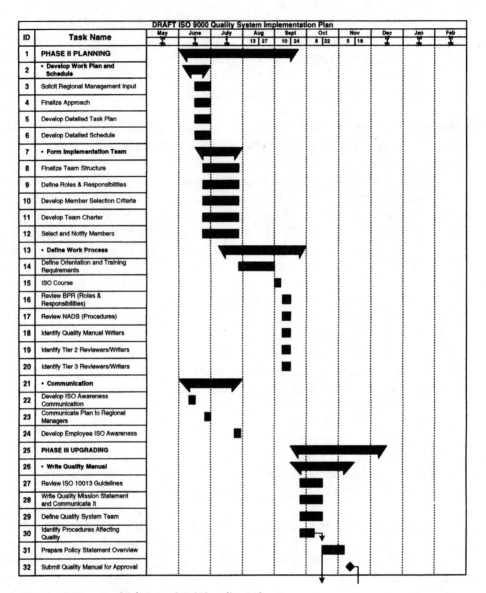

ID	Task Name	May	June	July	Aug 13 27	Sept 10 24	Oct 8 22	Nov 5 19	Dec	Jan	Feb
	DRAFT ISO 9000 Quality System Implementation Plan										
1	**PHASE II PLANNING**										
2	• **Develop Work Plan and Schedule**										
3	Solicit Regional Management Input										
4	Finalize Approach										
5	Develop Detailed Task Plan										
6	Develop Detailed Schedule										
7	• **Form Implementation Team**										
8	Finalize Team Structure										
9	Define Roles & Responsibilities										
10	Develop Member Selection Criteria										
11	Develop Team Charter										
12	Select and Notify Members										
13	• **Define Work Process**										
14	Define Orientation and Training Requirements										
15	ISO Course										
16	Review BPR (Roles & Responsibilities)										
17	Review NADS (Procedures)										
18	Identify Quality Manual Writers										
19	Identify Tier 2 Reviewers/Writers										
20	Identify Tier 3 Reviewers/Writers										
21	• **Communication**										
22	Develop ISO Awareness Communication										
23	Communicate Plan to Regional Managers										
24	Develop Employee ISO Awareness										
25	**PHASE III UPGRADING**										
26	• **Write Quality Manual**										
27	Review ISO 10013 Guidelines										
28	Write Quality Mission Statement and Communicate It										
29	Define Quality System Team										
30	Identify Procedures Affecting Quality										
31	Prepare Policy Statement Overview										
32	Submit Quality Manual for Approval										

FIGURE 4.12 Typical Overview Timeline Chart

With the complexity of the QMS redesign project, the large number of people normally involved, and the fact that many of the people will not be working on the project full-time, it is very important to develop and use an effective tracking system. Without this tracking system, the emphasis of sub-committee members is frequently redirected, causing the QMS project to slip

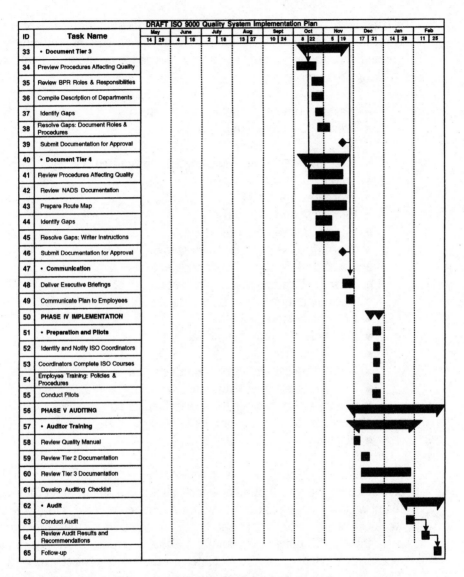

ID	Task Name
33	• Document Tier 3
34	Preview Procedures Affecting Quality
35	Review BPR Roles & Responsibilities
36	Compile Description of Departments
37	Identify Gaps
38	Resolve Gaps: Document Roles & Procedures
39	Submit Documentation for Approval
40	• Document Tier 4
41	Review Procedures Affecting Quality
42	Review NADS Documentation
43	Prepare Route Map
44	Identify Gaps
45	Resolve Gaps: Writer Instructions
46	Submit Documentation for Approval
47	• Communication
48	Deliver Executive Briefings
49	Communicate Plan to Employees
50	PHASE IV IMPLEMENTATION
51	• Preparation and Pilots
52	Identify and Notify ISO Coordinators
53	Coordinators Complete ISO Courses
54	Employee Training: Policies & Procedures
55	Conduct Pilots
56	PHASE V AUDITING
57	• Auditor Training
58	Review Quality Manual
59	Review Tier 2 Documentation
60	Review Tier 3 Documentation
61	Develop Auditing Checklist
62	• Audit
63	Conduct Audit
64	Review Audit Results and Recommendations
65	Follow-up

FIGURE 4.12 Typical Overview Timeline Chart (continued)

schedule and overrun budget. Many computer tracking systems are available on the market today, and most organizations are using one or more to track other projects that are being implemented within the organization. Almost any computer-based project-tracking program will meet the QST's needs. We like to use an on-line system so that the responsible person can upgrade his or her status as milestones are met. These milestones should be defined by each team and subcommittee as the individual project plans and milestones are defined. The following are typical milestones for an individual subcommittee working on a procedure:

- First meeting of the subcommittee held
- Project plan completed
- First draft completed
- First draft reviewed and comments submitted
- Second draft sent out for review
- Procedure approved by subcommittee
- Pilot evaluation started
- Pilot evaluation completed
- Third draft sent out for management review
- Third draft approved by management
- Personnel training materials prepared
- Documentation released and implemented
- OCM plan implemented
- Personnel training completed
- New process started
- Audit of document effectiveness started
- New process implementation completed
- Audit of document effectiveness completed
- New process survey completed
- Subcommittee disbanded

An effective tracking system reports much more than just what is behind schedule or over cost. It should report what the original target date was, what the new target date is, and what is due to be completed within the next two weeks. The tracking report should be customized to the individual who is receiving the document. The individual subcommittees are not interested in receiving detailed information related to the entire project every two weeks. They only need to be reminded about the status of their part of the project. Each of the executives should receive a report that provides the detailed status of the committees chaired by his or her employees, accompanied by a report that summarizes the overall status of the total QMS upgrade project, usually broken down to the functional level.

The QST should release an overview status report about every two weeks. The QST chairperson should contact each team or subcommittee chairperson who is more than two weeks behind schedule to find out how the QST chairperson can be of assistance and to develop a revised plan. Many organizations have established an escalation procedure for commitments that are more than four weeks overdue.

Step 13—Identify Who Will Do the Internal Audits

Before the QST can start this step, it must understand what an audit is. ISO 8402-1994, "Quality Management and Quality Assurance-Vocabulary," defines audits as:

DEFINITION | SYSTEMATIC AND INDEPENDENT EXAMINATIONS TO DETERMINE WHETHER QUALITY ACTIVITIES AND RELATED RESULTS COMPLY WITH PLANNED ARRANGEMENTS AND WHETHER THESE ARRANGEMENTS ARE IMPLEMENTED EFFECTIVELY AND ARE SUITABLE TO ACHIEVING OBJECTIVES.

Basically there are three kinds of QMS audits:

1. *First-Party or Internal Audits.* These are audits that are conducted by the organization to determine how well it is complying to its own procedures and imposed requirements and to identify opportunities for improvement.
2. *Second-Party or Supplier (Subcontractor) Audits.* These are audits of an organization conducted by an external organization that is considering, or is now purchasing, services or products from the organization being audited. The purposes of these audits are to define whether the supplier's or subcontractor's QMS meets the requirements set forth by the organization performing the audit, and whether the subcontractor has the capabilities to provide the desired products and/or services.
3. *Third-Party or Compliance Audits.* These are audits conducted by an external organization at the request of the organization being audited or by a governmental agency (e.g., OSHA safety audits). The objective of having a third-party audit of your QMS is to obtain a document from the auditing organization attesting that the audited organization is in compliance with a set of specific standards and/or set of requirements. To put it another way, a third-party audit (often called an assessment) is one that is undertaken by an independent body to establish the extent to which an organization meets the requirements of an applicable standard or set of regulations. In the case of ISO 9000, these assessments are conducted by an independent organization called a registrar. If

your organization wants to be registered, the QST needs to select a registrar that will perform an independent review of the upgraded QMS to determine its degree of compliance to the specific ISO 9000 documents (ISO 9001, 9002, or 9003). Successful completion of this assessment (audit) results in the registrar certifying that the organization met all of the requirements in the appropriate ISO 9000 documents. When this is accomplished, the registrar will provide the organization with a certificate of compliance and register the organization to the appropriate ISO 9000 standard. For the organization to retain the registration, the registrar will conduct additional assessments every six months and a detailed assessment every three years.

(Note: Third-party audits are not designed or capable of determining whether the subcontractor has the capabilities to produce the desired products and/or services. They are only designed to evaluate the QMS.)

Third-party assessments are not a new concept. They have been used in the United Kingdom for centuries. The concept began around A.D. 1140 with the use of hallmarks. Third-party audits of the financial systems of publicly held organizations have been a requirement for more than 100 years, creating organizations like Ernst & Young LLP and Deloitte & Touche LLP. Applying the concept of third-party registration of the QMS on a worldwide basis was a very important breakthrough.

First-Party Audits (Internal Audits)

First-party audits are often referred to as "internal audits." First-party audits can be divided into the following categories:

1. *Self-audits (often called self-inspection).* These are periodic reviews that are performed by the person doing the task to determine whether he or she is complying with the related instructions and/or procedures. They also are used to define whether the individual's output meets requirements. This category can be further divided into two subcategories:
   a. Employee self-audits
   b. Management self-audits

   Employee self-audits are normally defined in the job or work instruction and relate directly to the task being performed. They are not truly audits as defined by ISO 8402 because they are not conducted by an independent party.

Management self-audits are typically conducted every three months and evaluate whether the employees who report directly to the manager are following the related documents and whether their output meets their customers' requirements.

2. *Internal independent audits.* These are audits performed by individuals or a group that is not directly or indirectly responsible for the process or activities being audited. Internal independent audits can be further divided into the following:
   a. Product audits
   b. Activity audits
   c. Procedural or process audits
   d. Functional audits
   e. System audits

   Product audits can range from sampling parts during the production cycle by quality control to removing the product from the final shipping area and subjecting it to a series of environmental and stress test conditions.

   Activity audits are conducted by an independent internal group to determine whether an individual is performing his or her assignment in keeping with the work or job instructions. They are normally conducted in product-related areas of the organization by quality control.

   Procedural or process audits evaluate how well a group of departments is complying to the procedure and/or process and whether the desired results are being obtained. Typically the audit frequency and the audit checklist are included in the procedure. In some organizations, a special group or department is set up to conduct these audits. This group is sometimes called "Systems Assurance." In other organizations, the process owner is responsible for pulling together a group to conduct the audits of the process for which he or she is responsible. In multisite organizations, people doing the same activities at another site are often used to conduct these audits. In these cases they are called "peer reviews" or "peer audits."

   Functional audits are audits that review how well a specific function (finance, product engineering, production control, quality assurance, personnel, sales, etc.) is complying to all of the related procedures and whether its output meets requirements. These audits should be conducted at least once every two years and more frequently if the function is having problems in meeting cost, schedule, or customer-satisfaction requirements. They are normally conducted by a special department set up to conduct internal audits (Systems Assurance).

These departments are often the same ones used to conduct procedural or process audits. The peer-audit concept can also be applied to functional audits.

System audits are audits of a total system (e.g., quality management system, environmental system, safety system, financial system, procurement system, personnel system, development system, etc.) made up of many processes that may or may not be interconnected. These audits are the most complex and, to get meaningful results, require personnel who have a great deal of skill and experience. Large organizations set up a corporate audit staff to organize these audits and often call upon experts from a number of sites to participate on the audit team. In smaller organizations the departments that conduct the procedural and functional audits also perform this activity. If a very effective job is done at conducting the procedural audits, the resources required to perform this task can be greatly reduced, often making it possible for top management to perform this assessment. Of course, having top management conduct the system-level assessments is the ideal condition, particularly from the quality management system's standpoint. But a number of systems need to be audited, and it is often desirable for the top management team to audit many of them. The QST should consider which of the organization's systems top management should be involved in auditing (safety, quality, environmental, financial, etc.) and how much of their time it consumes before they define top management's role in auditing the QMS. There is no doubt about it. Top management must take part in auditing the QMS. The question is: How does the QST make the best use of the limited top management resource?

There are five types of internal auditors:

1. The employee doing the job
2. Management responsible for getting the job done
3. Internal independent activity auditors
4. Internal independent procedural and system auditors
5. Top management auditors of the total QMS

The QST should now define the combination of audit approaches that will be used within the organization and estimate the resources required to support these audits. Typically the self-audit requirements should already be in place because self-evaluation is part of everyone's job. In addition, product audits have been a responsibility of the quality control department in most organizations for the last 40 years and these resources should already be in place. As a result, in most cases the QST will only need to estimate the resources that will be required to do the work instruction, procedural, and QMS audits.

It is important that the procedural and QMS auditors be identified and assigned during Phase II. The lead auditor should be a certified auditor and a certified quality engineer by the American Society for Quality Control. If an individual with this type of background is not available, select the best candidate and develop a schedule to provide the required education so that he or she can become certified. The other auditors can be selected based on their specific process knowledge and their understanding of the QMS. Early in Phase III the internal auditors should start their training by attending a five-day ISO 9000 assessors' class. They will then prepare the procedures and job instructions that will be used to conduct the internal independent audits. These documents will include the QMS documents used by top management to conduct their audits. High priority needs to be placed on developing the audit procedures because these audit procedures will be used and refined during the pilot runs when the auditors verify the effectiveness and the degree of compliance to the redesigned QMS.

Step 14—Select a Registrar

Many small to midsized organizations do not pursue registration because they feel that it is too expensive and time-consuming. Nothing could be further from the truth; it is more advantageous to small and midsized organizations than it is to large organizations that have already established a reputation for producing high-quality products and services. Customers are often willing to accept a large, successful organization's QMS that is not exactly in line with the customer's idea of what a QMS should look like (e.g., GM evaluating IBM's QMS). But when the same customer looks at a small to midsized supplier, it often expects the smaller organizations to adjust their quality management systems to comply with the potential customer's view of the way quality should be managed. In the United Kingdom, the country that has the highest percentage of its organizations registered, the overwhelming majority of the organizations registered have between 60 and 250 people, and a number of organizations registered have less than 25 people.

Basically, the registrar performs an independent assessment comparing the organization with the appropriate ISO 9000 standard. If this assessment is conducted successfully, the registrar issues a certificate documenting that it has verified that the organization was operating in compliance with the appropriate ISO 9000 standard at the time the registrar evaluated the organization's process. The registrar will then list the organization as being in compliance with the appropriate ISO 9000 standard.

Although a lot of work has been done to standardize registrars around the world and within most major countries, there is still a degree of difference in how the ISO 9000 standards are interpreted by different registrars. One of the strengths, and at the same time one of the weaknesses, of the ISO 9000 series is the degree of interpretation that can be exercised and the variety of ways that can be used to comply with the standards. It is this flexibility that has been built into the ISO 9000 series that allows the standard to be applied in both the service and hardware industries. The disadvantage is that individual registrars (organizations) and registers (individuals) have slightly different interpretations related to some clauses in the ISO 9000 standards. It is very important to select your registrar (note: a registrar is an organization, not an individual) with great care, since this interface will grow into a long-term relationship. We see a number of approaches used in selecting a registrar. Typically, they are as follows:

1. The organization uses a registrar that the consulting firm has been working with.
2. The organization uses a registrar that has a reputation or left an impression during the interview that the registrar would be less stringent.
3. The organization uses a registrar that has a reputation or left the impression during the interview that it would be the most stringent.
4. The organization uses the registrar that has the most experience within the organization's industrial type.

Approach 1—Using the registrar that the consulting firm has been working with. The negative side of this approach is that both the consultant and the registrar will be looking at your QMS in the same way, and the organization does not get another independent view of its QMS from the registrar's standpoint. The advantage to this approach is that it is usually much faster and less expensive to get registered.

Approach 2—Using a registrar that is perceived to be less stringent. The advantage of this approach is obvious. It is easier to get registered. The disadvantage is that you probably will not have one of the better quality management systems and this registrar will be evaluating your QMS for years to come at a minimum standard. This approach is wrong for most organizations.

Approach 3—Using a registrar perceived to be the most stringent. This is a good approach because it ensures that your QMS is evaluated against the better quality management systems and that the registrar's comments over the years will help your QMS to improve. Its disadvantage is that it may take longer and cost more to get registered. It will also require more effort and resources to keep registered over the years.

Approach 4—Using the registrar that has the most experience in your industry. Using a registrar that has extensive experience in your industry has many advantages, because the registrar understands what your organization is doing and what is going on in similar organizations. The disadvantage is you must be very careful to ensure that the registrar does not share confidential information unintentionally with your competitors. In addition, using a registrar that just specializes in a single or limited industrial segment does not provide your organization with the broad-base view of what best practices are in the other industries. It is a lot like benchmarking an activity and just comparing it with organizations that are in your industrial sector.

It is very important not to make your selection based on the personality or credentials of the people who make the sales pitch. They probably will not be the people who will be doing the assessment or the follow-up assessments over the years. We suggest you take the following things into consideration when you are selecting a registrar:

1. In how many countries will the registrar's credentials be accepted?
2. In how many countries does the registrar have home offices, and are they the same countries that your organization has operations in?
3. Does the registrar's quality manual comply with the ISO 9000 requirements? (Ask for a copy of its quality manual.)
4. How long has the registrar been in business? (Consider whether it will still be in business 5, 10, or 20 years from now.)
5. How financially sound is the registrar?
6. What is the quality background of the key management personnel within the registrar's organization? Are they certified auditors or quality engineers by the American Society for Quality Control? How long have they been involved with quality management systems and do they understand how and why they developed? Have they held a job where they have managed the QMS for a minimum of ten years and was that organization successful?

7. How does the registrar measure customer satisfaction related to its operation? A minimum of 65 percent of the registrar's customers should rate it as outstanding.
8. Will the registrar provide copies of its assessment checklist?
9. What is the job description for the individuals who will be doing the assessment? Are these individuals full-time or subcontract employees?
10. How much will it cost and will this price include a preassessment review at your location?
11. How many people from the registrar's organization will be at your site and for how many days?
12. How soon can the registrar do the assessment? (Does this meet your time schedule?)
13. Will the registrar give you a list of organizations it has registered and is still providing surveillance activities over their QMS? (Randomly select from this list organizations and have the potential registrar provide contact names that you can check with to verify the quality of the registrar's performance.)
14. What is the cost of the full assessment and the follow-up assessments?
15. If there is a conflict between your organization and the registrar, what is the process to get it resolved?

Selecting a registrar is a very important decision and should not be taken lightly. Remember that a registrar is one of your suppliers. Take at least as much care in selecting the registering organization as you would a supplier that is providing a critical part to your most important product. The quality reputation of the registrar reflects directly on your organization. Organizations with long-term (ten years or more) excellent reputations are not going to risk doing a sloppy, inadequate assessment. Your customers will ask two questions:

1. Is your organization registered?
2. Who registered your organization?

Having the right answer to both questions is very important. Shop wisely for a registrar. First, for the quality of the registrar, then for their experience in your industry, and last for price.

Send out requests for quotations, and use the results to narrow down the potential registrars to two or three, then bring the finalists in for an interview. Ask them to bring to the interview the people who will be doing the assessment. The registrar should provide your organization with a list of the minimum credentials for the assessors who will be working with you. This is necessary due to the high turnover rates many registrars have in their assessment personnel. Look very carefully at registrars that use subcontract people to do the assessments for them.

The subcommittee should then carefully document the main advantages and disadvantages of each of the registrars and present these findings, along with its recommendation, to the top management team and the individual who was made responsible for the QMS. The final selection of a registrar should be made at this meeting.

The individual responsible for the QMS should notify in writing the selected registrar that it has won the contract.

When Should You Select a Registrar?

That is a hard question to answer. Selecting your registrar too early can have too big an impact on your QMS design. If you select your registrar too late, your organization may not be able to get the registrar you want to do the evaluation when you need it. The best registrars are very busy today, and their best auditors are even busier. We agree that when to select your registrar will depend on

- How busy the registrars are.
- When you want the registrar to do its first assessment.

We suggest that you select your registrar and define the person who will lead its assessment team 8 to 12 months before your target date to be registered, or before the end of Phase II, whichever comes first.

Step 15—Update the Project Plan and Review It with Top Management

Now the QST has all the information needed to update the project plan. This will include schedule, costs, and other resource projections. It should also include a detailed schedule for Phases II and III and the documentation subcommittee membership recommendations. The project plan should also now include the names of the people who will be teaching each of the classes.

After the project plan and the project file are updated, the QST should schedule a meeting with the top management team to review the details of the project and to obtain the team's authorization to assign the required personnel to the project and its subcommittees.

As a result of this meeting, the top management team should notify each individual that he or she has been assigned to work on a specific documentation subcommittee. The QST will also update the project plan and the tracking system to reflect the outcome from this meeting.

Summary

As a result of Phase II, the following was accomplished:

- The QST was assigned and trained.
- The major quality-related processes were block-diagrammed, and process owners were assigned.
- The documentation structure and format were established, and documentation subcommittees were assigned.
- Training plans to support the redesigned QMS were developed.
- A communication plan to support the QMS redesign effort was prepared.
- A list of required documentation was developed.
- Additional OCM assessments were conducted.
- An OCM plan was prepared.
- Internal auditors were assigned.
- The project plan was updated.
- A project file and tracking system were established.
- The registrar was selected.
- A consulting organization was selected, if needed.

Suggested Project Management/ Product Development Reading

F. Brooks. *The Mythical Man-Month.* Reading, MA: Addison-Wesley, 1975.

M. Cusumano and R. Selby. *Microsoft Secrets: How the World's Most Powerful Software Company Creates Technology, Shapes Markets and Manages People.* New York: Free Press, 1995.

T. Demarco and T. Lister. *Peopleware.* New York: Dorset House, 1987.

W. Humphrey. *Managing the Software Process.* Reading, MA: Addison-Wesley, 1989.

A. Johnston. *A Hacker's Guide to Project Management.* Newton, MA: Butterworth-Heinemann, 1995.

A. Randolph and B. Posner. *Effective Project Planning and Management: Getting the Job Done.* Englewood Cliffs, NJ: Prentice-Hall, 1988.

S. Wheelwright and K. Clark. *Revolutionizing Product Development.* New York: Free Press, 1992.

5 Phase III: Upgrading (Redesigning) the Quality Management System

Introduction

It has often been said, "Document what you do and do what you document. That's all that is required to comply with ISO 9000." That thought pattern is a gross oversimplification of what is required. Documenting and following bad procedures is not the intent of the ISO 9000 series. To meet the ISO 9000 series requirements, you must perform the key quality elements that are universally accepted as good business practices.

The purpose of documenting your QMS is not to create bureaucracy or to kill creativity with mountains of paperwork. The advantages of having a documented QMS that is effectively used far outweigh the documentation, installation, and maintenance costs. Some of the advantages are as follows:

- It provides an understanding of what management wants accomplished and who is required to do it.
- It provides a standard, proven approach to accomplishing activities and tasks.
- It encourages continuity of activities.
- It provides a base that improvement activities can be built upon.
- It provides a base for the audit activities.
- It provides a base for training newly assigned employees.
- It provides an excellent communication process.

- It provides employees and management with an understanding of what's going on around them in the interfacing departments.
- It defines the key business processes.
- It provides a way to measure performance and the positive or negative impact of change.

The reason an organization documents its QMS should not be to become ISO 9000 registered, but to help manage the organization better. As you approach documenting your QMS, focus on the documents that benefit the way your organization operates. ISO 9000 registration should always be of secondary consideration. The ISO 9000 series can be very helpful in considering what constitutes a modern QMS, but your processes and their supporting documents should always reflect the way your management team wants the organization to operate.

Documentation Tiers

The QMS is made up of documents from Tiers 2, 3, 4, and 5 (see Figure 5.1). Each of these tiers has already been discussed in detail in Chapter 4. In the ISO 9000 series, Tier 1 documents are not referred to. We believe, however, that the quality policy statement should be a Tier 1 document because it should be included in the organization's basic beliefs and should directly support the organization's vision.

The documentation system need not be complex and/or bulky to fulfill the organization's or ISO 9000's needs. The better documentation systems are concise, clearly written, simple, easily controlled, and very understandable for individuals with no more than a tenth-grade comprehension level. The QMS should get rid of documents that are not needed. Don't write documents just to satisfy an ISO 9000 auditor, if they are not value-added to the organization. You may have to write no-value-added documents for a customer, but never for an auditor.

ISO 10013—Guidelines for Developing Quality Manuals

ISO 10013—Guidelines for Developing Quality Manuals—was prepared to help organizations understand what should be included in their QMS documentation. It is an important document because it answers many of the most frequently asked questions related to QMS documentation.

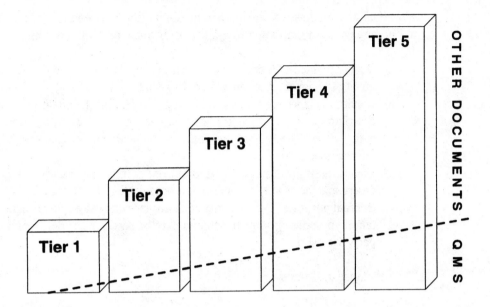

FIGURE 5.1 Documentation Hierarchy

Secondary Subclause 4.2.1 of ISO 10013 defines the purposes of quality manuals as follows:

4.2.1 Purposes of Quality Manual

Quality manuals may be used by organizations for purposes including but not limited to:

a) communicating the company's policy, procedures and requirements
b) implementing an effective quality system
c) providing improved control of practices and facilitation assurance activities
d) providing the documented bases for auditing quality systems
e) providing continuity of the quality system and its requirements during changing circumstances
f) training personnel in the quality system requirements and method of compliance
g) presenting their quality system for external purposes, such as demonstrating compliance with ISO 9001, 9002 and 9003
h) demonstrating compliance of their quality systems with required quality standards in contractual situations.

ISO 10013 makes a very important distinction between quality manual, quality management manual, and quality assurance manual. It explains

a) Quality manual—"A document stating the quality policy and describing the quality system of an organization" (ISO 8402).
b) Quality management manual—"A document stating the quality policy and describing the quality system of an organization which is for internal use only." *Note*—The quality management manual may contain proprietary information.
c) Quality assurance manual—"A document stating the quality policy and describing the quality system of an organization which may be used for external purposes." *Note*—A quality assurance manual would normally contain no proprietary information and may be used for customers and third-party assessors.

Subclause 4.3 states:

The simple term—*quality manual*—typically is used when the same manual is employed for both quality management and quality assurances purposes. In situations where a distinction of content or usage is needed, the more specific terms—*quality management manual* and *quality assurance manual*—should be used. It is essential that quality management manuals and quality assurance manuals describing the same quality system are not in conflict. The quality assurance manual may be offered for use by external auditors and/or customers in situations where the quality management manual contains material not relevant to those external purposes.

In practice, it is best to have just a quality manual. If proprietary information is required as part of the documentation system, we like to put the proprietary information in the related procedure and not include procedures in the quality manual. This minimizes the potential of conflicting directions.

ISO 10013, Secondary Subclause 4.2.3, Quality Manual Derivation, states:

A quality manual may:
a) be a direct compilation of quality system procedures;
b) be a grouping or clause of the quality system procedures;
c) be a series of procedures for specific facilities/applications;
d) be more than one document or level;

    e) have a common core with tailored appendixes;

    f) stand alone or otherwise;

    g) be other numerous possible derivations based upon organizational need.

It is obvious that the ISO 9000 series provides your organization with a great deal of latitude in defining the QMS documentation structure that best meets your specific organizational needs. In large organizations, the quality manual is usually limited to Tier 2 documents, with references to Tier 3 documents. A small organization can take on more of an operations-type manual format where Tier 2 and 3 documents are combined.

Is Documentation an ISO 9000 Series Requirement?

In the 1987 version of ISO 9001, a quality manual was not a specific requirement, but in the 1994 version, Secondary Subclause 4.2.1 states the following:

> The supplier shall establish, document and maintain a quality system as a means of ensuring that products conform to specified requirements. The supplier shall prepare a quality manual covering the requirements of this International Standard. The quality manual shall include or make reference to the quality-system procedures and outline the structure of the documentation used in the quality system.

As you can see, having a quality manual is a requirement for registration to any of the ISO 9000 standards. But even if it were not required, having a quality manual is just good business practice for the reasons already discussed. It is important to note that although a quality manual is required for the ISO 9000 standards, the standards do not dictate the format of your quality manual. This allows you to customize it to meet your organization's specific product customer set.

Quality Management Documentation System Structure: Three Generic Types

There are many right ways to organize an ISO 9000 QMS. The structure of the management system refers to how the various parts of the system relate to each other, and how the boundaries are defined for the procedures. This will become more clear shortly. There are three generic system structures. They are oriented around

- standards; or
- departments, functions, or organizations; or
- business processes.

In a standards-oriented system structure, your procedures would essentially follow the outline of the appropriate ISO 9000 standard. If ISO 9001 is the appropriate standard, for example, you would have a procedure covering Management Responsibility (Subclause 4.1 of the standard), a procedure covering Contract Review (Subclause 4.2 of the standard), and so on. In the simplest case, you would have a total of 20 procedures. In actuality, you may wish to address some of the sections of the standard in more than one procedure. For example, you may wish to have a procedure addressing Receiving Inspection and Testing (Secondary Subclause 4.10.1) and a separate procedure covering In-Process Inspection and Testing (Secondary Subclause 4.10.2). In any case, the standard guides the way the procedures are organized.

In a department-oriented system structure, your organizational structure is the primary guide for system development. You would likely have a procedure or multiple procedures for the Customer Service Department, procedures for the Production Scheduling Department, and so on.

In a process-oriented system structure, your procedures would align with the natural boundaries of your work processes. For example, you might combine production elements because they occur in sequence as part of the same larger process. You might combine the activities associated with printing a pick list for the day's shipments with the procedure for final packaging and shipping.

Each of these system structures has its merits and may be appropriate for a given organization. Figure 5.2 summarizes the advantages and disadvantages of the three generic approaches. Remember that these are only three models for QMS structures and that they have been presented as pure models (applying to the entire system). It is also often useful to combine elements of these pure models to form an effective hybrid. One of the most useful hybrids that organizations employ is to utilize the standards-oriented structure for the quality manual with the process-oriented structure for procedures, to get the best of both worlds.

These three generic system structures provide useful models for organizing the QMS. Whichever you choose, the process of examining the pros and cons of each of them in your environment will be very beneficial in clarifying your vision of the QMS.

Standards-Oriented	Department-Oriented	Process-Oriented
+ Easiest to ensure that all parts of the standard are addressed − May not fit what actually happens in your business	+ May be most natural for employees in some organizations + Easy to define implementation tasks − Do not address cross-functional processes • Mostly used in large organizations	+ Most useful for identifying improvements + Addresses inter-departmental links − Most effort to develop

FIGURE 5.2   Quality Management System Structures

Approaches to Documenting a Quality Management System

One of the decisions that needs to be made early in the documentation process is how the documentation system will be structured. There are four common approaches used:

1. Process-related
2. ISO 9000-related
3. ISO 9000 grouping-related
4. ISO 9000/process combination-related

All of these structures have their own advantages and disadvantages.

Process-Related Quality Management Documentation System

This approach parallels the documentation that already exists within your organization and is in line with your present business processes. It documents the way the existing processes flow. It is also very much in line with business process improvement methodologies (reengineering, redesign, and process benchmarking) that have been so effective at improving many organizations' efficiency, effectiveness, and adaptability. If your customers would like your organization's QMS to conform to a model other than the ISO 9000 series model, this is an excellent approach. In addition, it is usually easier to get the QMS accepted because it is designed around the way the organization is used to thinking about itself. It will also be in step with the organization's process redesign and reengineering activities. If this is the documentation system selected by your organization, the QST will need to construct a cross-reference list that relates the quality management documentation system to the appropriate ISO 9000 standard clauses before the organization can be registered.

ISO 9000–Related Quality Management Documentation System

This approach designs the organization's quality management documentation system around the specific ISO 9000 document that the organization has defined as applicable. The quality management documentation system will follow the same sequence as Clause 4.0 used in the appropriate standard. This approach makes it very easy for the outside auditor to follow. It is also an effective way to ensure that the organization's quality management documentation system meets all of the requirements specified in the appropriate standard. The disadvantage is that this approach is more difficult to implement than the process-related approach because it is difficult to relate it to the organization's normal business flow. Another disadvantage is that it usually does not fit in with the organization's other procedures.

ISO 9000 Grouping-Related Quality Management Documentation System

This approach is built around grouping individual, related subclauses in common clusters. For example:

- Core systems
- Operating systems
- Management support and control systems

The grouping of the individual subclauses brings like activities together, making it easier to understand and control the specific groups. It has the advantage of addressing each of the subclauses in a very systematic manner. Its disadvantage is that it is not laid out in the same order as the ISO 9000 standard, making it a little more difficult for the auditor to evaluate whether the QMS is in compliance with the appropriate ISO 9000 standard.

ISO 9000/Process Combination-Related Quality Management Documentation System

This approach develops the quality manual around the ISO 9000 series and the procedures around the organization's processes. This has the advantage of keeping the procedures in line with the organization's processes and provides a double check to ensure that all of the points defined in the relevant ISO 9000 standards are addressed. We particularly like this approach because it allows the quality management activities to be integrated into the organization's operating manual instead of being set aside as separate activities. This is a very important consideration because today's modern quality management systems are being integrated into the organization's normal management systems, thereby reducing the quality assurance and quality control support required to operate organizations.

Information Technology (IT)

In today's fast-changing world, the effective use of IT is required to be and stay competitive. The same is true for redesigning your QMS. We are not suggesting that you simply take a previously generated quality manual that is on a computer disk and just change the titles on the organization chart and the name of the organization. This concept will not work because there are major differences between organizations, products, and customer sets. Often, the differences between locations within the same organization make it necessary to have different operating procedures. Keeping in mind the need to have a very customized QMS, there is no need to reject the help that IT can provide. This will greatly reduce the efforts required to redesign the QMS and maintain it after it has been implemented.

The time of large three-ring binders of policies, procedures, and instructions is close to an end. These massive paperwork systems are frequently out of date and therefore are not used. In their place, a paperless information system is filling the organization's need to provide the required directions and help.

In upgrading or redesigning your QMS, some computer programs are invaluable in reducing the cycle time to perform Phases III and IV as much as 70 percent and work effort as much as 40 percent. These computer programs can also improve operational effectiveness after the new QMS has been installed.

Information Technology can help the QST by

- Providing an analysis tool that helps define the adequacy of the present QMS.

- Providing case studies.
- Providing expert advice.
- Putting the QST in touch with ISO 9000 knowledge databases.
- Providing sample documents and forms that are easily customized to meet the organization's unique needs.
- Providing consulting advice.
- Providing project management support to the QMS redesign project.
- Maintaining the documentation revision process.
- Providing a documentation interrelationship matrix.
- Routing documents for review.
- Providing QMS training.
- Providing a network with other organizations that are working on their quality management systems.

In the past, the best way to exchange information of this nature was in written form through books or standards, and this means of knowledge exchange is still effective. Today our written communication systems are being enhanced through the use of computers and videotapes to provide a more comprehensive learning experience. This is similar to the changes that our news media experienced as the newspapers were supplemented by the nightly news reports on TV and then by all-news TV stations like CNN.

The QST and the subcommittees should take advantage of supporting tools like CD-ROMs, videotapes, on-line documentation systems, and the Internet, for the previously mentioned reasons. The CD-ROM in the back of this book is an excellent example of how IT can support the exchange of information. The SystemCorp CD-ROM, "Harrington's ISO 9000 Step by Step," mentioned in the back of this book provides much more detail about quality management systems. To provide the same amount of information in book form that is available on the SystemCorp CD-ROM, it would take a book ten times larger than this book that could never be kept up-to-date like the IT approaches are able to do.

There are many advantages to having an on-line documentation and revision control system that should be considered by the QST. For organizations where this approach is practical, it should be used because it will prevent many of the problems that occur during the documentation, implementation, and maintenance phases.

The QST should not use IT as a way to drive the QMS redesign process but as an enabler that helps the QST develop an effective redesigned QMS in the minimum amount of time and at the minimum cost.

Designing an ISO 9000 Grouping-Related Quality Management Documentation System

Many business professionals, even those who have been through extensive ISO 9000 training courses, have said to us, "I need to explain to someone what the [ISO 9000] requirements are all about, but it would take all day." This perception develops for two reasons. First, the generic language of the standards makes it difficult for people with little experience implementing such systems to map the standards to a particular organization. This "mapping" is crucial not only for articulating what the requirements are but also for assessing an organization's current status relative to the standards and for planning an effective and efficient system implementation.

Second, when you read Clause 4.0 of ISO 9001 (the most comprehensive of the standards), you are introduced to 20 different subclauses (4.1 through 4.20). These 20 subclauses seem to be completely separate requirements, with little linkage between them. This makes it difficult to understand what value the organization will receive from implementing the standards. We have developed a simple framework that structures the requirements in an order that better shows the relationship of the various elements and makes the logic and the benefits of implementation more obvious.

The ISO 9000 requirements framework has three basic parts.

- *The core system* is the most fundamental part of the QMS. It includes the elements of the standard that are applied to all parts of the organization. These include Documentation Control, Training, Records, and Corrective Action (see Subclauses 4.1, 4.2, and 4.14, and Secondary Subclauses 4.1.3 and 4.1.7 in Figure 5.3).
- *The operating system* refers to the various parts of the value chain that are within the scope of the standards: Contract Review, Design, Purchasing, and so on. It also includes operations-support elements such as Statistical Techniques, Handling, and so on (see Figures 5.4, 5.5, and 5.6).
- *The management support and control system* refers to Management Responsibility and International Quality Audits. Management responsibility is specifically management's role in supporting the system, not to exclude management involvement from the other elements of the standard (see Subclauses 4.5, 4.16, 4.18, and 4.20 in Figure 5.7).

An in-depth discussion of ISO 9001 requirements was covered in Chapter 2 and will not be repeated here. However, since the core system impacts all

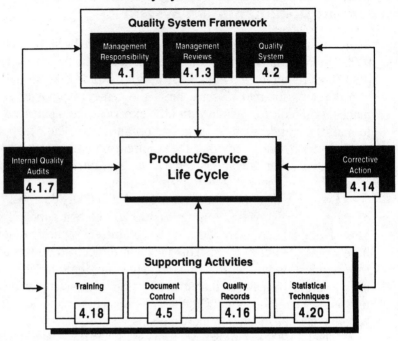

FIGURE 5.3   Core System Subclauses/Secondary Subclauses

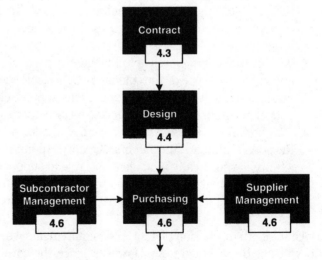

FIGURE 5.4   Operating System Subclauses

Product/Service Activities

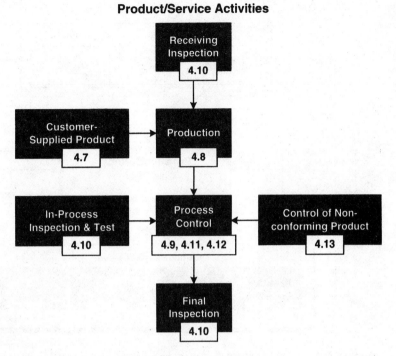

FIGURE 5.5   Operating System Subclauses (continued)

Product/Service Activities

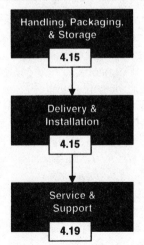

FIGURE 5.6   Operating System Subclauses (continued)

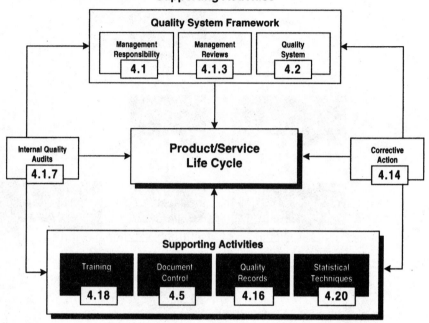

FIGURE 5.7 Management Support and Control System Subclauses

areas of the business, we will discuss it here in more detail. As already mentioned, the standards are primarily intended to help the organization consistently meet customer requirements. One of the basic premises that the ISO 9000 series is built on is that consistency of results starts with consistency of process execution. This consistency can be achieved through documentation, training, automation, or some combination thereof. Two subclauses of the ISO 9001 requirements are related to Document and Data Control (4.5) and Training (4.18), although the requirement for a documented system permeates the entire standard. In short, to achieve consistent process performance, *the way work is performed in all parts of the business should be planned and documented, and proper training should be provided.*

The next step is to execute the plan by performing work in accordance with the documentation and training. Next, there needs to be some mechanism in place to measure, or verify, whether the process is working; that is, whether it is producing the intended results, both in terms of customer requirements and internal needs. The Control of Quality Records portion of the standard

(4.16) addresses this need. Records are also referenced in various other parts of the standard. If records indicate that the system is not working properly, then there needs to be a mechanism in place for Corrective and Preventive Action (4.14). Corrective action directed at the system ensures improvement of the documentation and training that did not produce adequate results.

The message this framework provides is as simple as it sounds. In the ISO 9000 documentation, the relevant parts of the requirements that we call the core system are separated and not well linked (they are found in Subclauses 4.2, 4.5, 4.14, 4.16, 4.18). Reorganizing the standard into the core system, operating system, and management support and control system may provide you with a clearer understanding of the standard. You may have also noticed that the core system was put into the context of Walter Shewhart's Plan-Do-Check-Act cycle. Regardless of the labels used to convey the message, the framework provides a meaningful interpretation of the standards *for any business*. This interpretation should prove useful in examining, improving, or implementing your QMS.

As mentioned earlier, many people today interpret the ISO 9000 series as "Document what you do and do what you document." Though this is essentially a good guideline, don't be lulled into thinking that it is a sufficient rule. When addressing the various elements of the standards, there is definitely a judgment necessary as to the adequacy of procedures. For example, if you document your contract review process, but the present process does not ensure that the organization can meet the contract requirements, the new documentation is still inadequate. Perfect execution of an inadequate procedure results in inadequate performance.

Organizations that have pursued ISO 9000 registration have suggested that conformance to the documentation of the quality processes is all that is needed. Some consultants suggest that a key to getting registered is to avoid developing detailed documents so that auditors will not observe inconsistencies. Although some auditors might agree with this premise, the documentation should be at a level that ensures the consistent performance of processes and provides the needed level of direction when people are rotated into new assignments. We are using the ISO 9000 series as a basis for building a QMS that supports the organization's strategy; therefore, we should seek to apply the standard in a way that *ensures that an organization consistently meets customer requirements.*

Using this framework to guide your implementation can provide added focus to your effort. The other beauty of the requirements framework is that the core system can be applied to departments or processes that are not directly addressed by the standard. One of the necessary components of a

QMS is that it should be applied to all processes in the organization. For instance, you should use the same principles described in the core system to manage your finance, human resources, legal, or *any* other function, though it is not explicitly a requirement in the standards to do so. In some organizations, the capital allocation or personnel acquisition process is more important to their strategy and customer satisfaction than the manufacturing or order fulfillment process. Applying the framework will help you communicate the standard's requirements to the total organization and help you realize the intended benefits of ISO 9000 implementation.

Another effective approach is grouping subclauses under the following four major headings:

- Management Leadership and Involvement
- Quality Management System Support
- Process Management and Control
- Process and System Improvement

These four major headings provide an excellent way to group the individual subclauses within the ISO 9000 series.

- Management Leadership and Involvement
  - 4.1 Management Responsibility
    Quality Policy
    Responsibility and Authority
    Verification Resources
    Management Representative
    Management Review
  - 4.2 Quality System
  - 4.18 Training
- Quality Management System Support
  - 4.5 Document and Data Control
  - 4.7 Control of Customer-Supplied Product
  - 4.8 Product Identification and Traceability
  - 4.11 Control of Inspection, Measuring, and Test Equipment
  - 4.16 Control of Quality Records
- Process Management and Control
  - 4.3 Contract Review
  - 4.4 Design Control
  - 4.6 Purchasing
  - 4.9 Process Control

  — 4.10 Inspection and Testing
  — 4.12 Inspection and Test Status
  — 4.15 Handling, Storage, Packaging, Preservation, and Delivery
  — 4.19 Servicing
  — 4.20 Statistical Techniques
- Process and System Improvement
  — 4.13 Control of Nonconforming Product
  — 4.14 Corrective and Preventive Action
  — 4.17 Internal Quality Audits

Both approaches to grouping the ISO 9000 subclauses work well, and we don't see a specific advantage of one grouping over the other. Whether an organization uses three or four groups of the ISO 9000 subclauses depends on the unique situation within the organization.

Documenting Your Quality Management System

The purpose of the quality manual is to define the QMS, document the quality policies, and provide direction to management and employees. There are many options to the way you document your QMS, but, basically, the process of doing it is very straightforward. We suggest that you use the following 17 steps to redesign your QMS:

1. Define the documentation structure and the contents of the quality manual.
2. Form and train subcommittees.
3. Prepare individual sections of the quality manual.
4. Prepare flowcharts of the assigned processes.
5. Conduct process walk-throughs to verify the accuracy of the flowcharts.
6. Compare the present process to the ISO 9000 standards and identify discrepancies.
7. Change the process flowcharts to correct discrepancies and include suggested improvements.
8. Document the assigned processes.
9. Compare the draft procedures to the related document(s) in the quality manual to identify discrepancies and inadequacies. Then alter the documentation to correct any discrepancies and/or inadequacies.
10. Analyze each procedure and its supporting flowchart to identify activities that require documented instructions (Tier 4 documents).

11. Assign individuals or teams to generate the required instructions.
12. Prepare an interrelationship matrix and analyze it to identify missing documents.
13. Prepare missing documents.
14. Expand the Organizational Change Management activities.
15. Circulate the documents for comments and update them as required.
16. Send documents to the registrar for review and comments. Update the documents as appropriate.
17. Release the preliminary documentation for pilot studies only.

The results of Phase III will be a complete set of Tier 2, 3, and 4 QMS documents that are approved by the appropriate people to be modeled before they are implemented.

It is important to note that in the previous sequence of steps, the quality manual was prepared before the procedures. Sometimes procedures may be prepared before the quality manual. The sequence in which the documents are prepared is left up to the individual QST. In the long run, it will be an iterative activity where the quality manual and the procedures are aligned based on the ISO 9000 standards and the needs of the organization.

Step 1—Define the Documentation Structure and the Contents of the Quality Manual

As discussed earlier, the quality management documentation system can be structured in many ways. For example, the supporting procedures can be part of the quality manual or they can be in separate documents. It is rare to have the job or work instructions be part of the quality manual.

The QST needs to define what will be included in the quality manual. We suggest that the quality manual be limited to 25 to 40 pages. More and more organizations are moving to on-line manuals that use Object Linking and Embedding (OLE) to link the manuals with more detailed computer drawings or documents. We have seen manuals in the 10- to 15-page range that are far more useful than any 400- to 500-page manual. The manual should include the following:

- Title, scope, and fields of application
- Table of contents
- QMS statement of authority
- Quality policy and objectives of the organization

- Introduction to the quality manual and the QMS
- High-level organization chart
- Definitions and acronyms
- Individual quality manual documents (descriptions of the elements of the QMS)
- Cross-reference list between the quality manual and the procedures and/or work instructions
- Quality manual distribution control list

Remember, the quality manual is often provided to the external customer, so it is best to keep it very short, clear, and concise. For this reason, it is best to keep the procedures in another document set.

For purposes of our discussion, let's assume that we will be using an ISO 9000/process combination-related quality management documentation system. In this case, the quality manual follows the ISO 9001 Clause 4.0 layout. The procedures and the work or job instructions will follow the normal business process flow. We find this approach works best for most organizations.

During Phase II, the QST identified the supporting processes related to each subclause in Clause 4.0 of the relevant ISO 9000 standard. This action provides the information needed to define the documents that should be included at the procedural level (Tier 3). In addition, the plan and supporting budget developed during Phase II include the resources necessary for the formation of the required documentation subcommittees. At this point in this step, the QST should make a list of all the documents that will be included in the quality manual and all the supporting processes that will require procedures to be reviewed and/or prepared. A subcommittee and a subcommittee chairperson should be assigned to prepare or update each of these documents.

A member of the QST should be assigned to each subcommittee to act as the subcommittee's facilitator. This provides each subcommittee with an individual who has a good understanding of the ISO 9000 standards and expertise in team dynamics. If the members of the QST have not had facilitator training, they should attend a facilitator class.

At this point in the process, the QST should prepare a document that defines what the quality management documentation system will look like.

Quality Manual

The quality manual is normally divided into three sections, as follows:

Section I—Quality Management Documentation System Overview

1. Introduction to the Quality Manual/Statement of Authority
2. Table of Contents
3. Quality Policy and Quality Objectives
4. Organization Charts and Description of Management Responsibilities and Authorities
5. Overview of the Quality Management Documentation System

Section II—Quality Concepts, Philosophies, and Elements

- The individual quality concepts, policies, and elements are documented here. Often, they are aligned with Clause 4.0 of ISO 9001, or grouped in one of the two ways discussed earlier in this chapter.

Section III—References

1. Cross-Reference List to Other Documents
2. Quality Manual Distribution Control List*
3. Definitions and Acronyms*
   *Not required by ISO 9000 but considered good business practice.

Section I—Quality Management Documentation System Overview

Section I of the quality manual, entitled "Quality Management Overview/Statement of Authority," is divided into the following five distinct documents.

1. *Introduction to the Quality Manual.* This is usually a statement that defines why the organization developed a formal, documented QMS. Typically, this introduction would start with a statement something like: "The Walter L. Hurd Corporation has established a documented quality management system to provide all its employees with direction on how the organization expects them to operate related to the quality aspects of their assignments. This quality management system is our guarantee to our customers, both internal and external, that we will provide only high-quality products and service by faithfully executing these written directions. The quality management system also provides our external customers with an understanding of the way our organization performs on a day-to-day basis to ensure our customers receive the best products and services possible at a very competitive price."

   The overview will also include a statement that defines how the QMS is used within the organization and under what circumstances (if any) it is acceptable to deviate from the documented QMS. A typical statement that might be included to reinforce the adherence to the documentation might read: "Under no circumstance should anyone deviate from the documented quality management system. If the system needs to be changed, the proper paperwork should be processed before any change is made to the way we perform our work activities."

This introduction to the quality manual should be signed by the top-level manager within the organization (COO, CEO, senior partner, etc.). This document is necessary to legitimize the quality manual and the QMS.

2. *Table of Contents.* The table of contents for the quality manual should be divided into three sections, with a detailed list of each document contained within the section.

3. *Quality Policy and Quality Objectives.* The organization is required by ISO 9000 to have a quality policy statement in Secondary Subclause 4.1.1. Even if not required by ISO 9000, your organization should have its own quality policy.

The foundation for an improvement process is the "quality policy statement." It should clearly and concisely state what is expected of all employees, as well as the products or services that are delivered to the customers. This quality policy should be released over the president's signature. To delegate this action to a vice president or another executive detracts from the meaning and the priority it will have in the working environment.

The quality policy should be worded so that it applies to each employee's activities, not just to the product or service provided by the organization. It should also clearly state the quality performance standards for the organization and should cover the total aspects of the QMS, not just the organization's end output. That sounds like a big order, and it is. Nevertheless, a good quality policy must be short and easy to remember.

Let's take a look at a typical quality policy to see if it meets these requirements (see Figure 5.8).

- *Is it concise?* Yes. The policy, definitions, and implementation statement are confined to one page.
- *Does it apply to each employee?* Yes, each employee has some value added to the part of the operation being performed in his or her area. The policy clearly states that it applies to an individual's value-added activities.
- *Does it set the performance standard?* Yes, it states that the company expects error-free output from each employee. It does not state that the company expects each employee to be infallible but, rather, allows each employee the chance to detect errors and correct them

---

JOHNSON PLASTICS, INC.

Quality Policy

WE WILL DELIVER ERROR-FREE, COMPETITIVE PRODUCTS AND SERVICES
ON TIME TO OUR CUSTOMERS THAT MEET OR EXCEED THEIR
EXPECTATIONS.

Definitions

We	=	The company as a whole and each individual employee
Competitive	=	Provide the customer with more value for the investment than the competition does
Customer	=	The next person that receives our output, inside or outside of the company

Implementation

To implement this policy means that all employees will understand what their
customers expect and that they will provide the customers with products or services
that meet or exceed their expectations. All requirements must be continuously
evaluated and upgraded to reflect changing customer expectations. All work will be
performed to requirements and in keeping with the documented quality management
system.

Dr. John E. Johnson
   President, Johnson Plastics, Inc.

FIGURE 5.8 A Model Quality Policy

before the output is delivered to the customers. Nevertheless, the
ultimate aim would be for everyone to perform his or her assigned
tasks correctly every time, not just deliver error-free products or
services to customers.

■ *Does it cover the total aspects of quality?* Yes. In yesteryear, when
we spoke of quality, we talked about the quality of the shipped
product. Today, there is a "big Q" to quality. There is a quality of
schedule, of price, and of performance.

   a. *Quality of schedule.* We can provide the best-performing item
in the world, but if we do not deliver it to our customer when it
is needed, it is useless.

   b. *Quality of price.* What good is a product if your customer cannot afford to buy it? Included in the quality of price is the quality of worth. Even if your customers can afford to buy your
product, they may feel that it is not worth the price because

your competitors produce something that will perform the same function at a lower price.

c. *Quality of output.* This includes both product and service. Today, with greater and greater portions of our resources being used in the service industry, less than one-third of the American labor force is involved in producing durable goods. Even then, a large portion of this third is supporting the manufacturing process people—activities such as accounting, personnel functions, maintenance, and management. A ratio of five support people to one production worker is common in high-technology areas.

■ *Was it released over the president's signature?* Yes.

When this policy is put in the hands of both management and employees, it will provide some guidance in implementing the improvement process.

If you don't have a quality policy for your organization, now is the time to have the president release one. And if you do have one, take the time to review it to be sure that it meets the requirements described in this chapter.

Although we are suggesting that the quality policy be included in the quality manual, in many organizations it is also included in the organization's Tier 1 documentation. If this is the case in your organization, great care should be taken to ensure that the quality policy is worded exactly the same in both places.

4. *Organization Charts and Description of Management Responsibilities and Authorities.* This section of the quality manual includes high-level organization charts and the quality assurance function's organization chart. These charts should show the names of the individual departments and their interrelationships. The organization chart should not include individuals' names. The department head should be identified by job title only. This reduces the work required to keep the organization charts up to date. It is also a good idea to include in this section a short, one- or two-paragraph description of the quality responsibilities and authorities for each title on the organization chart. For example, "The Director of Procurement is responsible for planning, purchasing, expediting, and storing of all purchased items. The objective of the Director of Procurement is to provide the organization with a competitive advantage by procuring only high-quality items at competitive prices and having them available when they are required, while minimizing the amount of money tied up in component part inventories."

5. *Overview of the Quality Management Documentation System*. In this section the quality management documentation system is described briefly. It is important that the reader understands the documentation structure and how to use the documentation system. This section should also include a short overview on the change level control processes, defining the controls related to making a change to the quality management documentation system and the individual documents that make up the QMS.

Section II—Quality Concepts, Philosophies, and Elements

This section will include all of the quality concepts that impact the QMS. In the scenario that we are using, a minimum of one statement will be included for each of the subclauses in Clause 4.0 of the related ISO 9000 standard. For organizations that want to be registered to ISO 9001, this section of the quality manual can be divided into any one of the following combinations:

- The section can be divided into 20 different documents, each addressing an individual subclause in Clause 4.0 of ISO 9001.
- The section can be divided into three or four documents that group the individual subclauses as suggested in the ISO 9000 grouping approach discussed earlier in this chapter. In this case, each of the subclauses is discussed separately within the related grouping.
- The section can contain only one document with separate paragraphs discussing each of the 20 subclauses and how each applies to the organization.

All three approaches will work and meet the registration requirements. We like the first approach that results in 20 separate documents because it allows each clause to be addressed in greater detail and, in most cases, each clause can be documented on a single page. It also makes change control easier. The second approach is also good because it is usually more in line with the organization's processes. The third approach is good for small organizations with fewer than 100 employees, because it minimizes the size of the quality manual.

We recommend that the documents that make up Section II contain the following:

1. Document number
2. Version letter
3. Subject

4. Date of last release
5. Purpose
6. Scope
7. References
8. Definitions
9. Responsibility (the specific organization responsible for the document)
10. Requirements (concepts, policies or elements)
11. Supporting documentation
12. Change history

ISO 10013 suggests using the layout shown in Figure 5.9.

Organization		Title/Subject		Number		
Unit issuing		Approved by		Date	Revision	Page

POLICY/POLICY REFERENCE
Governing requirement

PURPOSE AND SCOPE
Why, what for, area covered, exclusions.

RESPONSIBILITY
Organizational unit responsible to implement the document to achieve the purpose.

ACTION/METHOD TO ACHIEVE SYSTEM ELEMENT REQUIREMENT
List, step-by-step, the details of what needs to be done. Use references, if appropriate. Keep in logical sequence. Mention any exceptions or specific areas of attention.

DOCUMENTATION/REFERENCES
Identify which referenced documents or forms are associated with utilizing the document, or what data have to be recorded. Use examples, if appropriate.

RECORDS
Identify which records are generated as a result of using the document, where these are retained and for how long.

FIGURE 5.9 ISO 10013 Suggested Documentation Layout

Although this approach will work for most organizations, we prefer to use different forms for the quality manual and the operating procedures. We suggest that this section of the quality manual be documented using forms similar to the ones shown in Figures 5.10, 5.11, and 5.12.

Each document in the quality manual can make use of these three different forms.

	QUALITY MANUAL	
TITLE:	**DOC. NO:**	**VERSION:**
	DATE: / /	**Page ___ of _____**
CONTROLLING FUNCTION:	**APPROVED BY:**	

FIGURE 5.10   Quality Manual Cover Page Form

	QUALITY MANUAL	
TITLE:	**DOC. NO:**	**VERSION:**
	DATE: / /	**Page ___ of ____**

FIGURE 5.11 Quality Manual General Form

	QUALITY MANUAL	
TITLE:	**DOC. NO:**	**VERSION:**
	DATE: / /	**Page ___ of _____**

DOCUMENT CHANGE HISTORY		
VERSION	**DATE**	**CHANGE DESCRIPTION**

FIGURE 5.12 Quality Manual Change History Form

1. Cover Page Form (Figure 5.10): The following defines each of the blocks in Figure 5.10.
   - Document number—The unique number that differs this document from all other documents within the organization.
   - Version—This indicates the change level of the document and is usually an alpha letter. For example, the release level of a document is usually assigned an "A" version. The first revision to the document would be assigned the "B" version. Each time the document is changed, the version level is changed. It is also called the change level or revision level.
   - Date—The date that the most recent version was released.
   - Title—The name of the document.
   - Controlling function—The name of the function (product engineering, quality assurance, purchasing, manufacturing engineering, etc.) responsible for coordinating the document. It is the only organization that can process a change to the document.
   - Approved by—The signature of the person designated by the controlling function as being responsible for the document.
2. General Form (Figure 5.11): The blocks on this form have the same meaning as the blocks on the cover page form.
3. Change History Form (Figure 5.12): Each time the document is changed, a short description of the change is added to this form. It provides a documented history of how the particular quality manual document has evolved.

Section III—References

This section contains backup information needed to understand, use, and control the quality manual. Three main documents usually make up this section.

1. *Cross-Reference List.* The cross-reference list connects the documents within the quality manual with their related procedures and, in some organizations, down to their related work or job instructions. In most cases, the quality manual document and/or clause is listed first, followed by the supporting procedures (see Figure 5.13). Some organizations also include the name of the function or department responsible for each of the quality manual documents.
2. *Quality Manual Distribution Control List.* This list defines who has been assigned copies of the quality manual. When the quality manual is sent or delivered to an individual, it is accompanied with an acceptance letter that states the requirements for maintaining and updating

	QUALITY MANUAL		
TITLE	DOC NO.	VERSION:	
	DATE: / /	Page____ of ____	

CROSS-REFERENCE LIST

DOC NO.	PAR. NO.	PAR. NAME	PROCEDURE NUMBER	WORK INST. NUMBER
QM0101		Management Responsibility		
	3.0	Quality Policy		
	4.0	Responsibility and Authority		
QM0101		Quality System		
	2.0	Quality Management System Procedures	P02001	W0201 W0202
	3.0	Quality Planning	P02001	
	4.0	Management Review	P01002	W0203 W0204 W0204

FIGURE 5.13 Typical Cross-Reference List

the quality manual. This letter defines the responsibilities that the individual receiving the quality manual must agree to accept in order to be issued a quality manual. This letter should be signed by the individual accepting the quality manual and returned to the individual who coordinates the quality management documentation system.

A similar list is maintained by the individual responsible for the quality management documentation system for manuals sent to customers or potential customers. Copies sent to customers should always be accompanied by a letter stating that the enclosed manual will not be updated unless the customer submits a special request.

Maintaining this list as part of the quality manual is often helpful in small to midsized organizations. In large organizations, the distribution list for the quality manual is so extensive that it is usually kept separate from the quality manual. Figure 5.14 is a typical example of a quality manual controlled copies record.

3. *Definitions and Acronyms.* This is a list of key definitions and acronyms used in the quality management documentation system. It should include all words and acronyms that could be misinterpreted in the quality manual, plus other key words and acronyms included in the related procedures and work instructions. It does not have to include all of the technical terms that the organization uses.

Service Industry Example

Too often we think of the ISO 9000 series as being manufacturing-related only. This is far from the truth. More and more customers are requiring the organizations that provide them service to have a good QMS. In addition, the service industry itself is beginning to see the value in having a documented QMS and is turning to the ISO 9000 series to provide it with the needed direction. Figure 5.15 is a table of contents for a quality manual for a service organization that has been registered to ISO 9001.

Figure 5.16 shows how a page in the quality manual cross-references the quality manual documents to the related ISO 9001 subclauses for a typical service organization's quality manual.

Step 2—Form and Train Subcommittees

The subcommittees should now be formed and trained. To accomplish this, the QST should hold a meeting of all subcommittee chairpersons and review the QMS upgrade plan created in Phase II. At this meeting, the expectations for each of the subcommittees and subcommittee chairpersons should be discussed and agreed to. In addition, the subcommittees' chairpersons will then develop a schedule of activities and the interrelationship between the subcommittees. Also during this meeting, the training that will be given to the subcommittees

	QUALITY MANUAL	
TITLE:	**DOC. NO:**	**VERSION:**
	DATE: / /	**Page ___ of ____**

QUALITY MANUAL - CONTROLLED COPIES RECORD

The **XYZ Corporation** Quality Manual is issued on a controlled copy basis to the following individuals. The Quality Assurance Manager or his/her designated representative are the only ones who are authorized to make copies of the documents or to issue additional manuals.

Manual #	Issued to:	Department:	Date Accepted:	Signature:
01	_____	President/CEO	_____	_____
02	_____	Quality Mgr.	_____	_____
03	_____	Mfg. Manager	_____	_____
04	_____	Materials Mgr.	_____	_____
05	_____	Engineering Mgr.	_____	_____
06	_____	Purchasing Mgr.	_____	_____
07	_____	Contracts Mgr.	_____	_____
08	_____	Marketing Mgr.	_____	_____
09	_____	Sales Mgr.	_____	_____
10	_____	Mfg. Eng. Mgr.	_____	_____
11	_____	Test Eng. Mgr.	_____	_____
12	_____	Personnel Mgr.	_____	_____
13	_____	Customer Eng. Mgr.	_____	_____
14	_____	Q.A. Mgr.	_____	_____
15	_____	ISO Registrar	_____	_____

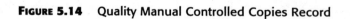

FIGURE 5.14   Quality Manual Controlled Copies Record

<u>**Quality Manual Table of Contents**</u>

SECTION
 Introduction
1 Quality Policy
2 Quality System
3 Management Representative
4 Management Review
5 Resources and Personnel
6 Document Control
  6.1 Document Approval and Issue
  6.2 Document Changes/Modifications
7 Contract Review
8 Design Control
9 Process Control
10 Purchasing
  10.1 Assessment of Subcontractors
  10.2 Purchasing Data
  10.3 Verification of Purchased Product
  10.4 Client-Supplied Product or Services
11 Inspection and Testing
  11.1 Receiving Inspection and Testing
  11.2 In-Process Inspection and Testing
  11.3 Final Inspection and Testing
  11.4 Inspection and Test Status
  11.5 Inspection and Test Records
12 Handling, Storage, Packaging, and Delivery of Deliverables
13 Servicing
14 Product Identification and Traceability
15 Control of Nonconforming Product or Services
  15.1 Nonconformity Review and Disposition
  15.2 Corrective Action
16 Quality Assurance Reviews/Internal Quality Audits
17 Quality Records
18 Quality Statistics
19 Training

APPENDIXES
A Responsibilities
  • Quality Director
  • Director of Risk Management
  • Head of Quality Services
B Nonconformity and Corrective Action
C Quality Assurance Reviews
D Quality Training

FIGURE 5.15 Typical Quality Manual Table of Contents for a Service
Organization

	QUALITY MANUAL	
TITLE:	**DOC. NO:**	**VERSION:**
	DATE: / /	**Page ___ of ____**

5.0 Cross-Reference List to ISO 9001 Subclauses

ISO 9001 Subclauses		Policy Manual Section Nos.
4.1	Management responsibility	1 to 5
4.2	Quality system	2
4.3	Contract review	7
4.4	Design control	8
4.5	Document and data control	6
4.6	Purchasing	10
4.7	Control of customer-supplied product	10.4
4.8	Product identification and traceability	14
4.9	Process control	9
4.10	Inspection and testing	11
4.12	Inspection and test status	11
4.13	Control of nonconforming product	15
4.14	Corrective and preventive action	15
4.15	Handling, storage, packaging, preservation and delivery	12
4.16	Control of quality records	17
4.17	Internal quality audits	16
4.18	Training	19
4.19	Servicing	13
4.20	Statistical techniques	18

Note: Subclause 4.11—Control of inspection, measuring and test equipment is not applicable.

FIGURE 5.16 Typical Quality Manual Cross-Reference List to ISO 9001 Subclauses for a Service Industry

will be discussed and a training schedule will be established. We suggest that all members of the subcommittees receive the following training:

- Eight-hour overview of ISO 9000 and the subcommittee's role in implementing and maintaining a QMS
- Four hours of Organizational Change Management
- Two hours document writing and evaluation
- Four hours of preparing training programs for adults
- Two hours of training related to the organization's Tier 1 documentation (mission, values, visions, critical success factors, etc.)

We are making the assumption that all the members who will be assigned to each subcommittee have already received team activity and problem-solving methodology training. If not, approximately 16 hours of training on these two subjects should be considered.

Each subcommittee chairperson will meet with the appropriate department managers to obtain the name of an individual who will be assigned to his or her subcommittee representing that department. The subcommittee chairperson will then prepare a meeting schedule and schedule training for the team members.

Step 3—Prepare Individual Sections of the Quality Manual

The trained subcommittees should now prepare the individual documents that make up the quality manual. High priority should be assigned to preparing the quality policy and the organization chart portion of the quality manual because they present concepts that need to be considered throughout the rest of the quality management documentation system. Normally, the quality manual is not completed until many of the operating procedures are completed. Often, an individual subcommittee will be assigned to prepare parts of the quality manual and the associated operating procedures. The subcommittee may choose to prepare the operating procedures first and then prepare the related parts of the quality manual. The sequence of preparing the quality manual and then the operating procedures, or preparing the operating procedures and then the quality manual, is left up to the discretion of the individual subcommittee. In reality, the subcommittees and the QST will learn that this is an iterative process in which one is refined, and the other is adjusted.

Step 4—Prepare Flowcharts of the Assigned Processes Being Documented

In Phase II, the QST block-diagrammed the key processes related to each subclause in Clause 4.0 of ISO 9001. These processes were then assigned to subcommittees to prepare the associated operating procedures. These subcommittees will now prepare a flowchart of the assigned processes that will define how the process flows through the various functions.

Introduction

"One picture is worth a thousand words." If we may modify this age-old proverb and expand it a little to cover your business processes, it might read, "A flowchart is worth a thousand procedures." Flowcharting, also known as logic diagramming or flow diagramming, is an invaluable tool for understanding the inner workings of, and relationships between, processes.

Flowcharting is defined as:

DEFINITION | A METHOD OF GRAPHICALLY DESCRIBING AN EXISTING PROCESS OR A PROPOSED NEW PROCESS BY UTILIZING SIMPLE SYMBOLS, LINES, AND WORDS TO DISPLAY PICTORIALLY THE ACTIVITIES AND THEIR SEQUENCE IN THE PROCESS.

What Are Flowcharts?

Flowcharts graphically represent the activities that make up a process in much the same way that a map represents a particular area. Some of the advantages of using flowcharts are similar to those of using maps. For example, both flowcharts and maps illustrate how the different elements fit together.

Consider Figure 5.17, a block diagram (a type of flowchart) of the process for hiring a new employee in the fictitious HJH Company. The process begins with recognition of the need to hire someone and ends with the employee reporting to work. This brief overview of the major activities in the process enables those who understand how to read this story, to quickly compare the ways in which HJH's hiring process resembles and differs from that of other companies. For example, you can easily see that HJH emphasizes hiring from inside the company. Another advantage is that constructing flowcharts disciplines our thinking. Comparing a flowchart with the actual process activities will highlight the areas where rules or policies are unclear, or are even being violated. Differences between the way an activity is supposed to be conducted

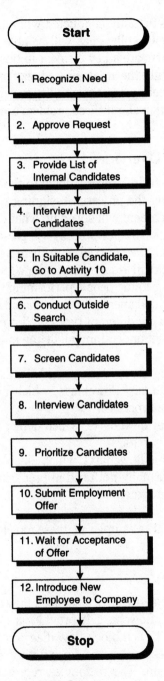

FIGURE 5.17 Hiring Process at HJH Company

and the way it is actually conducted will emerge. Then, with just a few short steps, you and your colleagues will be able to determine how to improve the activity. Flowcharts are a key element in business process improvement. Good flowcharts highlight the areas where fuzzy procedures disrupt quality and productivity. Then, because of their ability to clarify complex processes, they facilitate communication about these problem areas.

Flowcharting Overview

Flowcharting an entire process, down to the task level, is the basis for analyzing and improving the process. Assigning portions of the process to specific subcommittee members will speed up what can be a time-consuming task.

Every situation and/or process will present unique charting problems. The subcommittee will have to deal with them as they arise. For instance, existing documentation seldom is sufficient to allow flowcharting of every task and activity without talking to the people performing the tasks. Be careful to distinguish between what the documentation says should be done and what actually is done.

There are many different types of flowcharts, each with its own use. The subcommittee must understand all of the following techniques to be effective:

- Block diagrams, which provide a quick overview of a process
- ANSI standard flowcharts, which analyze the detailed interrelationships of a process
- Functional flowcharts, which depict the process flow between organizations or areas
- Geographic flowcharts, which illustrate the process flow between locations. (Normally not used in preparing the quality management documentation system.)

Figure 5.18 presents examples of these four flowchart techniques.

Block Diagrams

A block diagram, also known as a block flow diagram, is the simplest and most prevalent type of flowchart. It provides a quick, uncomplicated view of the process. Figure 5.17 is a block flow diagram that provides an overview of the hiring process. Rectangles and lines with arrows are the major symbols in a block flow diagram. The rectangles represent activities, and the lines with arrows connect the rectangles to show the direction of information flow and/or

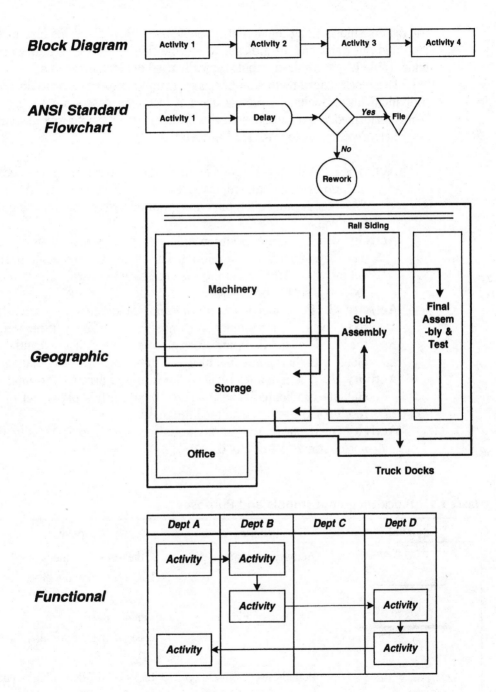

FIGURE 5.18 Types of Flowcharts

the relationships among the activities. Some block flow diagrams also include stop and start symbols to indicate where the flowchart begins and where it ends. Table 1.1 shows the symbols typically used in block diagrams.

Use block diagrams to simplify large, complex processes or to document individual tasks. Include a phrase in each rectangle describing the activity being performed. Keep these descriptive phrases (activity description) short.

Let's decode the story told in Figure 5.17.

Activity 1　A manager recognizes a need for another employee because of high overtime, an employee leaving, and so on. To fill this need, the manager must complete the required forms and get the proper approvals.

Activity 2　The appropriate people review the request for a new employee and approve or reject it. This approval may result in a budget increase. After obtaining the necessary approvals, the approved request is sent to personnel.

Activity 3　Personnel looks for internal candidates who have been recommended for promotion or transfer, who also meet the needs of the job. The HJH Company does not post jobs. A list of candidates, along with their personnel files, is sent to the requesting manager.

Activity 4　The manager reviews the files and arranges to interview suitable candidates. The manager then notifies personnel of the results of the review and the interviews.

Activity 5　If one of the candidates is acceptable, go to Activity 10. If not, continue to Activity 6.

TABLE 1.1　Block Diagram Symbols and Purposes

Symbol	Name	Purpose
▭	Activity (Operation)	Indicates that some change has occurred in the process.
→	Direction of Flow	Denotes the direction and order of the operation.
⬭	Boundaries or Start/Stop Symbols	Indicates the beginning or end of the block diagram.

Activity 6 Personnel conducts an outside search for candidates by running ads in newspapers, reviewing on-file applications, hiring a search firm, and so on.

Activity 7 Personnel reviews potential candidates' applications and conducts screening interviews with the best candidates. It then sets up interviews between the manager and the most promising candidates.

Activity 8 The manager interviews the candidates.

Activity 9 The manager prioritizes the acceptable candidates and sends this list to personnel.

Activity 10 Personnel submits an employment offer to the best candidate.

Activity 11 The company waits for the candidate's response. If the offer is rejected, Activities 10 and 11 are repeated for the next candidates on the priority list. Once the offer is accepted, go to Activity 12.

Activity 12 Personnel arranges for the employee to report to work, familiarizes him or her with company procedures, and presents the employee to the manager.

As you can see, many activities are performed within each rectangle. If desired, each rectangle can be expanded into a block diagram of its own. Figure 5.19 takes the first activity in Figure 5.17 and explodes it into a more detailed block diagram comprising the following activities:

Activity 1 The manager analyzes the amount of overtime in the department to determine whether a new employee could reduce it sufficiently to offset the cost of the new employee's salary and benefits.

Activity 2 The manager reviews the procedure for acquiring a new employee.

Activity 3 The manager asks personnel to send blank personnel requisition forms and budget variation forms.

Activity 4 The manager fills out the forms.

Activity 5 The manager prepares a job description for the new job.

Activity 6 The manager reviews the requisition form and job description with the second-level manager and gets a sign-off.

Activity 7 The manager mails the job description, budget change request, and employee requisition form to the controller for approval.

Even in Figure 5.19, some of the activities could be broken down into individual task flowcharts. For example, how to write a job description easily could be a separate block diagram.

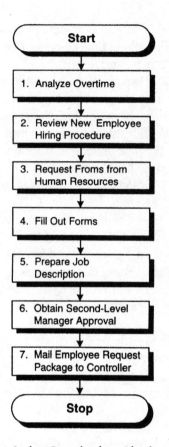

FIGURE 5.19 Management Action Required to Obtain New Employee Approval

Notice that the description of each activity begins with a verb. Although not mandatory, following this practice is a good general rule. Standard phrasing speeds understanding for the reader. In addition, all business activities can be described by a verb. Thus, by starting each block description with a verb, you ensure that the label does, in fact, describe a true business activity.

If there are conditional statements in your flowchart, you may not be able to begin every description with a verb. For instance, in Figure 5.17, Activity 5 begins with a conditional statement, "If suitable candidate, **go** to Activity 10." The rule of using a starting verb is still expected—immediately after the conditional statement.

Block diagrams provide a quick overview of a process, not a detailed analysis. Block diagrams can flow horizontally or vertically. Normally they are prepared first to document the magnitude of the process; then another type of flowchart is used to analyze the process in detail. Typically, many activities and inputs are intentionally not detailed in a block diagram so that a very simple picture of the total process can be drawn.

Figure 5.20 adds a new dimension to block diagramming. Here, responsibility for each activity has been assigned to a specific person or persons. The name or title of the person responsible for the activity is indicated in the open-ended rectangle. This symbol is called an **annotation symbol,** as it is used to provide additional information about the activities. A broken line leads away from the activity to the annotation symbol. The broken line is used so that the reader will not mistake it for a direction flow line. The arrow leads away from the block diagram activity and points to the person or persons responsible for that activity. When your organization uses block flow diagrams to chart a set of business activities, you may indicate responsibilities differently. You may use the name of a department, the job titles of employees and managers, or the actual names of the individuals in denoting responsibilities.

Although not considered proper procedure by flowcharting experts, Figure 5.21 presents another way of connecting an activity with the person(s) or area(s) responsible for performing that activity.

The purpose of flowcharting is to paint a picture that is easy for the subcommittee to understand and use. You can modify rules, such as starting each activity name with a verb, or using annotation symbols in place of the activity owner's name within the activity rectangle, if it significantly improves the understandability and use of the flowchart.

However, given that any nonstandard deviation may confuse other people within the organization using the flowchart at a later date, it is a good idea to have the QST establish a complete list of symbols at the beginning of the QMS update activity to minimize deviations.

It is good practice to start your business process flowcharting by block-diagramming the process. The block diagram can be used to help define which of the other flowcharts best provides a detailed understanding of the tasks within the process.

Block-Diagramming Activities and Information

A process is also likely to have a communication system with its own separate and distinct flow, superimposed on the flow of activities. This communication system must also be recognized, flowcharted, and understood as an integral part of the process operations.

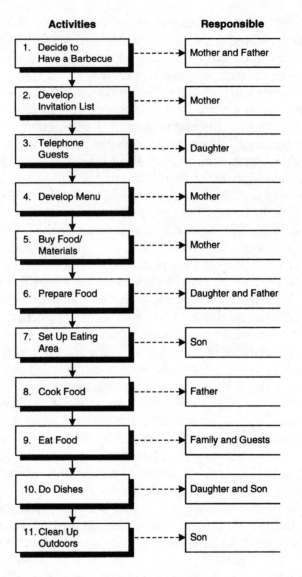

Figure 5.20   Block Flow Diagram with Assignment of Responsibilities

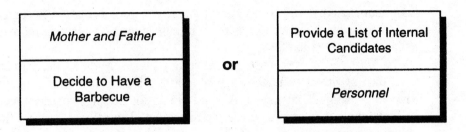

FIGURE 5.21   Another Way to Denote Ownership of an Activity

An organization chart is a type of block diagram. In this case, the reporting structure is pictured. An organization chart shows how authority, responsibilities, and activity are delegated down into the organization.

Figure 5.22 presents a typical organization chart. The organization flow is represented by solid lines, while the communication system is indicated by broken lines. The communication flow in most organizations is an essential, but complex, part of the organizational structure. A good communication system flows up, down, and sideways. Frequently, a communication flow line will have arrows on both ends, signifying two-way communication. A typical two-way

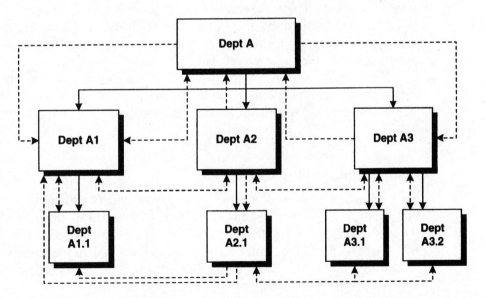

FIGURE 5.22   A Block Diagram with Its Communication Systems Added with Broken Lines

communication would be a meeting where everyone is invited to contribute to the discussion. As you can see, the communication flow is much more complex than the organization flow.

Figure 5.22 reveals some interesting patterns. Midlevel department A2 is not part of upper management's communication flow and, as a result, holds meetings with departments A1 and A3 in an attempt to communicate its department's concerns to upper management. Typically, A2 meets first with A1 to obtain a status report, then meets with A3 to verify the information obtained at the first meeting.

Unfortunately, this pattern is repeated at lower levels because, although the manager of department A2 communicates the verifying data to the first-line department A2-1 that reports to him or her, the manager never solicits input from A2-1, developing another communication void. As a result, the manager of department A2-1 has developed a very active communication system with the other first-line departments, in the hope that the department's activities and concerns reach upper and middle management.

Standard Flowchart Symbols

Before examining the remaining types of flowcharts, we should define some additional symbols. The most effective flowcharts use only widely known, standard symbols. Think about how much easier it is to read a road map when you are familiar with the meaning of each symbol, and what a nuisance it is to have some strange, unfamiliar shape in the area of the map you are using to make a decision about your travel plans.

The flowchart is one of the oldest of all the design aids available. For simplicity, we will review only 12 of the most common symbols, most of which are published by the American National Standards Institute (ANSI) (see Figure 5.23).

ANSI Standard Flowchart

An ANSI standard flowchart provides a detailed understanding of a process that greatly exceeds that of a block diagram. In fact, a block diagram often is the starting point, and a standard flowchart is used to expand the activities within each block to the desired level of detail. Each task in the process under study can be detailed to the point that the standard flowchart can be used as part of the training manual for a new employee.

Charting a business process requires careful attention. Consider a manager of a large retail store in a big city. The procedures he or she must follow

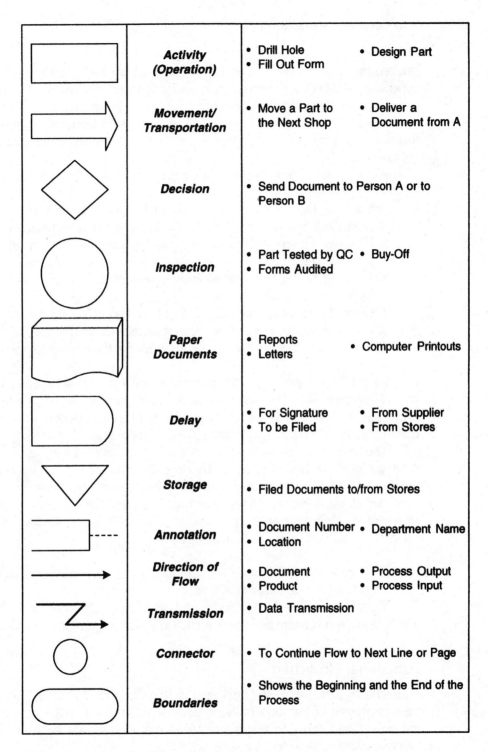

Activity (Operation)	• Drill Hole	• Design Part
	• Fill Out Form	
Movement/ Transportation	• Move a Part to the Next Shop	• Deliver a Document from A
Decision	• Send Document to Person A or to Person B	
Inspection	• Part Tested by QC	• Buy-Off
	• Forms Audited	
Paper Documents	• Reports	• Computer Printouts
	• Letters	
Delay	• For Signature	• From Supplier
	• To be Filed	• From Stores
Storage	• Filed Documents to/from Stores	
Annotation	• Document Number	• Department Name
	• Location	
Direction of Flow	• Document	• Process Output
	• Product	• Process Input
Transmission	• Data Transmission	
Connector	• To Continue Flow to Next Line or Page	
Boundaries	• Shows the Beginning and the End of the Process	

FIGURE 5.23 Standard Flowchart Symbols

can become quite involved. He or she may have a large staff, delegate authority, supervise various departments, and so on. Each supervisor has sales reports to complete and check against inventory changes. The manager must provide each supervisor with instructions to help ease the workload and promote uniformity among the different departments. This, in turn, helps the accounting department.

A typical set of procedures for a supervisor might include the following:

1. Choosing the weekly sales total for an employee; reading the value of price items from column X and the value of sales items from column Y
2. Figuring out the X commission by multiplying the value in column X by 10 percent
3. Figuring out the Y commission by multiplying the value in column Y by 5 percent
4. Computing the total due: $50 + X commission + Y commission
5. Entering the total pay opposite the employee's name in the payroll ledger
6. Returning to activity 1 and repeating this for the other employees

Figure 5.24 flowcharts the procedure for calculating an employee's weekly commissions. The activities in the procedure are listed beside each symbol in the flowchart to help people understand the details of the flowchart. Unfortunately, this is not usually practical on complex flowcharts.

The first activities on the flowchart follow activities 1 through 5 of the written procedure. Notice, however, that the flowchart allows for a procedure not accounted for in the written procedure (i.e., eventually, the weekly sales totals for all employees will have been processed, and the procedure need not be repeated). Flowcharting the process, in this case, helps us to discover that activity 6 should be rewritten as follows:

6. If the weekly sales totals for additional employees must be calculated, go to activity 1. Otherwise, stop.

This simple flowchart clearly and accurately depicts the activities involved in the procedure and the sequence in which they are to be carried out.

Functional Flowchart

A functional flowchart is the next step in flowcharting. It pictures the movement between different work units, an additional dimension that is particularly valuable when total cycle time is a problem. A functional flowchart uses either block or standard flowchart symbols.

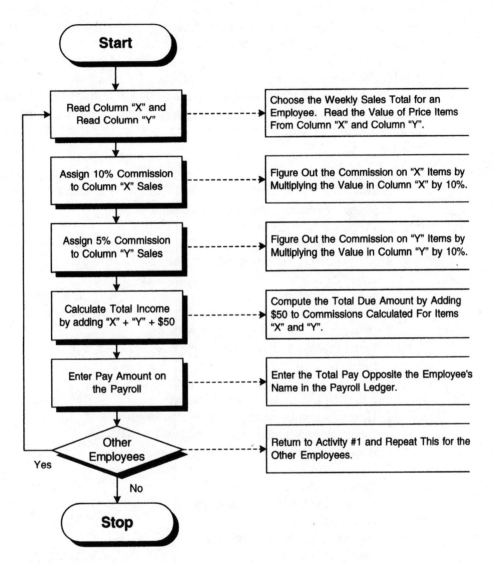

FIGURE 5.24 Paying Commission Flowchart and Procedures

A functional flowchart identifies how vertically oriented functional departments affect a process flowing horizontally across an organization. If a process was always contained within a single department, and didn't cross over to other territories, a manager's life would be much easier. However, in most companies, the functional or vertical organization is a way of life, because it provides a highly trained competency center that cannot be equaled using a process or product organization.

Figure 5.25 is a standard functional flowchart of the hiring process that was block-diagrammed in Figure 5.17 (activities 1 through 5).

To keep the flowchart simple, we have used only three of the standard symbols. We have also expanded the first 5 activities in Figure 5.17 to 15 activities and separated them by the area performing them. The 15 activities are:

Activity	*Responsible Area*
1. Recognize need. Complete payback analysis. Prepare personnel requisition. Prepare budget request.	Manager
2. Evaluate budget. If yes, sign personnel requisition slip. If no, return total package with reject letter to manager.	Controller
3. Conduct in-house search.	Personnel
4. If in-house candidates exist, provide list to management. If not, start outside hiring procedure.	Personnel
5. Review candidates' paperwork and prepare a list of candidates to be interviewed.	Manager
6. Have candidates' managers review job with the employees, and determine which employees are interested in the position.	Personnel
7. Notify personnel of candidates interested in being interviewed.	Candidates
8. Set up meeting between manager and candidates.	Manager
9. Interview candidates and review details of job.	Manager
10. Notify personnel of interview results.	Manager
11. If acceptable candidate is available, make job offer. If not, start outside hiring process.	Personnel
12. Evaluate job offer and notify personnel of candidate's decision.	Candidate
13. If yes, notify manager that the job has been filled. If no, go to activity 14.	Personnel

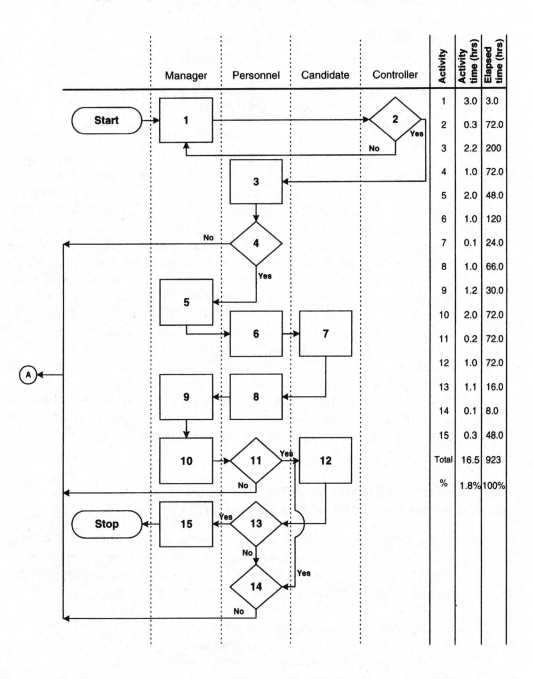

The following table accompanies the flowchart:

Activity	Activity time (hrs)	Elapsed time (hrs)
1	3.0	3.0
2	0.3	72.0
3	2.2	200
4	1.0	72.0
5	2.0	48.0
6	1.0	120
7	0.1	24.0
8	1.0	66.0
9	1.2	30.0
10	2.0	72.0
11	0.2	72.0
12	1.0	72.0
13	1.1	16.0
14	0.1	8.0
15	0.3	48.0
Total	16.5	923
%	1.8%	100%

FIGURE 5.25   Functional Flowchart of the Internal Job Search Process

14. Were there other acceptable candidates?
    If yes, go to activity 12. If no, start outside
    hiring process.   Personnel
15. Have new manager contact candidate's present
    manager and arrange for the candidate to report
    for work.   Manager

For purposes of preparing the operating procedures, flowcharting down to the activity level is very adequate. For work or job instructions, the activity level flowcharts need to be broken down to the task level. It is important to note that the ISO 9000 series does not require your organization to flowchart its quality processes, but we believe it is good practice because it helps the subcommittees understand and analyze how the portion of the QMS they are working on operates. A number of excellent computer programs are available to help you with your flowcharting activity. Two that we like are "ABC Flowcharter" and "ABC Graphics Suite for Windows '95." The entire Graphics Suite package sells for less than $300, and upgrade kits for less than $150. The ABC products are produced by Micrografx, 1303 Arapaho Road, Richardson, TX 75081, telephone number 800-454-7116. Another package that we like is "Work Draw/Professional," produced by Edge Software, P.O. Box 656, Pleasanton, CA 94566, telephone number 510-462-0543. We particularly like the "Work Draw/Professional" program, even though it is more expensive, because it has all the capabilities and backup systems required to support the simulation modeling needed when a process is reengineered or redesigned.

Step 5—Conduct Process Walk-Throughs to Verify the Accuracy of the Flowcharts

In Step 4, the subcommittee developed a flowchart of the process it is working with. Very often, however, the process documented by the subcommittee is not what is really happening in the organization. Employees deviate from the established procedures for a number of reasons. For example:

- They misunderstand the procedures.
- They do not know about the procedures.
- They find a better way of doing things.
- The documented method is too hard to do.
- They are not trained.
- They were trained to do the activity in a different way.

- They do not have the necessary tools.
- They do not have adequate time.
- Someone told them to do it differently.
- They don't understand why they should follow the procedures.

It is also possible that the process flowchart was constructed incorrectly by the subcommittee. The only way that the subcommittee can really understand what is happening in the assigned process is to personally follow the work flow, discussing and observing what is going on. This is called a **process walk-through.**

To conduct a process walk-through, the subcommittee should physically follow the process as documented in the flowchart from the end to the beginning. The subcommittee should observe the process at the task level. The subcommittee needs to know and understand what is being done, and why it is being done. While the subcommittee performs the walk-through it will be able to gather additional information about existing problems and roadblocks to change, as well as suggestions for improvements.

To prepare for the process walk-through, the subcommittee should assign team members (usually groups of two or three people) to different parts of the process. Typically, one member of the walk-through team (WTT) will be from the department in which the activity is being performed. When the team is made up of three people, it is also a good idea to have a customer of the department in which the activity is taking place as a member of the WTT. The people who are assigned to the WTT should have a good understanding of the activity they will be evaluating. This facilitates review and verification of the process flow. Each WTT should

- Become very familiar with all relevant, existing process documentation.
- Arrange with the department manager to interview his or her people.
- Interview a sample of the people performing the task to fully understand what is occurring in the process.
- Compare the way different people do the same job to determine which approach produces the overall best-value output.

Preparation is the key to a successful walk-through. The WTT must really understand what should be happening in the process and be able to talk in terms that are relevant to the person performing the activity. This requires a lot of work prior to the interview process.

To prepare for conducting the evaluations, the WTT should collect the detailed, documented work instructions for the activities that it is going to study. Each team member should become very familiar with these work instructions. If work instructions are not available, much more information will need to be recorded during the walk-through.

During the process walk-through, the WTT will have an opportunity to develop a list of the tasks required to support each activity. For example, let's look at the tasks required to support the activity of typing a letter.

1. Read handwritten memo.
2. Check punctuation.
3. Check spelling and proper names, and obtain mailing address.
4. Assign file reference number to document.
5. Ensure that proper letterhead paper is inserted in printer.
6. Turn on word processor, load program, and insert proper disk.
7. Type letter.
8. Use spell check.
9. Proofread letter.
10. Print letter.
11. Review printed letter to ensure that it is positioned correctly on the paper.
12. Place in manager's incoming mail.

Doing the task analysis often reveals new suppliers to the process. It also provides keys on how to improve the process. The task analysis should be prepared in conjunction with the person performing the activity, because that person has the best understanding of what is involved.

The subcommittee should prepare a **Process Walk-Through Questionnaire** to collect needed information about the process. Typical questions might be:

- What are the required inputs?
- How were you trained?
- What do you do?
- How do you know your output is good?
- What feedback do you receive?
- Who are your customers?
- What keeps you from doing error-free work?
- What can be done to make your assignment easier?
- How do you let your suppliers know how well they are performing?
- How is your output used?
- What would happen if you did not do the job?
- What would you change if you were the manager?

A member of the WTT should schedule meetings with the individual employees through the department managers. Care should be taken to ensure that the right types of input are at the workstation during the meeting so that the team can observe the activity under real conditions. In some cases, the subcommittee will set up a pilot run and follow it through the process.

Before the WTT starts the interview, the role of each team member should be defined. One member of the team should be a scribe; usually the team member from the work area makes the best scribe. The other team members should also record notes, but usually not in the same detail as the scribe, since their role is to interview the employees. These notes will be very helpful later, since the team members from the work area often have preconceived opinions about how the job is being performed. These preconceived opinions sometimes prevent him or her from noting important information that is obvious to a person not so involved with the process.

Another element of success is the way the interview is conducted. Many employees feel threatened and intimidated being interviewed by the WTT. The small walk-through teams help, but that is not enough. Dress to fit the environment. A black suit, white shirt, and tie are totally inappropriate for interviews conducted in a warehouse or service center. Take time to put the interviewee at ease. Before you ask questions, explain why you are talking with him or her. Show the interviewee the flowchart, and explain how he or she fits into the big picture. Interviewing is an art. You should have interview training to get satisfactory results. A four-hour class on interviewing methods is very helpful.

Immediately following each interview, the team should schedule a short meeting to review the interview and agree on the following items:

- Task flow
- Required inputs
- Measurements
- Feedback systems
- Conformance to procedures
- Conformance to other employees
- Major problems
- Training requirements
- Adequacy of work instructions

It is often helpful to flowchart the activity so that the team can gain a better understanding of the tasks being evaluated and be in a better position to report its findings to the subcommittee. The task-level flowcharts will also be used in preparing the job or work instructions.

We find it is good practice to review the findings with the interviewees to be sure the team did not misinterpret their comments. A summary of the interviews of all members in a department should be reviewed with the department manager before they are reviewed with the subcommittee. The department manager and the WTT should agree on what action will be taken to eliminate differences among employees and/or between practice and procedure.

Clearly identify any differences between what is supposed to occur and current practice. Determine why these differences exist. Analyze why everyone is not doing the same job in the same way. Standardization is the key to improvement, and the first task that must be undertaken. Select a way of performing an activity that provides the best results, and use it consistently until you make a major change to the process. It is important for everyone to do the same job in the same way. The output must be predictable before you change the process.

When the walk-through is complete, each WTT should present its findings to the subcommittee. This provides the total subcommittee with a better understanding of the process. Based on our experience, we find that the best way to present this data to the subcommittee is to follow the flowchart, starting at the beginning and working your way through to the end, marking up the flowchart as you go along.

It is important to be able to readily identify all activities and/or tasks not being performed per prescribed procedures or in different ways by different employees. One method is to circle these areas of concern on the flowchart using a yellow highlighter. Action plans should be developed to either change the procedure, or to bring the activity in line with the procedure. If no documentation exists and different approaches to the same job are used, the subcommittee should analyze the advantages and disadvantages of the different approaches and document the approach that best meets the intent of the QMS and represents the most value-added approach to the organization.

Step 6—Compare the Present Process to the ISO 9000 Standards and Identify Discrepancies

The subcommittee now has an excellent understanding of how the present process is operating and of the problems related to the present process. The subcommittee should now compare the present process (often called the "as-is model") to the requirements in the related clauses of the quality manual and the appropriate ISO 9000 documentation, noting any discrepancies. The subcommittee should then prepare a list of all of the discrepancies and define what changes have to be made to the documentation and/or process to eliminate the discrepancies. Often, any major problems or suggested improvements noted during the process walk-through are added to this list.

Step 7—Change the Process Flowcharts to Correct Discrepancies and Include Suggested Improvements

In Steps 5 and 6, the subcommittee made a list of discrepancies and suggested improvements to the process. The subcommittee should now address each of the discrepancies to define how the process and/or its documentation needs to be changed to eliminate the discrepancies. In addition, the subcommittee should also evaluate each suggested improvement to determine whether it is a value-added change and should be incorporated in conjunction with the new documentation. The process flowchart should then be updated to reflect the proposed changes. Because of time constraints, the subcommittee may not be able to include all the good suggestions that were identified during the walk-through. In this case, they should be recorded and addressed during Phase VI.

Step 8—Document the Assigned Processes

Using the updated flowchart and the information collected during the process walk-through, the subcommittee will prepare one or more operating procedures that define how the process should function and what organizations are responsible for performing each activity. Four forms are used to prepare each operating procedure.

1. Operating procedure cover page form (Figure 5.26)
2. Operating procedure flowchart form (Figure 5.27)
3. Operating procedure general information form (Figure 5.28)
4. Operating procedure change history form (Figure 5.29)

Figure 5.26 is a copy of an operating procedure cover page form. All of the fields in this form are the same as the fields in the cover page form for the quality manual discussed earlier. The exception is two new columns on the right-hand side of the operating procedure form. The column labeled "Responsible Dept." is defined as the department responsible for performing the adjacent clause. Usually, abbreviations are used (e.g., in Figure 5.27, DE stands for

	PROCEDURE		
TITLE:	**DOC. NO:**		**VERSION:**
	DATE: / /		**Page ___ of _____**
		RESPONSIBLE DEPT.	**CROSS-REFERENCE**
CONTROLLING FUNCTION:	**APPROVED BY:**		

FIGURE 5.26   Operating Procedure Cover Page Form

Development Engineering; M stands for Marketing; PO stands for Project Office; EB stands for Executive Board). The column entitled "Cross-Reference" is used to define any work instructions, job instructions, or forms that relate to the adjacent clause. This completely eliminates the need for any cross-reference page in the operating procedure, unless it is used to cross-reference upward to

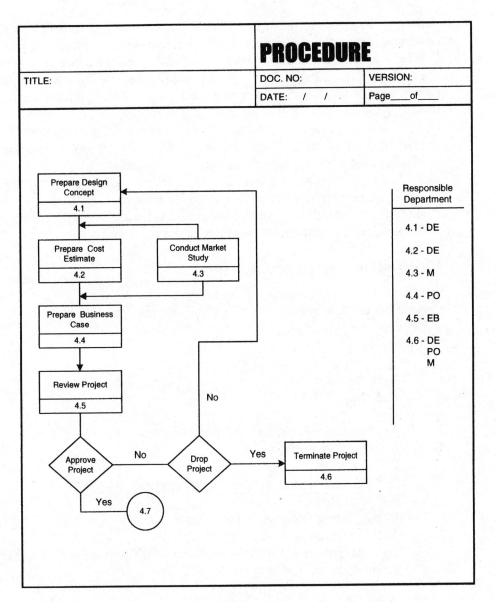

FIGURE 5.27 Operating Procedure Flowchart Page Form Example

the quality manual. The cross-reference documents recorded here are support-ing documents that are used to implement the operating procedure.

Figure 5.27 is an example of an operating procedure flowchart. The flow-chart provides a quick pictorial overview of the particular operating procedure. Each block contains a short description of a clause and the clause number. On the right-hand side of the form is a list of the organizations responsible for performing each activity. Flowcharting the procedures is not required by ISO 9000 standards, but we find this practice is very useful because it increases the document's readability. It also greatly reduces the time required to use the document because individuals can go directly to the clause in the document that they are looking for.

Figure 5.28 is an operating procedure general information form that is used for the body of the document. The headings on this form are the same as the ones used in the operating procedure cover page form.

Figure 5.29 is an operating procedure change history form. Each time a version level is changed, the new version level, the date it was released, and a short description of the change are recorded on this form. By maintaining this form, a complete change history for the document is available.

Operating Procedure Structure

Although the actual format of operating procedures can vary greatly from organization to organization, we recommend that the following sections be included in your operating procedures:

1. Purpose
2. Scope
3. Responsibilities
4. References
5. Definitions, Acronyms, and Abbreviations
6. *Process Flowchart
7. Process Description
8. *Prerequisites and Training Requirements
9. *Audit Requirements
10. Supporting Documentation/Forms
11. *Change History

*Sections that are not required by the ISO 9000 series but that we believe are good business practice.

Each of the 11 sections serves a very unique and different purpose.

1. *Purpose.* This section is usually the first section in the operating procedure. It defines, very distinctly, the intent and/or objective of the operating procedure (e.g., "This procedure defines the process used to control quality-related documentation review, release, change, and removal activities").

	PROCEDURE		
TITLE:	**DOC. NO:**		**VERSION:**
	DATE: / /		Page ___ of _____
		Responsible Department	**Cross-Reference**

FIGURE 5.28 Operating Procedure General Information Form

2. *Scope.* This section defines the departments, functions, organizations, and items that the operating procedure impacts and/or applies to (e.g., "This operating procedure covers all of the Tier 2, 3, and 4 documents that are in, or directly related to, the quality manual").

3. *Responsibilities.* This section lists all of the departments or functions that are directly involved in the operating procedure. The responsibili-

	PROCEDURE	
TITLE:	DOC. NO:	VERSION:
	DATE: / /	Page ___ of _____

DOCUMENT CHANGE HISTORY

VERSION	DATE	CHANGE DESCRIPTION

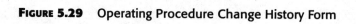

FIGURE 5.29 Operating Procedure Change History Form

ties related to each clause are further broken down adjacent to each clause in the process part of the operating procedure.

4. *References.* This section defines all of the quality manual documents and other operating procedures that relate to, have bearing on, or are referred to within the operating procedure.

5. *Definitions, Acronyms, and Abbreviations.* This section defines all key quality terms used within the operating procedure. It also defines what the acronyms and abbreviations stand for. We recommend that whenever possible, the definitions defined in ISO 8402 should be used. It is also good practice to have one operating procedure that lists all of the organization's quality-related definitions, acronyms, and abbreviations so that they are used the same way and have the same meaning in all of the quality-related documents.

6. *Process Flowchart.* This section uses a process flowchart to provide a pictorial overview of how the individual activities interrelate to each other (see Figure 5.27).

7. *Process Description.* This section defines the activities that make-up the process described in the operating procedure. It will explain what activities are involved and how, where, when, and why they are done. Each clause in this section should be written so that it can be audited.

8. *Prerequisites and Training Requirements.* This section defines any prerequisites and training requirements that the individuals using the operating procedure should have over and above the ones defined in their work or job instructions. It also defines the operating procedure–related training that will be provided to the involved employees when the procedure is released. All new employees who are assigned to the process described in the operating procedure should also receive the same training.

9. *Audit Requirements.* This section is based on the process section and usually takes the form of a list of questions that should be used by internal auditors to evaluate compliance to the operating procedure, to determine the effectiveness of the procedure, and to determine the process's level of compliance to the appropriate clauses in the related ISO 9000 standards. This section provides a general audit structure, but it should not limit the content of any individual audit that finds it necessary to probe deeper into the activities covered in the operating procedure. Including audit requirements within the operating procedure is not a requirement of ISO 9000 standards, but we feel it provides additional value added to your organization.

10. *Supporting Documentation/Forms.* This section lists all of the supporting lower level documentation (Tier 4 and Tier 5 documents). It will list the related job instructions, work instructions, and forms that are referred to in the operating procedure and/or are required to support the operating procedure. Copies or examples of all forms should be put into an appendix of the operating procedure. It is not necessary or advisable to include copies of all of the work instructions, job instructions, or job descriptions, although, on occasion, some of them are included where they provide increased understanding about the interfaces.

11. *Change History.* Each time the operating procedure is changed, this section is always updated to summarize the change activity. Recorded, on the change history form will be the new version level, the date the change was released, and a short description of the change. This section provides a history of all changes made to the operating procedure. It also provides traceability back to the original release (see Figure 5.29).

    Often the parts of the document that were changed are highlighted within the document to make it easier for the reader to understand the change. The next time the document is changed, the old highlighted parts of the document are printed in the normal print and the new changes are highlighted. This is good business practice, but the reader can still miss parts of the document that are removed. To eliminate this exposure, some organizations draw a line through words that are removed or changed but leave them in the document until the next change.

Based on the information provided in the previous paragraphs, the detailed explanation of ISO 9001 provided in Chapter 2, and the new process flowcharts, the subcommittee should be able to prepare the operating procedures. Following are some factors that should be considered during the preparation of the operating procedures:

- Involve the people affected by the operating procedure in preparing the operating procedure.
- Identify what you want to accomplish with the operating procedure and keep focused on that objective, not on the sophistication of the documentation process.
- Keep the process and the documentation as simple as possible.
- Consider how the documentation will help keep the process under control.
- If the operating procedure becomes too long (more than ten pages), consider dividing it into two operating procedures.

- Prepare the documentation so that it will be easy to read and understand for every person who will need to use the document. If English is a second language for anyone who will be reading the document, the document should be written at three grade levels lower than the individual's formal education level.
- The draft should be reviewed by the people who will be using the documents.

Step 9—Compare the Draft Procedures to the Related Document(s) in the Quality Manual

The draft operating procedures are now compared with the related documents in the quality manual. If discrepancies exist, the quality manual or the operating procedures should be revised, being careful to ensure that they are still in compliance with the related ISO 9000 standard. If the related quality manual documents have not been prepared, they must be created before continuing with Step 10.

Step 10—Analyze Each Procedure and Its Supporting Flowchart to Identify Activities That Require Documented Instructions (Tier 4 Documents)

When the operating procedures are in the draft stage, the subcommittee should review the operating procedure, its flowchart, and the results of the process walkthrough to identify which activities require that documented instructions (job instructions, work instructions, job descriptions, or form instructions) be prepared. The subcommittee should then develop a list of additional required documents and a plan to have these documents prepared. Whenever possible, the people performing the activity should be assigned to develop the Tier 4 documents.

Step 11—Assign Individuals or Teams to Generate the Required Instructions

In Step 10, a list of Tier 4 (instructions) document requirements was prepared. Now these Tier 4 documents need to be prepared. If the activity is undergoing a major change as a result of the QMS redesign, then a member of the subcommittee will probably need to be in charge of preparing the related documents. If the activity will remain relatively unchanged and all that is required is to document the present activity, the people performing the activity are best prepared to do the documentation. We have found that a team of people doing the activity with a documentation specialist is a cost-effective way of accomplishing this assignment. When this approach is used, the documentation specialist provides the team with information related to the documentation process. The team then discusses how the activity is performed and agrees on a standard approach. This is documented by the documentation specialist in a flow diagram with an accompanying draft instruction. This draft is then rewritten by the team as necessary. This approach provides the required buy-in from the people who need to implement the instructions and, at the same time, captures their experience and knowledge related to the activity.

There are many types of quality-related instructions (Tier 4 documents). Some of them are as follows:

- Work instructions
- Job instructions
- Job descriptions
- Task procedures
- Calibration procedures
- Set-up procedures
- Class curriculums
- Inspection instructions
- Maintenance instructions
- Audit instructions

As you can see, Tier 4 documents can take on many different formats. For purposes of this book, we will limit the example to the job (or work) instruction. This type of Tier 4 document was selected because it represents most of the items that should be considered in all of the other documents.

Job Instruction Preparation

Job instructions are used to define a common approach to performing an activity or set of tasks. They are usually written to define how an individual will perform these tasks. The job instruction uses forms similar to those used in the operating procedures. The only change is that the title "Operating Procedure" is replaced with "Job Instruction." In addition, the document identification system starts with different alpha letters. In some specific manufacturing job instructions, the document identification number is a combination of a specific part number and the routing activity number. (Figure 5.30 is an example of a job instruction cover page form.)

	JOB INSTRUCTION	
TITLE:	**DOC. NO:**	**VERSION:**
	DATE: / /	**Page ___ of _____**
		Cross - Reference
CONTROLLING FUNCTION:	**APPROVED BY:**	

FIGURE 5.30   Job Instruction Cover Page Form

The following are typical sections included in a job instruction:

1. Purpose
2. Scope
3. Safety
4. Precautions
5. References
6. Definitions, Acronyms, and Abbreviations
7. Equipment and Materials Required
8. *Activity Flowchart
9. Activity Description
   - Task descriptions
   - Test descriptions
   - Data flow and related instructions
10. *Prerequisites and Training Requirements
11. *Self-Inspection or Checklist
12. *Audit Requirements
13. Change History

*Sections that the ISO 9000 series does not require but that we believe are good business practice.

Each of the 13 sections serves a very unique and different purpose.

1. *Purpose.* This section is usually the first section in the job instruction. It defines very distinctly what the activity is and what it is intended to accomplish (e.g., "This job instruction defines how requests for quotations are prepared and distributed to potential subcontractors").
2. *Scope.* This section defines the boundaries that the activity operates within (e.g., "This job description defines how Department 972 processes requests for quotations that are projected to be less than $150,000").
3. *Safety.* This section describes hazards the employee might face while performing the work.
   Example:
   - Do not touch the tip of the soldering iron. The tip is hot.
   - Solder only under the ventilation hood. Make sure the fume hood sucks in all smoke from the iron. See the solder manual for further hazard information and precautions.
4. *Precautions.* This section describes precautions needed to avoid accidentally damaging or contaminating the product and/or equipment. Special instructions may need to be given, or referenced, in this section.

Example:

- These circuits are damaged by electrostatic discharge and by fatty substances. Please be sure to wear your antistatic bracelet and to thoroughly wash your hands before returning to the assembly line.

5. *References.* This section lists all of the quality manual, operating procedures, and Tier 4 documents that relate to, have bearing on, or are referred to in the job instruction. It will also include all of the form numbers that are used within the document. Copies of these forms should be attached in an appendix to the job instruction.

6. *Definitions, Acronyms, and Abbreviations.* This section defines all key quality terms used within the job instruction. It also defines any acronyms and abbreviations that are used within the document.

7. *Equipment and Materials.* This section lists all the equipment and materials the employee needs to do the job.

Example:

- A Braun soldering iron #AB123
- A Braun 1 MM taper point tim #AB003
- A jig fixture #C-56-791

8. *Activity Flowchart.* This section is a flowchart that pictorially shows how the tasks interrelate to one another. It is similar to the flowchart used in the operating procedure, only it typically expands one block in the operating procedure flowchart down to the task level.

9. *Activity Description.* This section defines the tasks that make up the activity described in the job instruction. It will also include how the data related to the job are collected, the form the data will be collected on, and what the employee does with the forms. It will also explain how, where, when, and why the tasks are done.

10. *Prerequisites and Training Requirements.* This section defines the prerequisites that all individuals should have before they are assigned to the job. It would include

- formal education requirements,
- experience requirements, and
- specific job-related training requirements (must be able to read blueprints, must be able to program in Fortran, etc.).

It will also include the formal and on-the-job training that will be provided to the individual that is specific to the job. Often it will include the level of proficiency requirements that must be met to allow the newly assigned employee to be certified on the job. (Certification in this case means that the person is no longer in the training classification.) Often this section of the job instruction will define how the employees' activities and output will be monitored until they are certified. This section should also define the performance requirements that the individual must reach to be certified.

11. *Self-Inspection or Checklist.* Checklists and self-inspection of the individual's output are used by the individual performing the job to ensure that the job is successfully completed. A checklist is made up of a list of tasks that the individual should perform to evaluate the quality of his or her work and be sure that the output is ready for the individual's customer. The employee signs off on the checklist, indicating that each of these tasks has been completed (see Figure 5.31). Self-inspection instructions provide individuals with direction on how to evaluate the jobs they are performing. The job instruction may require that a self-inspection be conducted each time a job is completed, or it can be based on a time interval (e.g., weekly or monthly).

The self-inspection instruction defines how the individual evaluates the activity to be sure it has been completed correctly.

Example:

Examine the solder joint for defects. The joint should be shiny and penetrate to both sides of the circuit board. Refer to the workmanship standard section of the operator's manual to see examples of acceptable and unacceptable solder joints. Solder joints with excess flux are not rejected at your workstation. The excess flux is removed at the next workstation.

The self-inspection is often based on the internal auditor's requirements, and its documented results are usually part of the internal auditor's review plan.

12. *Audit Requirements.* This section usually includes a list of questions that could be used by internal auditors or the area manager to evaluate compliance to the job instruction, to determine whether the activity was effectively conducted and whether it was conducted in compliance with the related clauses in the ISO 9000 standards and the job instruction.

13. *Change History.* Each time the job instruction is changed, the version identification number, the date of the version change, and a description of the changes within the job instruction are added to this page. Over a period of time, a history of all changes to the job instruction will be documented. This provides traceability back to the original release.

Based on the information provided here, the process information provided in the relative operating procedures, and the activity flowchart prepared

	JOB INSTRUCTION	
TITLE:	DOC. NO:	VERSION:
	DATE: / /	Page ___ of ____

REPORT AND PRESENTATION CHECKLIST

ISSUES TO BE CONSIDERED WHEN REVIEWING REPORTS AND PRESENTATIONS

Customer: **Assignment:**

TITLE: **UNIQUE ID (e.g. version no.):**

	Tick ✓	
General points	Yes	No
• Is there a clear explanation of		
- the objectives of the assignment (or this part of it)?	☐	☐
- the source of any data used in the preparation of the results?	☐	☐
- details of any assumptions used and whether they have been approved by the customer?	☐	☐
• Has the content of the report or presentation been approved by the customer?	☐	☐
• Is the format of the report the same as the in-house style?	☐	☐
• Has the customer reviewed a draft of the report?	☐	☐
• Has the report or presentation been reviewed by the assignment partner?	☐	☐
• Does the assignment's security classification require any special arrangements for printing, storing, packing, handling or delivery of the document?	☐	☐
Interim reports and presentations		
• Are the facts/arguments based on sound evidence rather than perception/belief?	☐	☐
• Do the facts/arguments used in the report support the conclusions?	☐	☐
Does the report provide an accurate analysis of the work undertaken and the conclusions reached for this stage of the assignment?	☐	☐
Final report		
• Has the customer signed off the interim report(s), if any?	☐	☐
• Are the facts/arguments based on sound evidence rather than perception/belief?	☐	☐
• Do the facts/arguments used in the report support the conclusions?	☐	☐
• Has the customer been informed of the contents of the report or reviewed a draft?	☐	☐
• Does the report address all of the issues in the terms of reference?	☐	☐

COMMENTS (To be completed if any NO's are answered above)

Prepared by: ....   Date: ....

REVIEWED BY:

Assignment manager ....   Date: ....

Partner (if appropriate) ....   Date: ....

Client (if appropriate) ....   Date: ....

FIGURE 5.31   Typical Checklist

by the team, the team should be able to prepare the job instruction. Sample work and job instruction forms can be found in Appendix VII.

Step 12—Prepare an Interrelationship Matrix

As the documents are prepared, an interrelationship matrix should be developed. Documenting the interrelationship matrix on one sheet of paper can be very confusing and complex. To simplify this task, we suggest that you prepare one matrix for each subclause in Clause 4.0 of the related ISO 9000 standard (Figure 5.32).

It is important to note that a quality manual document can be applied to more than one clause in an ISO 9000 standard. Likewise, operating procedures can relate to more than one document in the quality manual and/or more than one clause in the ISO 9000 standard. We like to store the individual interrelationship matrices in a computer base to simplify the job of analyzing and changing the matrix. We like to change the color of the individual boxes to visually show status of the document.

- Clear—unassigned
- Blue—assigned and on schedule
- Yellow—behind schedule
- Red—behind schedule and critical to the success of the project
- Orange—document released for piloting
- Green—document formally released

The interrelationship matrix is used to review the quality management documentation system with the objective of identifying missing or behind-schedule documents. The interrelationship matrix should be prepared and maintained by the QST.

Step 13—Prepare Missing Documents

During Step 12, the QST identified documents that were behind schedule or missing. Now the QST should prepare a corrective action plan to correct the discrepancies and get the document back on schedule. This corrective action plan should be tracked very closely because these are often the documents that cause the total project to miss schedule. Unfortunately, your organization cannot be registered if only 90 percent or even 98 percent of your quality management documentation system is complete.

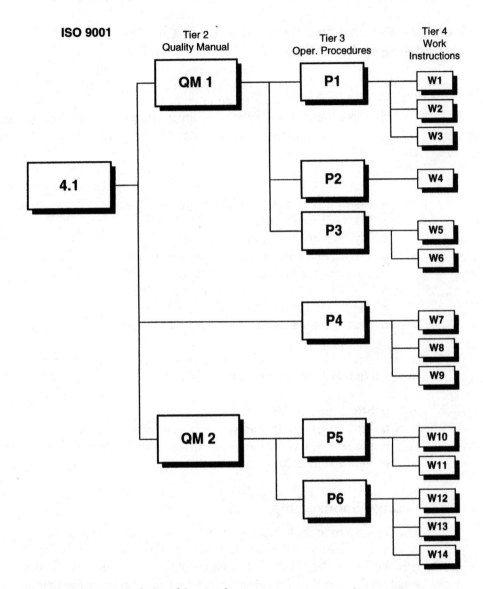

FIGURE 5.32 Interrelationship Matrix

Step 14—Expand the Organizational Change Management Activities

While documentation activities are under way, a number of Organizational Change Management activities initiated during the previous phase(s) should be expanded, and several new ones initiated. By this step, documentation will have added sufficient clarification of the extent and nature of the change to allow refinement of previous work based on new information obtained:

- Risk assessments, both QMS-wide, and specific to this change
- The QMS OCM plan
- The change readiness assessment
- The organizational alignment assessment
- Enablers and barriers assessment
- The tier-level transition management plan
- The communication plan
- More complete and accurate role maps

In addition, sufficient information should now exist to permit meaningful progress in regard to the following:

- Strengthening cascading sponsorship
- Providing OCM training for sponsors, change agents, and others
- Forming sponsor, change agent, and advocate teams
- Implementing the communication plan

Change Sponsorship

Developing strong sponsorship for change is the key to success in any business change implementation effort. Committed, effective sponsors are those who truly believe in the value of the change and who use their positional and personal power over the life cycle of the change process to ensure that any barrier to implementation is removed. These activities assist the development of effective sponsorship in two ways: (1) educating and coaching individual sponsors on how to perform the public and private roles necessary to legitimize the change; and (2) developing an unbroken "cascade of sponsorship" by which authority and responsibility for implementation are rolled down through the organization.

Use sponsorship activities to accomplish these goals:

- Educate and coach sponsors on how to perform their public and private roles.
- Begin to build a cascade of sponsorship.
- Maintain the sponsor motivation necessary to sustain the change.
- Manage the sponsorship issues that arise out of multiple change projects.

As a result of the sponsorship activities, sponsors should be willing and able to perform effectively as leaders and sustainers of change, a network of sponsors should be established, and the responsibilities for managing multiple projects should be clarified.

Change Communications

In business change, communication activities serve to build commitment to the change by providing information necessary to help organization members understand the need to change, the vision for the change, and the implications for them. The groups and individuals affected by the change are identified, a coherent communication plan is developed, and appropriate communication channels are chosen. "Four-way communication" is fostered, by creating avenues for dialogue between all parties in the change process. The overall goal of this strong emphasis on communication is to ease the implementation process by reducing resistance to change that is often related to lack of information about business reasons for change and what is expected of them. Now is the appropriate time to begin implementation of appropriate elements of the communication plan developed earlier.

Step 15—Circulate Documents for Comments and Update Them As Required

A list of functions that should receive and approve the individual documents before they are released should be prepared. At a minimum, it should include all of the functions that are defined on the related block diagram. Often, a section within each document is set aside to define the functions that must approve the document before it is released or changed.

As the documents near completion, they should be reviewed by the functions that are required to approve the document for release. Each area should comment on the document, and a list of suggested changes should be prepared by the subcommittee. The suggested changes should be included in the document, or the function that suggested the change should remove its suggestion. When the suggested changes are resolved, the documents should be circulated again to the functions that must approve the document for their signature, indicating that the document is ready for preliminary release. These preliminary release documents will be used for piloting purposes only. If piloting is not required, the sign-offs indicate that the document is ready for formal release.

Step 16—Send Documents to the Registrar for Review and Comments

Some organizations include in their registrar's contract an agreement that as document sets reach this stage, they will be reviewed by the registrar to identify any major omissions. This is also a good point in the QMS redesign process to get constructive suggestions related to the QMS from the registrar. All the registrar's suggestions should be reviewed by the subcommittee responsible for the document set, and the suggestions they agree with should be implemented. If subcommittee members do not agree with some of the suggestions made by the registrar, they should discuss them with the QST and then with the registrar. All disagreements should be resolved before the document set is preliminarily released. (Note: Read Chapter 6 for a better understanding of document sets.)

Step 17—Release the Preliminary Documentation for Pilot Studies Only

Now the document can be preliminarily released for piloting purposes only. In some cases where the document does not need to be piloted, the document can be formally released for use. This does not mean that the formally released document can automatically be implemented right away, because its implementation often has to coincide with the release of other documents and supporting training before it can be implemented.

Tips and Traps

Figures 5.33, 5.34, and 5.35 list tips and traps related to documentation control used by Ernst & Young LLP that we find useful. A similar approach can be effectively used for each subclause in ISO 9001, Clause 4.0, to double-check the redesigned process and its supporting documentation.

Key Documentation Points to Remember

The following are some suggestions related to writing any type of document. In the case of the QMS, these points are very important:

- Write to the audience that will be using the document.
- Write in the second person (you should do, you can do, etc.).

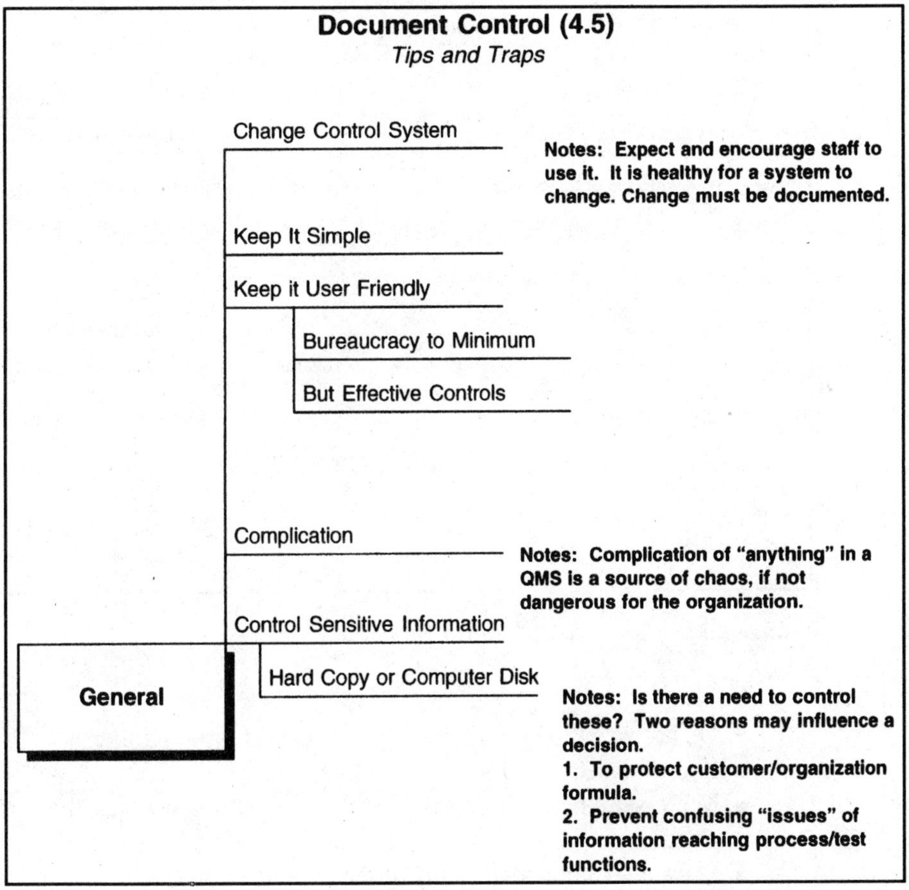

Document Control (4.5)
Tips and Traps

Change Control System
— **Notes:** Expect and encourage staff to use it. It is healthy for a system to change. Change must be documented.

Keep It Simple

Keep it User Friendly

Bureaucracy to Minimum

But Effective Controls

Complication
— **Notes:** Complication of "anything" in a QMS is a source of chaos, if not dangerous for the organization.

Control Sensitive Information

General

Hard Copy or Computer Disk
Notes: Is there a need to control these? Two reasons may influence a decision.
1. To protect customer/organization formula.
2. Prevent confusing "issues" of information reaching process/test functions.

Figure 5.33 General Tips and Traps

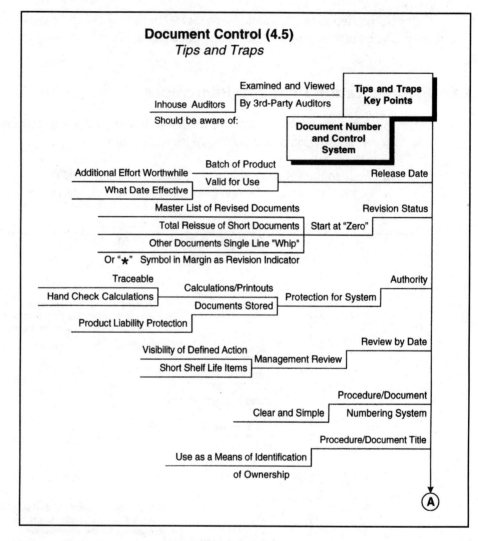

FIGURE 5.34   Document Control Tips and Traps

- Do not write in an autocratic or condescending manner.
- Keep the document as short as possible.
- Make sentences short and concise. Reword sentences that exceed 20 words.
- Separate major ideas into different subclauses, and minor ideas into different sentences.

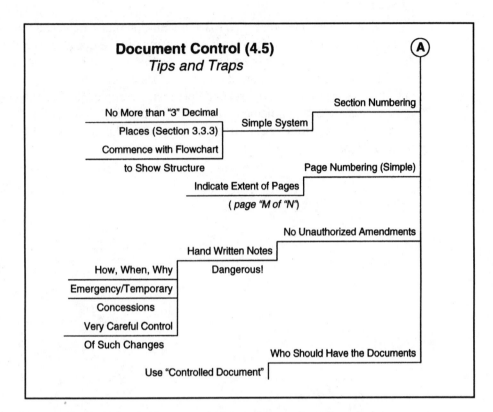

FIGURE 5.35   Document Control Tips and Traps (continued)

- Try to avoid words of more than three syllables.
- Make the document read like you are talking to a friend.
- Try to minimize the number of abbreviations. Only use abbreviations if they are repeated numerous times throughout the text.
- Last, but not least, always live by the KISS principle—Keep It Short and Simple.

Summary

During Phase III, all of the documents were prepared and released for pilot evaluations. Piloting the redesigned QMS documents is one of the first activities addressed in Phase IV—Implementation.

The way this book presents the documentation phase may lead the reader to believe that all of the documents have to complete the documentation phase before the implementation phase can start. Nothing could be further from the truth. In practice, the implementation phase goes on in parallel with the documentation phase. As groups of related documents complete the documentation phase, they should be implemented as soon as possible. This will reduce the culture shock to the total organization and speed up the implementation of the redesigned QMS.

6

Phase IV: Implementation

Introduction

This is where the rubber meets the road. Planning is fun and documenting is difficult, but the real work starts when the subcommittee starts to implement the redesigned QMS. This is the phase that separates the committed organization from the interested organization. Phase IV is where all the good-sounding words and phrases are translated into behavioral patterns. The most frequent reasons for the failure of improvement processes are not poor planning and not because the problem could not be solved. They failed as a result of poor or nonexistent implementation of the defined solution. You see, everyone is for change. I would like to see you change. We both would like to see them change. But should I change? No way! I am comfortable where I am. My expectations are being met. If I have to change, I will put it off as long as I possibly can. Yes, consciously or unconsciously, we all resist change.

The implementation phase of the QMS redesign is the point where organizations must translate their words into actions. They must stop talking about quality and start to change the way they act and react to the quality concepts. Employees will listen to the tongues in management's mouths, but they believe based on what the tongues in management's shoes do. As a project starts into the implementation phase, top management must increase its involvement and the amount of personal time it devotes to the QMS upgrade activities. Top management needs to show interest by closely following the implementation plan status, by visiting the pilot departments to determine firsthand how the project is going, and by actively communicating the implementation status to the rest of its team. The redesigned QMS should be an agenda item for every staff meeting during the implementation phase.

This is the phase where a good consultant really earns his or her money. An organization can find almost everything in books that it needs to know to document its QMS, but the transformation of theory into practice is where most organizations need help. A good consultant will have extensive knowledge about Organizational Change Management. A great deal of his or her effort will be devoted to how the documented processes are implemented, greatly increasing the probability of the processes being accepted and used by the people who need to live with the documentation and the processes it supports.

To enable the organization to smoothly move from the current state to the future state, support structures must be designed and put in place. Steering committees and design and implementation teams perform this function by providing support and guidance to the people affected by the change, ensuring the necessary resources are available, and finally, assessing, planning for, and dealing with enablers and barriers to change. These support structures become the means for cascading sponsorship. The activities in this cluster include: chartering the steering committee (sometimes called the transition council) and the design and implementation teams (sometimes called change agent teams); educating and training the members; monitoring and improving team performance; and establishing and maintaining communication channels between all the teams and the transition council.

Although the QMS upgrade process is defined in six distinct phases, one after another, in reality a great deal of overlap occurs between the documentation phase and the implementation phase. For most organizations just beginning to implement a documented QMS, there will be a considerable initial effort to document current procedures in order to achieve consistency without even trying to improve the present processes. Although there is a wide variation in the amount of time organizations require to develop the documentation (two months to two years, depending on several variables), let's be optimistic and say it is a four-month effort. If the organization begins its documentation in January, it will document some processes in January, some in February, more in March, and eventually wrap it up in April. Then they can implement them in May. The problem is that if your organization is like many others, your processes are not remaining stagnant for four months. By the time May rolls around, some of the documents you produced in January or February may no longer be accurate, and you will need to update them before implementing them. The cycle of updating may never end. It creates a moving target.

An alternative implementation plan can avoid the frustration associated with moving targets as they relate to documentation development and implementation. The alternative is to simply implement the procedures and work instructions in sets as they are developed. There are other benefits to using this approach. It reduces system shock that can be associated with a one-day cutover to the use of the redesigned QMS. By slowly introducing the use of documented procedures and instructions to the various work areas, there can be an adaptation period that allows for more comfort with the redesigned QMS. The staggered implementation approach provides you with feedback in the early stages that can be used to improve other procedures or future implementation activities. This approach also allows you to prioritize the processes so that the ones that have the highest benefit to the organization are implemented first without waiting for the others to be completed.

By this point in the process, the OCM activities are well under way, and key managers have been trained and understand the roles that they must play. During the implementation phase, the change agents and sustaining sponsors play a key role in having the redesigned QMS accepted.

The following is a list of the steps that will lead the organization through the implementation phase:

1. Define the documentation distribution and control system.
2. Determine when sets of documents are ready to be implemented.
3. Expand the QMS and individual OCM activities.
4. Develop a document set implementation plan.
5. Define pilot area and prepare the pilot study plan.
6. Execute the pilot study plan.
7. Review the pilot results and alter the processes if necessary.
8. Circulate the revised documentation for formal release.
9. Implement the formally released document set.
10. Evaluate the new processes to identify weaknesses and correct them before they become problems.
11. Conduct internal audits.
12. Measure the performance level of the new processes.
13. Analyze the total QMS.

Implementation starts as soon as the documents have been preliminarily released and is completed when the subcommittee verifies that the updated process is working as intended. You will note that it is completed before the new QMS has become internalized into the organization, because this can take many years.

Throughout the implementation phase, we will be working with processes, although the documentation that will be used includes conceptual, procedural, and instructional documents (Tiers 2, 3, and 4). This is a legitimate approach because the concepts that the organization embraces affect the way an organization operates. It is the organization's processes and related procedures that define how the organization operates. By focusing on implementing the new documented procedures that support a process, the adequacy of the total documentation system can be evaluated simultaneously.

Step 1—Define the Documentation Distribution and Control System

During Phase IV, first priority must be given to defining how the documents will be distributed and controlled. These decisions must be made before the actual implementation of the new documented QMS can be started. This means that the first procedure that must be implemented is the document control distribution and maintenance procedure, which includes such key decisions as

- How will the documentation be distributed?
- Who will have them?
- How will outdated documents be handled?
- How will individuals know what the correct version level is?
- How will the documents be stored?
- Where will the document masters be stored, and how will they be controlled?
- How will the documentation be updated?

An on-line data system can solve many of the problems related to change level and revision control. A good on-line document control system not only will provide the latest approved document to the user but also will control the revision and approval cycle. With these computer programs, the revision generation, approval, and release activities are all controlled within the computer program. In most cases, this approach works well for manuals and operating procedures, but it may not be practical at the instructional level if the people who use the instruction documents do not have ready access to an on-line computer. The other problem is that people feel more comfortable with hard-copy documents. To offset this problem, many organizations allow hard copies of their documents to be printed and use the on-line system to define current levels and to facilitate the revision cycle. This approach has a built-in problem of removing obsolete documents from the user operations.

Although all of the approaches have problems, we believe that an on-line document control system is the best way to manage your document process for the following reasons:

- It provides a single point of reference.
- Only the latest revision is available.
- All the masters are in one place.
- A detailed document change history can be maintained.
- Only properly approved documents can be released.
- The document approval process can be customized to the individual document.
- It greatly reduces cycle time because reviews can be conducted in parallel.
- It does not increase the exposure to having outdated copies of the document in use over the other approaches.
- It minimizes the work required to maintain the documentation system.
- It minimizes the possibility of marked-up documents being used.

"H. James Harrington's ISO 9000 Step by Step" CD-ROM package is an excellent example of a document control system that meets these performance requirements. Of course, this is not the only software package available that can fulfill these needs.

What if you don't have an on-line computer system available in all the areas? Well, unfortunately, we will have to chop down more trees. The best approach that meets the needs of all organizations is the storage of documents in a series of loose-leaf notebooks. There is a seemingly endless number of ways that loose-leaf notebooks can be used to organize the documentation. The one that we find effective uses a combination of bound books and loose-leaf binders.

- A bound book is used to hold the quality manual. To start with, this can be a loose-leaf binder, but it can be replaced with a bound book when the Tier 2 documents become well defined. Normally, this is shortly after the organization is registered. The advantage of having the quality manual in a bound book is that the total book can be replaced when a change is made, providing better control of the quality manual. Often this approach is combined with a serialized quality manual assigned to individuals. The obsolete manuals are turned in when a new manual is released.

- One or more loose-leaf binders are used to hold all of the operating procedures (quality, safety, finance, personnel, engineering, IS, etc.).
- Each area has a loose-leaf binder of Tier 4 documents that relate to the activities in that specific area.

In this case, a function (document control center) is assigned the responsibility for maintaining the masters for the quality manual and the operating procedures. Usually this function also coordinates the revision process for these documents. When a revision to a document has been approved by the appropriate functions, copies are sent out to all manual holders instructing them to remove the old document and return it to the document control center, where it is destroyed. The more effective document control systems number each document with the individual loose-leaf binder identification number and require that each obsolete document be returned to the document control center. In this case, the document control center takes on the responsibility for identifying individuals who have been assigned loose-leaf binders and are not complying with the document control procedures. With the loose-leaf binder number on each document, the person that the loose-leaf binder has been assigned to has accepted the responsibility for removing all copies from the work area that were made from the document assigned to him or her when they become obsolete. In some organizations, each page of the documents is stamped "DO NOT COPY." In these cases, additional copies are provided by the document control center upon request. This helps control the proliferation of copies throughout the organization.

The major exposure to the loose-leaf binder approach is that documents can be readily removed and copied for use in the workplace. By marking the loose-leaf binder identification number on each document, copies can be readily traced back to their source so that problems can be eliminated.

The loose-leaf binders used to store the documents should be clearly identified on their covers and spines so that their contents can be readily identified without having to look inside.

What we have presented here is a much better document control system than ISO 9000 standards require. A minimum document control system would not require a document control center. In this case, the individual organizations perform the role of the document control center for their own documents. Usually in these cases, the people who receive the documents are obligated to dispose of the outdated documents when they receive new documents. Although this approach works, it requires a great deal of discipline on the part of the entire organization's management and employees.

Step 2—Determine When Sets of Documents Are Ready to Be Implemented

Phase III ended with preliminary documents being released for pilot evaluation. This does not mean that the piloting activities are ready to begin. For the piloting activities to start, a complete set of preliminary documents must be collected that thoroughly defines an individual process. Typically, a set of documents will be developed around a procedure that defines an important part of the QMS. For the document set to be considered complete, the procedure, all of the related instructions, and the related quality manual document should be at least at preliminary release levels. We will refer to this combination of documents as a document set throughout the remainder of this chapter. Usually, the piloting of a document set will be the responsibility of the subcommittee that prepared the procedure. As a result, the subcommittee should track the status of the document set to determine when all of the documents in the set have completed their required reviews. When this occurs, the set is ready to start the implementation process.

Step 3—Expand the QMS and Individual Organizational Change Management Activities

The process of actually implementing business change brings to bear all the activities from the other OCM plans as needed to deal with the inevitable and unanticipated twists and turns on the path to change. The business case and the vision for change must be clarified and reiterated often, sponsorship must be monitored, and the transition plan and commitment approach must be modified as necessary due to emergent internal or external events. Finally, evaluation against the critical success factors for the change effort must be done. It is crucial to monitor all of the implementation risks during the full life cycle of the change and recognize when an intervention is appropriate to ensure that the project is on target. It is in this stage of change that the "art" of managing the people dimension of business change implementation becomes crucial.

Implementing change is challenging and requires the ability to recognize when to intervene or to step in to do the following:

- Clarify roles, responsibilities, and membership in the executive sponsor team, steering committee, and change agent teams to meet the demands of implementation

- Provide training to members of those teams to enable a high level of fulfillment of their roles and responsibilities
- Bolster waning sponsor commitment through coaching and feedback
- Rebuild an ineffective team
- Reinforce the need for change by communicating the business case for change
- Implement organizational alignment enablers that have been determined as key to driving required behavior

Other OCM activities initiated earlier are frequently expanded or accelerated during this phase.

As a result of performing the implementation activities, the organization will have a realized return on their investment of the time and resources made to implement a change and achievement of agreed-upon business results. In addition, the organization will have smoother transition from current state to future state, and opportunities for other improvement efforts that can add value and contribute to meeting business strategy.

Step 4—Develop a Document Set Implementation Plan

The subcommittee should now develop a plan that defines how the document set will be deployed (implemented). This plan should define the following:

1. Process measurements before, during, and after implementation
2. Prerequisites for implementation
3. Training
4. Detailed timeline implementation plan and chart
5. Support during process start-up
6. Problem and suggestion handling
7. Process analysis and qualification

Process Measurements Before, During, and After Implementation

The first thing that the subcommittee needs to address is how to measure the efficiency, effectiveness, and adaptability of the process before, during, and after the redesigned process is implemented. To accomplish this, the flowcharts prepared to support the procedure development activities provide a good starting point. A well-designed process should reduce the resources (people, cycle time, dollars, space, etc.) required to operate the process while simultaneously improving the satisfaction level of the individuals and organizations that receive its output. It is very important that the measurement system be defined and implemented before the redesigned process is implemented so that the old process characteristics will be well defined before the process is changed. Often, organizations will run a control sample in parallel with the changeover to compare the new process to the old one. We do not recommend this approach because it greatly complicates the situation. We do support the use of control samples during pilot studies.

During implementation, the process's performance often decreases as the people using the process go through a learning curve (see Figure 6.1). This decrease in performance should be anticipated, and the subcommittee should project how long the learning curve will have a negative impact on the process, as well as the magnitude of this impact. As Figure 6.1 indicates, the actual performance of the new process cannot be measured until the process has become stable.

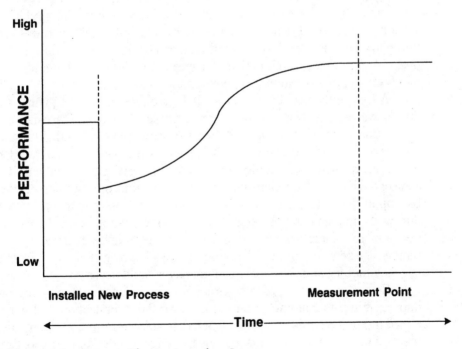

FIGURE 6.1 Process Change Learning Curve

Define the Prerequisites for Implementation

The subcommittee must define all the items that must be in place and the minimum quantities that should be available before the new process is implemented. Prerequisites include such items as classrooms, equipment, computers, Tier 5 documents (recording documents), training programs, trainers, backup personnel, and so on. Another key prerequisite to implementation is the agreement of the affected department managers on the implementation plan and schedule. Don't implement a process change that affects manufacturing at the end of the month, or one that impacts finance during the budget cycle. Be sure that all the prerequisites are available before you start to implement the document set.

Training

Training related to the process should be included in the related documents. If it is not, the associated training programs need to be defined. Even if the requirements are included in the document, the training syllabus is usually not included and must be developed. We find that the use of photographs and videotapes provides an effective way of delivering training that is more uniform, and often less expensive, than on-the-job training. The problem with working with an experienced employee to learn a job is that the trainee is introduced to all of the experienced employee's bad habits as well as his or her good ones. We find that a combination of conceptual, off-line training, followed by hands-on, in-process training, works best for most applications.

A frequently asked question is, "If I am only documenting what is going on, do we need to train anyone? For example, if only Joe is using a work instruction and Joe wrote the work instruction, why do we need to train him in the use of the work instruction?" The answer is you don't need to train Joe, but this is an excellent opportunity for some job enrichment assignments. Choose someone who is not familiar with that job and train him or her to serve as a backup for Joe when he is out. Reassigning a new employee to a particular job during the implementation phase has many advantages. Not only does it provide a more comprehensive evaluation; it also establishes a cross-training initiative. The new employee will also verify the adequacy of Joe's job instruction in a way that Joe and the department manager could never do.

Here is an example of how Grace Specialty Polymers (GSP) approached implementing its training program. Because the organization had not maintained training records, it pretty much had to start from scratch. It first defined the minimum job requirements and the training required for each job. Employees who had been in the same job function at GSP for a minimum of five years were certified based on past performance. Employees with less than five years had to provide evidence of training that covered the requirements. If the documentation was not available, the employees were allowed to continue to work on their present assignments, if a personal training program was defined that would provide the required training in a reasonable period of time. We believe that the GSP process is a very stringent one. A more typical approach would be to certify all employees who have been on the job for six months and have performed acceptably. The organization should also look at how many months employees can be off the job before they are decertified, requiring them to be retrained before they perform the specific assignment.

Detailed Timeline Implementation Plan and Chart

The subcommittee should develop a detailed timeline implementation plan and chart, which should be reviewed with the department managers who are impacted to obtain their agreement and support. Where practical, the names of the individuals involved with each document and the training classes should be identified. We recommend that an estimate of how the workflow will be affected and suggestions on how to contain the additional workload be included in this work plan.

Support During Process Start-up

The period after the new process is installed and the employees are institutionalizing the process is a very critical point in the implementation phase. During this time period, the subcommittee members should be very visible throughout the process, probing for problems, potential problems, and identifying improvement opportunities. The subcommittee should audit the activities to be sure that the documented process is being followed, that the data are being recorded correctly, and that the equipment is working as projected. The subcommittee members should have an ongoing dialog with the employees, probing to define ways that the process can be simplified. Each idea should be evaluated and the action that was, will be, or will not be taken should be reported back to the individual employee within 24 hours.

Problem and Suggestion Handling

Once the turmoil of starting up the newly documented process is over, the subcommittee needs to put into place a system that will allow employees to suggest improvements to the process that the subcommittee can investigate.

Each suggestion submitted by an employee during this time period should be answered within 48 hours. In addition, a hotline should be established so that the subcommittee is immediately notified of a critical problem and can take immediate corrective action. Typically, this quick reaction process is kept in place for approximately three months.

Process Analysis and Qualification

The subcommittee should continue to measure the process's performance until the process stabilizes and sufficient data have been collected to define the new process's performance level. These data should be reviewed with the QST to be sure that the new process is performing at a level that is acceptable from management's standpoint. If the performance of the new process is acceptable, the process is classified as qualified. A qualified process is one that the subcommittee has verified is operating in accordance with its documentation and its output meets the customer's requirements.

Step 5—Define Pilot Area and Prepare the Pilot Study Plan

The subcommittee should now define whether the document set should be piloted before it is totally implemented. If the redesigned QMS reflects new concepts, requires new equipment, or is a major change from past approaches, it probably is a good idea to select a small part of the affected departments in which to pilot the process. This approach helps ensure that all potential problems have been considered and corrected. The pilot study will evaluate the following:

- The adequacy of the training program
- The effectiveness of the process
- The efficiency of the process
- How adjustable the process is
- How understandable the documentation is
- How complete the documentation is
- How user-friendly the process and documentation are
- How complete and interconnected the documentation is

The pilot study plan should define what measurements will be recorded to evaluate the previous questions. In addition, the pilot plan should define the sample size and the way the data will be recorded. Typical items that would be included in a pilot plan are the following:

- Start and end dates
- Areas that will be used to do the evaluation
- A measurement plan
- The data collection forms
- The roles that the supporting people will play
- How the as-is status will be measured so that the impact of the change can be measured
- The control sample (if needed) will be defined
- The pass/fail criteria for the pilot study

If the new process includes the use of new equipment, it may not be cost-justifiable to purchase or rent the equipment. For example, the redesigned process may make use of a new computer-controlled recall system for the recalibration of instruments. In this case, a mock-up model is often used with a lot of behind-the-scenes work going on to simulate the equipment. This approach is an effective way of evaluating the effect that new equipment will have on the process without a major expenditure for equipment and software support. This approach is often called conference room modeling.

How do you select the pilot areas? Do you select the most-experienced part of the organization so that the individuals involved can identify improvements in the new process, or do you select the weakest part of the organization to ensure that the new design will work anywhere? Each of these approaches has its pluses and minuses.

We like to take the conservative position and run the pilot study in the weakest areas, thereby ensuring that the process will work in any area. Another reason for selecting the weakest area is that usually the best people are used to prepare the work instructions, so they have been involved in developing the redesigned process. Having them model the process provides little added value. We even find that it is a good idea to bring brand new people into the area so that the training and documentation system can be thoroughly analyzed.

It is important to understand that not all document sets need to be modeled. A lot of time and money can be wasted if an organization blindly charges into the modeling activities. The important thing is that you cannot take extensive risks with any of the organization's management systems, let alone the QMS.

Step 6—Execute the Pilot Study Plan

Execute—a good word for the pilot evaluation. Sometimes this is exactly what happens when the subcommittee implements the pilot process. These pilot studies can literally kill or destroy some of the concepts that the subcommittee thought were very sound.

Great care should be taken to minimize the process distortion that always impacts pilot studies if the targets are aware of the study. It is just human nature to try a little harder, work a little faster, and do just a little bit better whenever someone is watching what you are doing. It is often impossible to continuously operate at the same rate you did when the industrial engineer conducted the time and motion study. That's why it is considered good practice to add an X-factor to the actual measurements, taking into consideration that there are times of lost productivity. It is for this reason that a pilot program often makes use of a control sample that is run in parallel with the pilot study to collect as-is performance data to compare with the pilot results.

The pilot study usually starts by the subcommittee holding a meeting and explaining the purpose of the study to all individuals who will be involved in the study. That is followed by training the employees who will be involved in the pilot study using the training documentation plan plus any special data control or procedural training that relates only to the pilot study. During the study, the subcommittee members should conduct regular reviews of the process to ensure that the plan is being implemented correctly. The subcommittee should personally collect the related data and review it each day to identify abnormalities. This will allow the subcommittee to review the data with the person who recorded it while the situation is still clear in the individual's mind.

By the end of the pilot study data collection stage, the subcommittee, with the aid of the people in the pilot area, normally will have identified a number of improvements that should be made before the documents are formally released. Often, the effectiveness of these suggestions will have already been evaluated in conjunction with the pilot process. If the pilot process, when compared with the original process and/or the control sample, meets the performance requirements established by the process's customer and management, the documents are upgraded to reflect the suggested changes and prepared for formal release.

Step 7—Review the Pilot Results and Alter the Processes If Necessary

At the end of the study, the subcommittee should prepare a document set pilot evaluation final report. This report should include the following:

- Sample size
- Performance comparison

- Data confidence limits
- Suggested changes to the process
- A recommendation of future activities (documents should be released, change documents, repeat pilot study, etc.)

The subcommittee should also revise the document set implementation plan to reflect the lessons learned during the study.

Step 8—Circulate the Revised Documentation for Formal Release

Once the documentation is updated to reflect the pilot study, the revised documentation and the documentation implementation plan should be circulated for approval. Usually the pilot study final report will accompany the document review package to provide additional assurance that the documents should be formally released. When all approvals have been received, the formal installation process is ready to start.

Step 9—Implement the Formally Released Document Set

With the experience gained in the pilot process and the resulting corrections, the implementation of the formally released documentation should go relatively smoothly, allowing much of the subcommittee's efforts to be directed at implementing the OCM part of the installation plan. This does not mean that all of the precautions and suggested follow-up activities described in the pilot program should not be used in the formally released document set implementation activities. When the implementation plan is fully implemented, the subcommittee should prepare an installation report comparing the formally released process to the pilot process and the previous process's performance. This report often will include a list of suggestions that should be considered during Phase VI, the continuous improvement phase.

Step 10—Evaluate the New Processes to Identify Weaknesses and Correct Them Before They Become Problems

Once a process is implemented, the subcommittee should continue to work closely with the people using the process and the process's customers. This should allow the subcommittee to identify weaknesses in the process and get them corrected before they become major problems. This close monitoring activity should continue until the process stabilizes.

Step 11—Conduct Internal Audits

As soon as the subcommittee believes that the process is in compliance with the formally released documentation, it should ask the internal audit group to do an audit of the document set. This will provide an independent process assessment as well as a means to debug the audit procedures. The internal audit team should conduct its audit of the process exactly as it would conduct a normal process audit. At the end of the audit, the audit team should prepare a final report documenting its findings and submit it to the subcommittee. The subcommittee and the internal audit team should be careful not to blindly accept the internal audit team's report and start changing the process documentation, because the audit team documentation could be the real problem. Remember, the audit is used to prove out the audit team procedures and related checklists, as well as the process being evaluated. Frequently, the audit procedures are rewritten based on the results of the document set audit activities. All discrepancies noted by the audit team should be resolved, either by changing the document set, the audit procedures, or retraining the employees as required.

Step 12—Measure the Performance Level of the New Processes

When a process has stabilized and successfully completed the internal audit, the subcommittee should prepare a final report that will be reviewed with the QST. This report will be a complete review of the subcommittee's activities and the resulting impact that the documented process had on the performance of the process. Typical things that make up this report include the following:

- Total cost to redesign the process
- Before-and-after performance evaluation
- Time required to recapture the investment
- List of major problems faced by the subcommittee
- List of potential additional improvements
- List of suggested improvements to the redesigned process

■ List of process-related measurements that should be followed by management

If the final report is accepted by the QST, the subcommittee should be rewarded for its contribution, and then disbanded.

Step 13—Analyze the Total Quality Management System

The approach of document set analysis is continued until all documents have been formally released and implemented. After each document set has successfully completed implementation, the total QMS should be intact. Now the QMS needs to be evaluated to ensure that it all links together without creating conflicts, and that there are no voids in it when it is compared with the appropriate ISO 9000 standard. This is achieved by three very different approaches:

■ QMS assessment
■ QMS audit
■ QMS preassessment

The QST should repeat the assessment conducted in Phase I to be sure that the new QMS is capable of meeting the minimum necessary requirements to have an effective QMS. In addition, the organization's audit team should conduct a complete audit of the new QMS. These audits will be used to ensure that the QMS is being followed and is adequate to meet the ISO 9000 requirements. Another way of accomplishing this activity is to have the organization that was selected to register the QMS perform a preassessment audit. Often, this preassessment audit is part of the price the registrar quotes in its contract with your organization. The preassessment audit provides an independent view of the new QMS and allows the organization to make final adjustments to the QMS before the formal assessment. We recommend using all three approaches to ensure that the organization has an effective QMS. At a very minimum, the first two approaches should be used.

Any deviation discovered during these different types of evaluations should be corrected. When the identified discrepancies are corrected, the QST should document the results of the analysis and schedule a meeting with the executive team to notify it that the new QMS has successfully been implemented and is now ready to be assessed by second- or third-party organizations. At this meeting, the QST should report what effect the new QMS had on the organization's performance and project a three-year return on investment.

Summary

During Phase IV—Implementation—the following was accomplished:

- All of the documents were formally released, evaluated, and successfully implemented.
- A final report was prepared for each document set that records the set's performance level.
- The total QMS was evaluated to ensure that it met minimum requirements for a good quality management system.
- The new QMS was evaluated to determine whether it improved the efficiency, effectiveness, and adaptability of the organization's quality processes.
- The QMS was classified as being ready for external organizations to evaluate its adequacy and compliance to the related parts of the ISO 9000 series.

If the QMS is not scheduled to be registered by a third party, the QST will be rewarded for its contributions to the organization's future and then will be disbanded. If the organization is pursuing third-party registration of its QMS, the QST will not be disbanded until the end of Phase V.

Note: Parts of this phase were taken from Chapter 5 of *Total Improvement Management* written by Ralph Ott, published by McGraw-Hill in 1995.

Phase V: Audits

Introduction

We want to address one major misconception about audits right at the start. Audits are conducted to confirm that the activity being evaluated is conducted correctly. That means that the best audits are comprehensive audits that define no deviations. Too often, management and the audit team itself are disappointed if the audit does not find major problems. As a result, when two or three audits are conducted that confirm that the procedures are being followed, management stops the audits, thinking they are a waste of time and money. Nothing could be further from the truth.

Audits are an effective way of reinforcing desired behavioral patterns. Audits are a lot like that police car you see sitting around the corner from a stop sign. The average driver sees the police car and will carefully pull up to the stop sign and come to a full, complete stop, wait 10 to 15 seconds, then proceed across the road. The next day, when the same driver comes to the same cross street, the driver, once again, comes to a full stop. If the driver repeats this process for the next six months and does not encounter a police car near the cross street, the driver has a tendency to stop for shorter and shorter periods and, in time, does not come to a complete stop before he or she presses down on the gas pedal. Often, employees and managers know what they should be doing but take shortcuts or put off doing the things they should. Stopping at a stop sign is important, so the city conducts audits to be sure that this process is being followed. Likewise, audits should be conducted to ensure that the procedures that are used to run your organization are followed. If it isn't necessary to follow the procedure, get rid of it. Management should show their commitment to the remaining procedures by establishing an effective audit process.

During and following the implementation activities, we assist in determining whether the human, process, and technical objectives have been attained on time and within budget. The activities and deliverables from this work provide a structure to manage the transition; track, refine, and evaluate the initiative; and ultimately, to sustain the change effort. Contingency plans are developed on an ongoing basis to address any "gaps" in the initiative. Finally, change implementation activities help you frame the organizational learning that has taken place during the project.

Specific OCM elements that should be included in most audit activities include the following:

- Monitor and measure implementation effectiveness (including such elements as communications, training, commitment levels, behavior changes required).
- Monitor schedule adherence.
- Determine what, when, and where corrective action is indicated.
- Modify the transition plan.
- Communicate findings to those who can take corrective action.

Figure 7.1 provides a view of a comprehensive audit system for an organization. As Figure 7.1 indicates, an audit activity can be put into motion in two different ways. Winning organizations today use both types: internal (self) audits and external audits.

Internal (Self) Audits

The following four types of internal audits provide a comprehensive audit program for most organizations.

- Employee self-assessments
- Management self-assessments
- Internal staff audits
- Executive audits

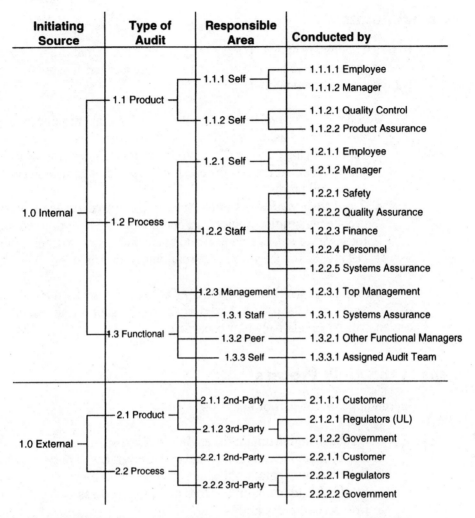

Audits of the Quality Management System cover 1.2.3, 1.2.2, and 2.2.2 only. The others, we believe, are good business practices.

FIGURE 7.1 Organizational Audit Overview

A great deal could be written about how to design and implement each of these audits, but we have decided to only discuss in detail management self-assessments. Management self-assessments were selected because they are such a powerful tool—one that is largely underutilized by most organizations.

External Audits

External audits are audits conducted by organizations that are not part of the management structure of the organization being audited. There are two different types of external audits:

- *Second-party audits*—Audits conducted by an organization that is directly purchasing products or services from the supplier or potential supplier being audited. These audits assess not only the QMS but also the process that creates the end products and may include evaluations of the end products.
- *Third-party audits*—Audits that are conducted by governmental or private registration bodies (e.g., operational safety audits conducted by the government, or financial audits conducted by Ernst & Young LLP, Deloitte & Touche, or other accounting audit firms).

Second-party QMS audits have been in use for more than 50 years, so we will concentrate on the use of third-party audits in support of ISO 9000 registration, which is a relatively new concept.

Steps in the Audit Process

The audit phase consists of six steps.

1. Establish and maintain the employee self-assessment process.
2. Establish and maintain the management self-assessment process.
3. Establish and maintain the internal staff audit process.
4. Establish and maintain the executive audit process.
5. Host second-party audits.
6. Host third-party audits.

Step 1—Establish and Maintain the Employee Self-Assessment Process

Employee self-assessments are audits that are conducted by the employees related to their own activities. (An assessment is a type of audit.) Often they take the form of check sheets that are filled out as a requirement defined in the job instruction (e.g., design review check sheets, inspection check sheets, supplier evaluation check sheets, etc.).

The self-assessment tasks and schedule should be defined in the related instructions that have already been verified and released. The employees should have been trained to perform the self-assessment as part of their job training. All that remains to do now is to follow the related instructions and document the results of the assessment.

The employee is responsible for ensuring that corrective action is taken to correct any deviation he or she finds. Often this means changing the way that the employee is doing an assignment or contacting the proper individual who can implement the required changes. The employee should not continue performing the activity until the problem has been corrected.

Step 2—Establish and Maintain the Management Self-Assessment Process

Management self-assessments are audits of the QMS and other management systems that the manager is personally responsible for. Usually these assessments are conducted once every three months using an assessment plan developed by the individual manager and approved by his or her immediate supervisor. Immediate action plans are developed for each detected discrepancy. The results of the assessments are documented by the managers and submitted to their immediate supervisors. These reports are summarized by the executives and presented to the executive committee.

No one is in a better position to know whether the job is being done correctly than the employee who is doing it. The next person best prepared to evaluate a department's output is not quality assurance or a staff audit team, but the department manager. We normally think of department managers as working so closely with the employees that they always know what is going on, so without any research they can provide an accurate assessment of the department's quality level. Often, however, the manager becomes part of the problem. What the manager needs is a systematic and objective way of assessing the department's activities, allowing undesirable situations to be corrected before they become problems. One way of accomplishing this is for the manager to conduct a quarterly self-assessment.

Department Self-Assessment Checklist

The manager has the primary responsibility of ensuring that all the department's activities are managed in accordance with the organization's practices, procedures, and good business judgment. Each manager must understand the organization's control documents, the intent behind each of them, and how to implement them. The control aspects of each job should be part of the training package for that job. Each manager must periodically review with all employees the control aspects of their jobs and ensure that all employees clearly understand them. The manager should also conduct systematic audits to ensure that employees are in compliance with these requirements.

A self-assessment checklist can be used to evaluate how effectively the department is adhering to control requirements and to identify requirements that are needlessly complex, restrictive, time-consuming, burdensome, or demotivating.

The self-assessment checklist should identify key control items related to the department's activity. It will usually cover much more than just the QMS items. Typically, it will also include environmental, safety, security, and financial issues. It should specify how the item can be evaluated, the size of the sample that will be audited, and what constitutes acceptable performance. The manager's draft of the self-assessment checklist should be submitted to the next higher-level manager to be sure it is comprehensive and that the performance standards are reasonable. Figure 7.2 contains items that might be found on the self-assessment checklist of the manager of an accounting department responsible for travel expense account validation. You will note that the self-assessment goes beyond the quality-related requirements.

Self-Assessment Procedure

Each manager should personally conduct a self-assessment at least once every three months. Adequate data should be collected and maintained to ensure that an independent audit can verify that the self-assessment was conducted. All items that fail the self-assessment performance standard must have corrective action plans developed and implemented that will prevent them from recurring.

When the self-assessment form and corrective action plans have been completed, the manager should meet with the next higher-level manager to review the self-assessment. The higher-level manager will verify that the assessment was conducted, that the results are valid, that problems are classified correctly, and that the corrective action plans are adequate. He or she will then sign off on the form.

The functional-level manager will summarize, on a quarterly basis, all the unsatisfactory items that were detected in the area and present the action plans at an executive team meeting.

It is very important that the self-assessment process be presented to the managers as a tool to help them identify problems and develop plans to correct them, not as an ax to be held over the manager's head. Each manager should also be told that failure to record the true findings of the self-assessment could lead to dismissal from the organization for falsification of data. The self-assessment process helps to develop and maintain an effective preventive system of management controls. It brings the exceptions to the attention of management,

---

1. Review twelve travel expense accounts that have already been processed by the department to ensure they are filled out correctly and the calculations are accurate.

   PERFORMANCE STANDARD: One error is marginal if another error has not been recorded in the last three audits. Two errors is unacceptable performance.

   ASSESSMENT DATA: Number of errors found in each expense account.

   1. _____   5. _____   9. _____
   2. _____   6. _____   10. _____
   3. _____   7. _____   11. _____
   4. _____   8. _____   12. _____

   Total number of errors: _____

   • STATUS: Passed _____ Failed _____

2. Check eight employees in the department to see what jobs they are performing. Ask them if they thought their training was adequate. Check the training log to verify that each person was trained for the job actually being performed.

   PERFORMANCE STANDARD: Zero errors is acceptable. One error is marginal if no errors were recorded in the previous three assessments. Two errors is unsatisfactory.

   ASSESSMENT DATA: Names of the employees evaluated

NAME	NO OF ERRORS	NAME	NO OF ERRORS
1 _____	_____	5 _____	_____
2 _____	_____	6 _____	_____
3 _____	_____	7 _____	_____
4 _____	_____	8 _____	_____

   Number of employees not trained for the jobs they were doing: _____
   Number of employees not satisfied with training: _____
   Number of errors in records: _____
   • STATUS: Passed _____ Failed _____

FIGURE 7.2 Typical Accounting Department Manager's Self-Assessment Checklist

3.   Security
     (a)   Check your records to see if a security awareness meeting has been held in the last six months. Record the date of the last meeting.
     (b)   Check 5 combination locks to be sure they have been changed in the last 12 months.
     (c)   After working hours, check 8 office cubicles to be sure the desks and files are locked and that no confidential material has been left out.

PERFORMANCE STANDARD: Zero errors is acceptable. One error in the last four assessments just meets requirements. Two errors in the last four assessments is unsatisfactory.

ASSESSMENT DATA:
(a)   Date of the last meeting: _____
(b)   Record serial numbers of locks checked and date the combinations were changed.
1. _____
2. _____
3. _____
4. _____
5. _____

(c) Record the location number of the cubicles that were audited.

NAME	NO OF ERRORS	NAME	NO OF ERRORS
1 _____ _____		5 _____ _____	
2 _____ _____		6 _____ _____	
3 _____ _____		7 _____ _____	
4 _____ _____		8 _____ _____	

• STATUS: Passed _____   Failed _____

Assessment Performed by _____ Date _____

FIGURE 7.2   Continued

where the problems can be resolved, allowing the organization's procedures to be modified as business and customer needs change.

No auditor can do a more effective job of assessing an area's operation than its immediate manager. No one knows more about its people, its customers, its strengths, its weaknesses, its pressures, and its compromises than the manager directly responsible for the area. We have chosen to highlight this audit approach because we believe it is one of the most effective audit approaches available and that it is underutilized.

Step 3—Establish and Maintain the Internal Staff Audit Process

Internal staff audits are conducted by a department within the organization that has been assigned the responsibility for auditing the organization's compliance to practices and procedures. These audits usually follow a set schedule over a number of months that allows the organization to be completely audited once every two years. The department responsible for the internal staff audits usually releases a quarterly standard audit schedule. The standard schedule is usually supplemented with special audits that focus on areas that are having problems and/or are implementing changes to the related management systems.

The standard internal staff audit instructions were evaluated and released during Phase IV. The standard internal staff audit instructions should be closely aligned with the individual assignment audit instructions, ensuring that the employee is not surprised with the results of the audits.

In addition to the standard audit, the internal staff audit department often conducts special audits to identify weaknesses in processes that are creating problems. These special audits are usually initiated by management's request. Because these audits are typically one of a kind, their procedures are not usually formally released. The results of these audits often drive changes in the standard internal staff audit and management self-assessment instructions that are formally released.

The internal staff audit team should always review its findings with the management team responsible for the area being audited before the report is formally released. This prevents a great deal of misunderstanding and hard feelings for both the management team and the internal staff audit department.

Often the quality organization is assigned responsibilities for staff audits of the processes to ensure that they are following established quality, safety, environmental, personnel, and financial procedures. This new quality organization is often called "Systems Assurance." (See McGraw-Hill's book *The Improvement Process,* Chapter 10, published 1987.)

Step 4—Establish and Maintain the Executive Audit Process

Executive audits (management reviews) should be conducted of the total QMS, placing particular emphasis on customer-related quality data and processes.

The ISO 9000 series requires that management reviews be conducted at regular intervals.

Secondary Subclause 4.1.3 of ISO 9001 states:

4.1.3 Management review
The supplier's management with executive responsibility shall review the quality system at defined intervals sufficient to ensure its continuing suitability and effectiveness in satisfying the requirements of this standard and the supplier's stated quality policy and objectives (see 4.1.1). Records of such reviews shall be maintained (see 4.16).

Note: Supplier's management, of course, is your management.

We prefer the term *executive audits* because we believe that it is extremely important for the executives to obtain firsthand, personal knowledge of the QMS and not rely solely upon audits conducted by internal employees or external organizations. At a very minimum, the executive committee should include in its schedule a complete review of the results of all major internal staff audits and external audits of the QMS. Particular emphasis should be placed on the corrective actions proposed to eliminate discrepancies. Often the executive committee will focus its audits on personally evaluating how effective the corrective actions were at eliminating these discrepancies. This provides an excellent way for the executive committee to demonstrate its support of the QMS and, at the same time, ensures that discrepancies are handled expeditiously. As a result of the executive audits, the executive team should be able to answer the following questions based on the team's personal knowledge:

- Is the present QMS providing the organization with a competitive advantage?
- Is the present QMS aligned with the organization's business plan?
- Are activities under way or planned for that will require the QMS to be modified?
- Is the organization achieving the goals defined in the quality policy and its supporting objectives?
- Is the present QMS working effectively?
- Is the present QMS preventing errors from occurring?

Step 5—Host Second-Party Audits

Second-party audits are audits conducted by an organization of its subcontractor's (supplier's) or potential subcontractor's (supplier's) QMS to ensure that the subcontractor's QMS meets the minimum requirements defined by the purchasing organization. These audits are usually conducted prior to issuing a contract to a new subcontractor, and every 6 to 12 months for currently active subcontractors. Usually the semiannual audit of currently active subcontractors goes beyond the QMS to include audits of the product and/or service processes and outputs.

Step 6—Host Third-Party Audits

Typically, third-party audits can be classified into two subcategories:

1. Legally required audits such as financial audits of a public organization's financial records, or government audits usually focusing on issues like safety, health, and product quality for the protection of the general public (audits of food manufacturers, etc.)
2. Audits conducted by registration bodies at the request of the organization to provide documented independent evidence of the organization's compliance to a specific standard

The third-party organization provides a written report that defines how well the organization that is being evaluated complies to a specific standard. These documents, published by the third-party organization, are used to ensure interested parties that the organization is in compliance with a specific standard, policy, and/or legal requirements (e.g., yearly audits of the financial records for a publicly owned organization, or Underwriters Laboratory safety approval, or registration of the organization to one of the ISO 9000 documents). ISO 9000 registrars must not provide consulting services or training, either directly or indirectly, on quality-related activities. It is unethical for a registrar to be financially connected to an organization that provides Total Quality Management training or assists in establishing quality management systems, since this presents a major conflict of interest.

One of the ISO 9000 series' advantages is that third-party registration has been closely linked to the standards on a worldwide basis. We believe that the cost of having your QMS registered is more than offset by the many advantages that registration brings to most organizations. Assuming that you decide to register your QMS, it is very important that you understand what it involves and how the organization should interface with the registrar. As a result, we are providing the following prescription to assist an organization in interfacing with a registrar.

It's 8:05 in the morning. You just sat down with your coffee, and the receptionist calls. "The auditors are here." Panic? Only if you have waited until now to read this chapter. A third-party audit, by definition, is a planned, systematic method for reviewing whether your QMS has been implemented effectively. This section of this chapter addresses what to do when

a. You are being audited.
b. You have been asked to participate in an audit of another department or organization.

There are a number of key activities to focus on before the auditors arrive at your door. These include the following:

- Preparing and debugging the procedures referenced in the QMS
- Training the staff auditors
- Conducting internal audits per agreed-to schedule
- Preparing the executive audit procedures
- Training the executive team
- Conducting executive audits per agreed-to schedule

If you are pursuing registration, you have already had a number of interactions with the registrar's personnel before they arrived at your door. In general, the following three separate sets of activities are associated with any audit:

1. Preaudit activities
2. On-site activities
3. Postaudit activities

Preaudit Activities

The preaudit activities consist of the following action items:

1. Make initial contact with the registrar, or registrar's organization.
2. Assemble the information.
3. Follow up with the lead auditor.
4. Brief the management and staff in your organization.
5. Conduct an internal audit.
6. Confirm final details with the lead auditor.
7. Perform final check.

Activity 1—Make Initial Contact

The better registrars are fairly busy; hence, early contact is best. It can take up to eight months' lead time to get the best, particularly if a sizable amount of technical expertise is necessary, so start contacting the registrar early.

Most registrars provide a checklist that needs to be filled out and returned with a copy of your quality manual. Typically, the registrar will return comments on the quality manual, and related documentation, that need to be addressed before an audit will be scheduled. Take this as an opportunity for dialogue, but don't lose sight of the fact that when the auditor puts the ball back in your court, it is your turnaround time that will determine the earliest audit schedule.

Activity 2—Assemble the Information

In the preaudit phase, the auditors are concerned with scheduling the audit, selecting the audit team, making logistical arrangements, gathering background information, and developing an audit plan. Most of the essential information needed for preliminary planning will already be in your quality manual. However, additional detail may be needed on:

- The size of your facilities (how many buildings, at what locations, and how many employees, etc.).
- The scope of work (i.e., whether auditors with specific technical expertise, such as engineering design, software development, nondestructive testing, welding, etc., will be required for the audit).

Your objective at this stage is to assist the lead auditor in organizing an effective audit, which uses the audit team's time (and your money) efficiently.

Typically, your organization should have a minimum of six months of documented data that can be used to verify how well your organization is following the new QMS before the audit is scheduled. This is often a gating factor in defining when the audit is scheduled.

Activity 3—Follow Up with the Lead Auditor

About eight weeks before the audit, the lead auditor should be in contact with you. If the time is getting close, pick up the phone and give him or her a call. Details need to be worked out at least this far in advance of the audit, because in the case of the larger registrars, like QMI and BSI, auditing is a full-time job, and the auditors typically work in a cycle of two weeks on the road, and two weeks in the office.

The specific details should include the following:

- The exact timing of the planned audit
- Any documents that need to be sent to the auditors before the audit
- The types of documents that the team will want to review on-site
- The arrangements that need to be made for a tour of your facilities
- The arrangements that need to be made for introductory meetings and interviews

It is important that you also advise the lead auditor if safety equipment (such as safety glasses and boots) or CPR training is required for people entering your buildings, and so on. It may also be necessary to allow time for briefing on security precautions, electrostatic discharge concerns, or emergency evacuation procedures.

An audit team usually requests that a meeting room be made available as its workstation. It is also a good idea to plan for word-processing support and to provide for photocopying, as needed. If your organization runs more than one shift a day, you may need to arrange for the auditors to conduct audits on each shift.

Activity 4—Brief the Management and Staff in Your Organization

It's a good idea to roll out a communication campaign in preparation for the audit. The audit is your organization's opportunity to put its best foot forward. Part of it means thinking like a customer. Imagine if you went into your bank branch, and everywhere you looked, you saw piles of paper spilling out of in baskets onto the floor, out-of-date brochures, tellers eating their sandwiches at the windows, and people randomly wandering in and out of the safety deposit box area. As good as the service might be, you would probably be left with an impression that mistakes might be made on some of your transactions, and your valuables might not be as secure in the safety deposit box as they could be. Now, imagine that a customer is taking a tour of your facility or is participating on the audit as an observer. Obviously, poor housecleaning does not ensure that there are problems with the organization's QMS. However, it is the kind of thing that puts the auditor on high alert.

Start with a "heads up" memo to management and supervisors to provide an outline of the purpose of the audit, and its timing. Ask for their support, and use the opportunity as a reminder that, by now, all workstations should have the most up-to-date documentation and/or work instructions. This memo should also request that each supervisor review the organization's quality policy statement with the employees and ensure that each employee's training records are up to date.

Activity 5—Conduct an Internal Audit

Conduct your own preliminary audit at least four to six weeks before the formal audit, using either members of the QST or an outside consultant. This will allow enough time for corrective action to be implemented, before the formal audit. Also, having recently gone through and maintaining the records for an internal audit will help in meeting Subclause 4.17 of ISO 9001 or 9002. During the audit, keep the perspective of the outside individual in mind. Look carefully for trouble signs such as the following:

- Uncalibrated equipment in use at workstations (don't forget the equipment used in the development laboratories)
- "Unofficial" paper record-keeping systems that staff feel are needed to fill the gaps in the "official" on-line systems
- Invoicing errors that may be indicative of systemic problems, such as order entry (or other gaps in the "contract review" system), shipping/ receiving, and so on
- Files of customer complaints that have yet to be addressed
- Managers who have been "waiting for the opportunity to argue" with an ISO 9000 auditor
- Managers who believe a showy presentation, followed by an expensive lunch, is all that's necessary to ensure a successful audit

Your objectives at this stage are to clarify and verify; that is, *clarify* the formal audit goals, objectives, and procedures, and *verify* that the management, staff, and facilities are ready to withstand the scrutiny of an outside audit. Your internal audit should provide the advance opportunity for questions or clarifications to be raised on the applicable ISO 9000 standard, or on the process documentation in use within the facility. The internal audit should also provide management and staff the opportunity to gain some experience in the interviewing and fact-finding processes.

Activity 6—Confirm Final Details with the Lead Auditor

Two weeks before the audit, the lead auditor should be contacted to ensure the audit team's travel arrangements are clear and confirmed. This is a good opportunity for you to ensure that the key people the auditors may need to interview will be available, and to communicate any constraints on availability. At this stage, the lead auditor should be in the final stages of developing the audit plan.

Activity 7—Perform Final Check

Follow up with a reminder to management and supervisors. Check on meeting room availability, coffee, and lunch arrangements. Make sure the QST's schedule is clear, and interruptions can be managed.

On-Site Activities

The on-site activities start when the receptionist calls. These activities are largely the responsibility and under the control of the external audit team. They consist of the following action items:

1. Hold the opening meeting.
2. Conduct the orientation tour.
3. Refine the audit plan if necessary.
4. Conduct interviews to understand your organization's QMS.
5. Review quality records (Tier 5 documents).
6. Perform observation and verification testing.
7. Review audit team findings (audit team only).
8. Present final findings to the organization's management.

The QST's role is to ensure that the appropriate people are available for interviews, for conducting the tour, and the opening and closing meetings.

Activity 1—Hold the Opening Meeting

The first morning should start with an opening meeting that

a. Gives the auditors the opportunity to provide key personnel in your organization with an overview of their objectives and methodology.

b. Gives you an opportunity to provide the auditors with a brief introduction to the facility, the QMS, your organization's quality management practices, and the organization's executives.

The meeting is usually chaired by the lead auditor and attended by all members of the audit team. Also in attendance should be your organization's quality manager, senior/functional managers who would most likely be in a position to implement corrective action, and the staff who will accompany the audit team during the audit.

Activity 2—Conduct the Orientation Tour

Plan for a one- to two-hour orientation tour. The objective is for the auditors to get an overview of the facility's layout and operations. Cover the basics of the operations. Try to follow logical process flows, as outlined in the following examples:

- For materials, work from the receiving dock through the production and test areas to final packaging and shipping.
- For the administrative processes, work from receipt of the order to production scheduling to dispatching to invoicing.
- For support processes (such as calibration, control of quality records, document and data control, etc.), a walk-by of control points should be sufficient at this stage.

Be prepared to intersperse audit team members with your personnel, since each auditor will want to ask questions and move along at his or her own pace.

Activity 3—Refine the Audit Plan If Necessary

The audit team members will want to reconvene, by themselves, shortly after the orientation tour. The purpose is to revisit the audit plan and determine whether any adjustments or reassignments are necessary, to ensure that the team is most effectively deployed.

Activity 4—Conduct Interviews to Understand Your Organization's Quality Management System

Your quality manual, and related documentation, will have provided the audit team with a paperwork understanding of your QMS and the roles and relationships of key individuals in the system. The next step in the audit process is for the team members to obtain a living, more three-dimensional understanding of your QMS, particularly for their assigned clauses of ISO 9001, 9002, or 9003. If the auditors are from a registrar, expect that all elements of ISO 9001, 9002, or 9003 will be fully audited. Even if you have indicated that certain clauses are not applicable, the auditors will take the opportunity to clarify and verify that those clauses are, in fact, not applicable.

Typically, registrars work with an audit checklist. Typical audit checklist questions can be found in Appendix VIII. The checklist provides a consistent means for auditors in the field to keep track of findings, and report back to their management. It is up to the auditor(s) to answer those questions. Note that in the actual audit, the auditor(s) generally does not ask those questions directly. He or she will answer the checklist questions using one or more of the following techniques:

- *Inquiry*—Asking situation-specific questions, both formally and informally
- *Observation*—Collecting audit evidence through physical examination
- *Verification testing*—Starting with final records and moving back to original documents

The auditors will want to interview key people involved in the execution of relevant clauses of the ISO 9001, 9002, or 9003 standards. During these meetings, the auditors will strive to obtain information related to the who, what, and how questions given in Appendix VIII. These audit questions typically focus on items such as the types of procedures, plans, and record-keeping measures used by individuals. The auditors will query the staff's understanding of the systems used to identify and correct deficiencies, as well as their understanding of how customer and quality issues are considered in proposed process or product changes. In addition, the auditors will probe people on how responsibilities and accountabilities are defined, communicated, and reinforced.

Activity 5—Review Quality Records (Tier 5 Documents)

The confirmation of information is an essential element of the audit and differentiates it from a simple inquiry. Documentary evidence provides a visible "paper trail" that allows the auditors to see your organization's practices through the quality records. Don't confuse quality records with quality documents. Your quality documents are the basis of the inquiries in Activity 4; that is, procedures, work instructions, quality plans, and so on. The quality records are the fact base that provide evidence that an activity has been done. For example, after the plant manager asserted that "everyone is fully trained in ..." (SPC, or metrology, or root cause analysis, or whatever), the auditors would proceed to probe staff on their training, their understanding of its application, and the follow-up provided. Then, in terms of reviewing the quality records, the auditor would cross-check against employee records in the Human Resources department.

The quality records should provide evidence that your QMS meets the requirements of ISO 9001, 9002, or 9003 and should be available for the following activities:

- Management review
- Contract review
- Design review
- Design verification
- Design validation
- Supplier records and list of acceptable suppliers
- Lost or damaged customer-supplied product
- Traceability, product date codes, and so on
- Qualified processes, equipment, and personnel
- Positive recall records
- Inspection authority for release of product
- Inspection, measuring, and test equipment calibration
- Contractual repair records
- Customer complaints
- Investigations of the causes and results related to product, process, and QMS nonconformances
- Internal audit results and follow-up audit activities
- Employee qualification and training
- Service records
- Statistical data or results

It is important that you and the other staff accompanying the auditors on the orientation tour know exactly where each set of records is kept, particularly if they are not maintained centrally. It is not unusual for the auditor to ask to see "customer files." By this, he or she means the complete trail of the following:

- Purchase orders
- Product schedules, or work orders
- The product inspection and test records for the product ordered

- Shipping documents
- Any customer complaints or correspondence related to the purchase
- Invoices, credit memos, and adjustments if applicable
- Corrective action taken, if applicable, relative to any of the preceding

It is not unusual for people within organizations to believe that corrective action is something that is only applicable for the production line. You may find the auditor taking a close look for administrative problems in the following areas.

Order Entry	Wrong quantity, wrong product
Scheduling	Wrong delivery date, or even worse, everything is a rush order
Shipping	Wrong address—a particularly big problem for government departments
Invoicing	All of the above, from wrong quantity and product, to wrong address, and including wrong currency, particularly when cross-border (Canada–U.S.–Mexico) transactions are involved

Activity 6—Perform Observation and Verification Testing

The auditors are looking for consistency in what has been presented, from the QMS documentation, through the messages that the auditors pick up in the interview process, to the trail of evidence in the quality records. Observation and verification testing refers to a wide variety of activities that may be employed by the auditors to increase their confidence in the audit evidence gathered thus far. Examples include the following:

- Physical observation of people, process, product, and perhaps customer interaction
- Taking independent measurements, recomputing arithmetic calculations, and retracing data back to sources
- Confirmation of externally generated documents, such as calibration reports, by the independent third parties involved

Activity 7—Review Audit Team Findings (Audit Team Only)

Depending on the size of the audit team and the number of potential nonconformities observed, the audit team may need to meet by themselves to consolidate their findings. This can take from a few hours to a full day. Don't be alarmed; they are not plotting against your organization. They are summarizing their individual findings, exceptions and observations, to ensure that all findings and exceptions are significant and have been substantiated. As a team, they review all audit findings to determine which ones are to be recorded on the nonconformance reports and reported, both to your organization and theirs. The nonconformances will be identified in terms of the specific requirements of the ISO 9001, 9002, or 9003 standards, and supported by evidence.

It is advisable for the QST to remain available for consultation, so the audit team can verify that evidence of compliance has not been overlooked. The audit team will very likely want to give the QST a briefing on what will be reported to the organization's management team. This is a time for the QST to raise any legitimate questions and concerns that need clarification before the final meeting.

Activity 8—Present Final Findings to the Organization's Management

After the nonconformances have been documented on nonconformance reports, the audit team meets with your organization's management. Again, this meeting is chaired by the lead auditor. His or her report should provide

- A statement regarding the judgment of the audit team regarding your organization's compliance with the applicable standard.
- A review of any nonconformance reports, to ensure that your organization's management fully understands their content and context.
- An outline of the follow-up process after the audit.

Don't expect the report to provide specific suggestions on how to meet the ISO 9001, 9002, or 9003 standards, or to cover subjective topics, like how you are doing relative to your competitors. Strictly speaking, the purpose of the audit is to help you understand where your organization stands with regard to compliance with ISO 9001, 9002, or 9003.

Most auditors are experienced quality professionals who have had the opportunity to audit and observe a wide variety of organizations in operation. As professionals, most auditors are as concerned as you are that your organization does not interpret the ISO 9000 standards in a narrow, "just get me a certificate" fashion. The auditor's objective in all of this centers on evaluating whether your organization can satisfy your customer's requirements, and whether your organization will continue to maintain these capabilities. Pay attention to cues that "you meet the requirement, but...." Your objective should be to ensure that you are getting the maximum benefit from your QMS in all parts of your organization, even if it does not meet the formal relevant ISO 9000 requirements.

Postaudit Activities

The audit process continues after the external audit team leaves your organization. These activities are largely the responsibility and under the control of your organization. They consist of the following action items:

1. Review the nonconformances raised by the audit team.
2. Draft an action plan.
3. Implement the corrective action.
4. Follow up with the lead auditor.

Activity 1—Review the Nonconformances Raised by the Audit Team

The audit team will prepare a final report that more formally communicates the findings of the audit. However, the basic information will already have been presented at the final meeting. While the audit team is preparing its report the corrective action planning process should be initiated by your organization.

Although it is the responsibility of the auditors not to overstate the facts, it is your responsibility to draw the appropriate conclusions. For example, if the auditors have not found any evidence of training in SPC, or any specific subject that the plant manager stated that everyone needs to be fully trained in, the audit might report that "requirements for qualification of process operators were not specified, and related training was not documented (ref. 4.9, and 4.18)." It may be up to you to analyze the root cause of the nonconformities. For example, perhaps

a. the quality records simply need to be updated; or
b. your customer typically expects some form of qualification to be held by your staff, like a welder's certificate or professional engineer's designation, for the process under question; or
c. gaps should be filled in routine staff training.

Activity 2—Draft an Action Plan

This process includes determining potential solutions to the nonconformances raised by the audit team, preparing recommendations, assigning responsibility for corrective action, and establishing timetables. It is useful, at this stage, to conduct a short-risk analysis, along the following lines.

Priority	On the Basis That It	Timing
1.	Would cost us a customer	Next 30 days
2.	Would tighten up our business practices and save money	Next three months
3.	May cost us a customer	Next six months
4.	May tighten up our business practices and save money	At some future point

From the perspective of a registrar, you should assume that all nonconformances hold equal weight, in terms of getting (and keeping) your certificate. Many organizations will send copies of their corrective action plans to the lead auditor.

Activity 3—Implement the Corrective Action

It is important to ensure that corrective action hasn't simply taken place on paper. It may be necessary to go back through the manual, and make revisions to all levels of documentation. Then retrain your employees on the updated documentation.

Activity 4—Follow Up with the Lead Auditor

The final activity in the audit process is to provide the lead auditor with your action plan that corrects the documented nonconformances. It is not unusual for the lead auditor to return to your facility to audit the implementation of corrective action. Usually, the auditor will thoroughly evaluate the long-term impact of the corrective action during the semiannual recertification audits.

Conclusions about Third-Party Audits

Auditing provides a measure of how well your QMS conforms to a specified set of criteria; for example, ISO 9001, 9002, or 9003. Auditing by an independent third party also provides a fresh look at the way you are doing business and the incentive to implement corrective action on nonconformances found.

Unlucky 13—The Most Frequent Reasons for Failing a Registration Audit

1. Lack of the proper level of documentation
2. Poorly documented receiving inspection results
3. Failure to segregate good from bad products
4. Actual training activities fail to comply with the documented requirements
5. Poorly documented management reviews
6. Receiving inspection work instruction not complete
7. Contract changes not reflected in the documentation
8. Lack of equipment capability data
9. New staff not trained properly
10. Documentation in use at the wrong change level
11. Product engineering change level and work instruction change level not in agreement
12. Process control procedures not being followed
13. Approved supplier list not being followed or not tracking supplier performance

Summary

As a result of implementing and maintaining an effective QMS audit process, the organization will be able to hold the gains that it has made and the ones that will result from the continuous improvement phase (Phase VI).

During Phase V, the following audit activities were put in place:

1. An employee self-assessment process was established.
2. A management self-assessment process was put in place, with quarterly upper management reviews.
3. Internal staff audits were scheduled, conducted, and appropriate corrective action was implemented.
4. The executive team became actively involved in verifying that the QMS was operating per documentation and in an effective manner.

5. Second-party audit plans were developed to ensure that the organization's QMS was in line with customer requirements and that the product production process was ready for second-party audits.

6. The organization's QMS became registered.

Regardless of the worthy concepts embodied in, and the underlying intent of your organization's QMS, auditing is a valuable management tool for spotting weaknesses or potential problems in the deployment of your QMS. It provides a means by which the organization can recognize and correct deviations before they become major problems.

8

Phase VI:
Continuous Improvement

Introduction

Becoming registered is a major milestone, and your organization should take pride in this accomplishment, but it is not the end of your improvement journey. Registration just gets you up to the starting blocks for the competitive race. It will not win the race for you. To win the race, you need to continuously improve your organization's performance. Now that the upgraded QMS is in place and working effectively, you have a platform that your organization can build on to improve its performance. But the QMS must continuously change to keep pace with the changing environment. If not, instead of being a life jacket, it will become a millstone around your organization's neck. This means that the QMS change process must be integrated into the organization's Total Improvement Management efforts and become a supporting part of the total improvement plan.

The 1980s and 1990s have been a period where organizations around the world have been focusing on improving their effectiveness and efficiency. Every manager's bookshelf is stuffed full of books on teams, problem-solving applications, redesign methods, visioning, gain sharing, activity-based costing, and so on. Today our list of improvement tools exceeds 400 different, or seemingly different, tools. In an effort to change the organization's culture, management has randomly embraced these tools. This random focus on performance improvement has cost organizations billions of wasted dollars. Frequently, teams that were trained to do problem solving never used these skills. Statistical process control charts were implemented but didn't improve process operations because they were misapplied. People pulled away from meaningful work to attend classes whose theories were never put into practice. Truly, management is faced with a challenge of changing the way they act, talk, and think. Once management has changed, employees need to be convinced to change their behavioral patterns. To accomplish this, a major change in the workplace environment has to take place. This drastic environmental change needs to occur if organizations are going to meet the international competitive situation that presently exists and will become more intense in the twenty-first century.

Culture Is Not the Problem

Everyone is talking about the need for a cultural change, but we believe that focusing on it is the wrong answer to today's problems and does not prepare most organizations to enter the twenty-first century. Culture is defined as your background, your history, your heritage, your religion, your beliefs. Most organizations should want to hold on to their culture; in fact, they should be worried about losing it. America should be proud of its culture. It is a culture rich in imagination, hard work, caring, risk taking, and accomplishment. It is a culture that made us the richest, most powerful, most productive nation in the world. Our culture is not the problem. It is the personality of today's managers and employees that is the problem.

We talk about "workaholics" like *work* is the worst four-letter word in the English language. People work overtime begrudgingly if they are notified 72 hours in advance, and if not, they refuse. It is the personality of today's workforce and our children that needs to be changed. *Personality* is defined as an individual's or group's impact on other individuals or groups. We need to change the personality of our people before we lose the culture that our forefathers worked so hard to create. The personality of our key managers dictates the personality of the total organization. When a new CEO is appointed, the total organization adapts to his or her personality. If the CEO is a basketball fan, you would be surprised at how many people know last night's basketball scores.

We cannot go back to what we used to do, for "this old world" has changed. The amount of information available to an individual doubles every five years. According to Richard Worman in *Information Anxiety,* the weekday edition of the *New York Times* contains more information than the average person was likely to come across in a lifetime in seventeenth-century England.

How do we create a change in the personality of our people? We do that by changing the environment in which they live. Our personality is molded by an ongoing series of environmental impacts that we are subjected to. It starts at birth and ends with our last heartbeat. The biggest impact occurs during the formative years of children's lives—the period before they enter school. It is interesting to note that the period between birth and age five, when our young children start school, has a bigger impact on their personalities than everything that happens to them for the rest of their lives. But this is the same period in their young lives that many American parents are turning their backs on them. This is the time when a child should be spending half of the time he or she is awake with at least one parent. Parents today don't have time to devote to their children. Most parents are too busy with their careers, golfing, the Internet, TV, and so on to help their children develop a personality that reflects good work ethics and high moral standards. Is it any wonder that we have runaway crime rates and our teachers are asking for hazardous-duty pay? But the purpose of this book is not to correct society's personality problems or to convince parents that they should devote more time to their children, so let's get back to what an organization can do to change the personality of its managers and employees.

Let's focus on what we can do to influence and change the environment that impacts the personality of today's workforce. What the organization needs is to develop a plan that will change the environmental factors that affect the personality of the employees, placing special emphasis on the management team. If we sustain a positive change in the personality of the organization for a long enough period of time (about 5 to 10 years) or two changes in organizational leadership, the organization's culture will reshape itself in the desired direction.

Business Plans versus Environmental Change Plans

There is a big difference between a business plan and an environmental change plan. The business plan sets the product and service strategy for the organization—the markets that it hopes to penetrate, the new products that will be introduced, the production strategy, and so on. It is a plan that directs and guides the business. The business plan is primarily directed at meeting the needs of only two of the stakeholders associated with the organization—the customer and the stockholder. It is a plan that is primarily focused on the external opportunities.

The environmental change plan, on the other hand, is an internally focused plan designed to transform the environment within the organization, thereby changing the organization's personality (behavioral characteristics) so that the needs of all of the organization's stakeholders will be met. It takes into consideration the needs of all of the organization's stakeholders from an improvement standpoint. The environmental change plan defines how the organization's personality will be transformed. It provides an orderly passage from one state or condition to another. The environmental change plan supports the business plan, so both plans, although different in content and intent, must be kept in close harmony.

Why Do You Need an Environmental Change Plan?

One of the questions we are asked most frequently is, "Why does my organization need to develop an environmental change plan to improve? I know a lot of problems that we can start working on right now. In fact, we are already working on them." Don't stop working on your problems. You cannot afford to stop putting out the fires that your present organization is fueling, but as long as you continue to do what you have been doing, you will continue to get the results that you have been getting. Unfortunately, your competition is probably not content with their status quo and they are changing, so if you don't change, your competition will soon be ahead of you and, eventually, will drive you out of business. The twenty-first century will be dominated by those organizations that improve the most and can change the fastest.

Most organizations, in their hunger to improve their performance, have embraced many different improvement tools. It seems like each time someone went to another conference they came back with another improvement tool. Our research shows that more than 400 different improvement tools exist that will provide a positive impact on parts of the organization. Each of these tools works under the right conditions. Many solve the same types of problems. The following is a list of 10 of the more than 44 different tools used to improve the environmental category called Management Leadership and Support:

1. Management Self-Audits
2. New Performance Standards
3. Improvement Policy
4. Improvement Visions
5. Annual Strategic Improvement Plans

6. Leadership Skills Development
7. Self-Managed Work Teams
8. Responsibility Charting
9. 7-S Model
10. Risk/Opportunity Analysis

No organization can afford or effectively utilize all 400+ improvement tools. Many of the tools overlap in approach and the problems that they solve. Many of them are not applicable or have little effect on your organization.

Just as individuals differ, organizations differ in many ways. They have different management personalities, customers, products, cultures, locations, profits, quality levels, productivity, technologies, and core competencies.

Add to this complexity the fact that winning, surviving, and losing organizations have to do a very different set of things to improve. It becomes readily apparent that no one approach to improvement is correct for all organizations or even for different sites within an organization.

What Creates Your Organization's Culture?

The organization's culture is created over a long period of time as a result of the way management implements the organization's basic beliefs, combined with the way employees react to management's stimulation.

There is a great deal of confusion about which term or terms to use: values, beliefs, or principles. We don't care what you call them, but every organization should have a set of statements that communicate to management and the employees an understanding of what the organization's culture is based on. These statements provide direction to management that governs their performance. To the employees, they provide a promise of conditions that the organization is built upon. They are truly the employees' "bill of rights" and should be reflected in every decision and action made by management and employees.

Ford Motor Company's guiding principles are as follows:

- Quality comes first.
- Customers are the focus of everything we do.
- Continuous improvement is essential to our success.
- Employee involvement is our way of life.
- Dealers and suppliers are our partners.
- Integrity is never compromised.

The following is a quote from IBM's Manager's Manual:

> An organization, like an individual, must be built on a bedrock of sound beliefs if it is to survive and succeed. It must stand by these beliefs in conducting its business. Every manager must live by these beliefs in making decisions and in taking action.

The U.S. government has had a set of basic principles since the beginning. They are called the "Bill of Rights" and they have helped guide the United States for more than 200 years.

These fundamental statements, which we will call basic beliefs, are the things that attract new employees to your organization. They define the rules that the organization will not compromise. Since they are the employees' bill of rights, they should be changed only when they have become obsolete because of social and/or external environments. I (H. J. Harrington) worked for IBM for 40 years and its basic beliefs remained constant throughout that time period.

Management's job is to live every business minute complying with the organization's basic principles. This is the first obligation of every manager. No employee should be appointed to a management position unless he or she has already lived up to these basic principles, and no manager should be left in a management role unless he or she lives up to these basic principles. Employees have a responsibility to work in support of the basic principles, refusing to compromise them. Managers who ask their employees to bend the basic principles are not doing their job, and this condition should be brought to the attention of upper management. Conducting yourself during business hours in a manner that supports the organization's principles is a condition of employment for managers and employees alike.

How Do You Change an Organization's Personality?

Change is difficult under the very best circumstances. Western nations' change activities have been primarily driven out of fear—fear of losing market share, fear of losing jobs, fear of not making enough profit to keep stock prices up, and fear of failure. Eastern nations, on the other hand, are changing because they see an opportunity. It is too bad that most American organizations had to get into trouble before they got serious about improvement. For example,

- Xerox and General Motors lost more than 30 percent of their market.
- IBM began posting record-breaking financial losses.

- The U.S. government got so far in debt that there seemed to be no way out.

All organizations, not just the losers, need to have an improvement plan. It's unfortunate that our leaders have been so slow in realizing this. It has to be discouraging to the nation as a whole when the U.S. government is just starting to eliminate a quarter of a million jobs by improving its effectiveness, when the potential has been there since the early seventies. Even Japan is increasing its focus on improvement as corporations start downsizing (e.g., Toshiba eliminating 5000 jobs, and Fuji eliminating 6000 jobs).

What needs to be done to make improvement possible and long lasting? What needs to be done to bring about a change in the way we think, the way we talk, and the way we act? The following is an effective model for change:

1. Everyone must feel that change is necessary.
2. There has to be a common vision of how the change will affect the organization's environment.
3. Everyone should feel ownership in the improvement plan.
4. Management must change first and be the model for the rest of the organization.
5. Barriers must be broken down and removed by management.
6. The impact of the change must be openly communicated to each of the stakeholders.
7. Everyone needs to be trained to perform well in the new environment.
8. A measurement and feedback system needs to be put in place.
9. A risk-taking environment must be provided.
10. Directing and coaching must give way to leading.
11. Desired behaviors must be rewarded.

Organized Labor Involvement

It is strongly recommended that if some of the employees in the organization are represented by organized labor, the union leaders get involved as early as possible. We recommend that the appropriate union leaders become active partners in developing the environmental vision statements and the plan that will transform the organization. This will help to align organized labor's goal with the environmental vision statements. Early involvement of these key people in the planning process often slows down the process a little, but in the long run, more time will be saved because the plan will be better and more effectively implemented.

Continuous Improvement Organizational Change Management

It is extremely important that the OCM concepts we introduced you to during Phase I through Phase VI activities be practiced during Phase VI, as all continuous improvement processes are based on the need for an organization to continuously change in order to stay competitive.

Organizations that have demonstrated an uncommon capacity for continuous improvement establish a lessons-learned methodology with respect to every improvement effort. This is no less true with respect to OCM best practices. Take the time to discuss, capture, and share information and insights that will improve your OCM process by asking questions like the following:

- What worked well, and what didn't?
- How was sponsor commitment obtained and sustained?
- What obstacles were most difficult to overcome?
- What modifications were most effective?
- What would we do different next time, on the next process?
- What other process, technology, or people changes have to occur during implementation in other parts of the organization?
- What is the next significant change initiative we need to accomplish to attain the business objectives?

Developing and Implementing a Continuous Improvement Process

The following steps should be taken to develop an environment that will propagate the growth of a continuous improvement environment:

1. Assess today's organization's personality.
2. Establish environmental vision statements.
3. Set performance improvement goals.
4. Define desired behavior and habit patterns.
5. Develop individual three-year improvement plans.
6. Develop a combined three-year plan.
7. Develop a rolling 90-day implementation plan.
8. Implement the improvement plan and measure the results.

Step 1—Assess Today's Organization's Personality

In developing our improvement plan we need to define the "as-is" status of the organization related to the following:

- Competitive position
- Core competencies
- Core capabilities
- Basic beliefs
- Customer satisfaction
- Employee satisfaction
- Quality management systems
- Successful and unsuccessful improvement activities
- The organization's commitment to improve
- Major new programs
- Management style
- Training
- Supplier partnerships
- Measurement systems
- Business planning

To do a complete assessment can be very time-consuming and expensive, but when you take a look at the alternatives, it usually is less expensive in the long run. If the organization is relatively advanced, most of these data should be readily available within the organization. If this is the case, it is best to take the time to do a comprehensive analysis and define any voids and improvement opportunities in the as-is organizational structure. The advanced organizations will typically already have benchmarked their competitors' products, defined and compared their core capabilities and competencies, calculated the customer satisfaction index, held focus groups with customers, conducted employee opinion surveys, and have a business plan that is being actively followed.

If this is not the case, a minimum analysis may be the right answer for your organization rather than completing a more thorough analysis before starting to prepare your three-year improvement plan. This allows the organization to start the improvement process sooner. The downside of this approach is that the plan often needs to be modified when additional data is made available. At a minimum, the assessment would include the following:

- Review of customer-related data
- Review of competitor-related data
- Review of the business plan and critical success factors
- Review of upper management measurements and performance
- Review of the organization's measurements and performance
- Review of quality management system's audit data
- Review of past and planned-for improvement activities
- Review of grievances
- Private interviews with all top management to identify potential improvement opportunities and/or problems
- Focus group meetings with middle management, first-level management, and employees to define the present personality of the organization, compliance to business principles, and to identify roadblocks to change
- Customer round tables
- Improvement-needs survey

This type of assessment will provide a good definition of the as-is status. It will also identify many improvement opportunities that should be included in the three-year improvement plan. In addition, the focus groups and the surveys will identify the differences between management's and employees' priorities. Some surveys provide a measure of the organization's dedication to improvement that can be used to predict the probability of successfully implementing the improvement process. We find that this approach is very useful and greatly decreases the chance of failure.

It is very important that the data collected during the private interviews, focus groups, and surveys be kept absolutely confidential. This is one of the best reasons for using a third party to do the assessment. The third party also provides an unbiased view of the organization, which is needed to define a true as-is picture. When individuals live in a problem situation for a long time, they become used to it and begin to consider it normal, rather than the exception that it really is. Do not rely only on management to define improvement opportunities, because they are the ones that created the organization's personality and most of the problems.

Once the assessment is complete, the results should be reported back to management and, at a minimum, to every employee who took part in the assessment. If you ask anyone for their suggestions and/or to evaluate present status, you have an obligation to get back with them to show them how their inputs were used and reported to upper management.

Step 2—Establish Environmental Vision Statements

Management has control over relatively few things. They do not control the economy, their customer, their competition, their suppliers, government regulations, the stock market, and so on. The only things that management can change are the environmental processes that make up the organization. If you want to bring about change in the organization, the environmental processes within the organization that impact the desired results must be changed.

An Executive Improvement Team (EIT) should now be formed. This EIT should be made up of the highest officials in the organization (e.g., president and all vice presidents) plus the key union leaders. The EIT should be limited to about 8 to 14 people.

The EIT now needs to define the five to ten environmental processes that have the most impact on the organization's performance. The following are typical processes that influence organizational performance:

1. Measurement processes
2. Training processes
3. Management support and leadership processes
4. Customer partnership processes
5. Supplier partnership processes
6. Business processes
7. Production processes
8. Employee development processes
9. Reward processes
10. After-sales service processes

The EIT should set aside two or three days to define key environmental processes and develop a set of preliminary visions of how these processes will evolve during the next five years. To accomplish this, the meetings should be held off-site in a sterile environment where no one is interrupted by phone calls. The time spent during the day discussing visions of how the organization will function five years in the future is important, but equally important are the evening activities where the EIT gets to socialize and informally interact with each other.

The EIT should define the key environmental processes that impact the organization's performance by brainstorming to make a comprehensive list, and then consolidating and prioritizing the list down to a maximum of ten environmental processes. Once the key environmental processes are defined, the EIT should review the as-is analysis and define the present state of each of the processes. Then they should discuss each process to define if it needs to be improved over the next five years. If the process needs to be improved (and most of them will), the EIT should develop a vision statement for each environmental process that defines how the process will function in the future (desired future-state vision statement).

The EIT needs to think beyond the present boundaries to define the desired future-state vision. After the EIT has brainstormed a list of phrases that best represents the future state of the specific environmental process it is discussing, the EIT should prepare a vision statement for the specific environmental process. This five-year vision statement should clearly define the desired way the organization is operating five years in the future.

Jack Welch, CEO of General Electric, says in *AQP-ISO 9000 Collection*, vol. II, "Leaders—and take everyone from Roosevelt to Churchill to Reagan—inspire people with clear visions of how things can be done better. Some managers, on the other hand, muddle things with pointless complexity and detail. They acquaint it with sophistication with sounding smarter than anyone else. They inspire no one." Father Theodore Hesburgh, former president of Notre Dame University, stated, "The very essence of leadership is that you have to have a vision. It's got to be a vision you articulate clearly and forcefully on every occasion. You cannot blow an uncertain trumpet."

A typical example of a five-year vision statement for management support and leadership is:

> Management fosters an environment of open communication where opinions and suggestions are encouraged and valued; visions, plans, and priorities are shared throughout the organization.
>
> Management provides the necessary time, tools, and training for employees, which enables everyone to contribute their personal best toward the mission of the organization.
>
> Teamwork is stressed; decision making is accomplished at the lowest appropriate level. Bidirectional feedback occurs on an ongoing basis to measure results and provide input for a continuous improvement process.

Stakeholders' Involvement with Vision Statements

The EIT develops the preliminary vision statements. These statements reflect the way management interprets the data it has and the way it pictures the evolution of the organization's environment. But management is only a small part of the people who are affected by these vision statements. There are at least four more stakeholders who also need to influence these vision statements.

They are (1) the customer, (2) the employee, (3) the suppliers, and (4) the stockholders.

Each executive should take the preliminary vision statements back to his or her organization and hold a series of focus group meetings with his or her direct reports, first-line managers, and employees. Each focus group should review all the vision statements to determine the following:

1. Is this the type of environment you want to live in?
2. Is this different from today's environment?
3. Do you understand the vision statement and what each word means?
4. How could it be improved?
5. Do you think it is achievable?
6. What would keep us from achieving it?

Often these sessions are kicked off with the person who did the assessment reviewing the findings. This helps everyone obtain a better picture of the as-is condition.

Flip charts should be used to record all comments, negative or positive. This is an effective way to document the discussion and come to common agreement on key issues. Somehow things look different in print.

Procurement should ask the major suppliers to attend a focus group meeting where all the vision statements are reviewed, but most of the supplier focus group's time would be directed at the supplier partnership vision statement. Marketing should do the same thing for its major customers, with particular emphasis focused on present customer partnership status and on the customer partnership vision statement. The CEO and COO should hold focus group meetings with the stockholders to get their inputs related to the preliminary vision statements. With the suppliers, customers, and stockholders, it is better to review the vision statements with too many, rather than too few.

This is one of the most exciting parts of the entire improvement process. In most organizations, it is the first time that management has ever asked the employees what type of environment they would like to spend their lives in.

Preparing the Final Vision Statements

When the results of the focus groups are available, a second meeting of the EIT is held to develop the final vision statements. At this meeting, each executive presents his or her team's inputs related to the desired future state and the vision statements. Big arguments may break out over small points; that is, which synonym to use, which adjective to use, where the comma goes, and so on. After some agonizing debate, a final group of vision statements is agreed to. Now each word in each statement has a common meaning to the members of the EIT.

The outcome from this meeting is a new, final group of vision statements. In our experience, most of the final vision statements are very different from the preliminary vision statements. This difference is very important. Even when an individual employee's suggestion was not included, he or she is able to see that the executives changed their visions after they talked with the employees. This makes it very obvious that management is listening and really cares about the employees' opinions.

Organizations tap the full potential of their employees when meaningful, common visions are created jointly. Management's job is to promote these agreed-to, common visions. "Promote" does not mean to only talk about them or to support them. It means to live them, to sell them, to be enthusiastic about them. Confusion reigns supreme when management talks and writes one message but acts and lives another. If management cannot live and act the visions, for heaven's sake, don't talk or write them.

The management of a bank in Arizona felt so strongly about its vision statements that it rented billboards on the route its employees traveled to and from work. On these billboards, the bank's mission and visions were posted. The message was not there for its customers. The customers would see the results of these visions. The message was there for the employees. It showed the employees that management was firmly committed and that with the employees' help, they could bring about the major environmental changes that the visions pictured.

Step 3—Set Performance Improvement Goals

The executive team should now define how it will measure the success of the improvement effort. All of the executives have expectations of what should be accomplished in their individual functions and the organization as a whole as a result of the continuous improvement activities. But often each executive measures success differently. To guide the improvement planning cycle, the executive team needs to focus on setting goals for only a few critical organizational measurements, such as the following:

- Return on investment
- Market share
- Customer satisfaction

- Error-free performance
- Response time
- Dollars saved
- Value-added per employee
- Morale index

We suggest that the executive team select four to eight organizational measurements and set yearly goals for them that will be used as the focal points in designing the improvement process. The ultimate design of the improvement process will be greatly impacted by how aggressive these performance improvement goals are.

Step 4—Define Desired Behavior and Habit Patterns

To start the personality change, the organization developed a set of vision statements. If these vision statements are worthwhile and are embraced by management and employees alike, then individuals' feelings and thought patterns will need to change to reflect the new environment. If the organization and the individuals involved are rewarded personally and socially as these new feelings are embraced, over time these feelings will transform into normal behavior and/or habit patterns. For example, if part of your management support vision statement was to "empower your employees at all levels," this part of the vision could first be reflected in your employees as they begin to feel that they don't have to get management approval to take action on unplanned events. They would begin to gain confidence that they could make the right decisions in many cases without management's help. With time and continuing management support, they will begin to feel confident that they will not be hurt because they make a decision, and their behavior patterns will change. Then more and more, they will take the needed action, often telling management after the fact about the problem and how it was handled. They will start to come to management explaining how they are going to correct the problem instead of asking management how to solve it. Positively reinforced behavior and actions become habits. At some point in time, these special patterns become a natural pattern. "It's just the way we do things around here; it's nothing special."

For every vision statement, a list of habits and behaviors should be prepared that would exist in the organization if the vision was realized. To accomplish this, the EIT may decide to focus on key words or phrases in the vision statements, or on the vision statements as a whole. The following are typical key words or phrases that might be included in your vision statements:

- Empowered employees
- Streamlined operations
- Customer-driven
- Quality first
- Process focus
- Technology-driven

Using "empowered employees" as a key phrase, the following is a list of some of the behavior and habit patterns that would be observed in an empowered workforce:

- Self-managed work teams are used effectively.
- Wild ideas are encouraged and discussed.
- Unsolicited recommendations and suggestions are often turned in.
- Business information is readily available to all employees.
- Management defines results expected, not how to get them.
- Decisions are made more quickly and at lower levels.
- There is less second-guessing.
- People define their work process and time schedules.

Now the EIT needs to select key behavior and habit patterns and establish a way of measuring how they are changing within the organization. For example:

- Self-managed work teams could be measured by the percentage of people who are part of these teams.
- The degree to which wild ideas are encouraged and discussed could be measured by reviewing brainstorming lists to determine what percentage of the items stretch the imagination.
- How often unsolicited recommendations and suggestions are turned in can be measured by the number of performance improvement ideas and suggestions that are turned in per eligible employee.

Using this type of thought pattern generates a very extensive list of behavior and habit pattern measurements, many of which are not being measured in most organizations. The EIT should include many of them in creating its continuous improvement measurement plan.

Step 5—Develop Individual Three-Year Improvement Plans

Organizations that want to eliminate the piecemeal, flavor-of-the-month approach to improvement are stepping back and looking at all their improvement options before committing a course of action. It takes time up front, but it saves total cycle time, cost, and effort over a three-year period. In addition, it produces much better results. Properly designed, it will create an organization that is creatively bringing out the best each employee has to offer. Work becomes a rewarding, enjoyable, exciting experience. The environment promotes a team spirit without taking away the individual's sense of accomplishment, achievement, and self-esteem. The excitement of belonging and achievement creates an electrifying air that snaps like lightning bolts between management and employees alike, breathing new life into the entire organization.

David T. Kearns, chief executive officer of Xerox, stated, "Our primary motivation in applying for the National Quality Award was to find out how we could improve. Sure, we wanted to win. But we wanted to learn even more. We spent the last year using the award process to identify areas in which we can improve. And we're using what we learned to kick off a second 5-year plan for quality improvement at Xerox worldwide."

Yes, a multiyear improvement plan lies at the heart of every successful improvement activity, and not just for the large corporations. We reviewed Globe Metallurgical's "QEC Continuous Improvement Plan." (Globe was the first small business to win the coveted Malcolm Baldrige National Quality Award.) Globe's continuous improvement plan contained 96 different objectives, with multiprojects for most of the objectives, with target completion dates distributed over a two-year period.

Factors Impacting the Three-Year Improvement Plan

An organization must consider many factors before finalizing the three-year improvement plan. It can be divided into two categories: impacting factors, and influencing data. Impacting factors are things like the organization's mission, values, performance goals, business plans, and so on. Influencing data are things like customer feedback, opinion surveys, poor-quality cost, competitive performance, and so on.

Certainly the environmental influencing data can have a major impact on the final three-year improvement plan. Some of the things included in these considerations are technologies, standards, desired pace of change, competitive environment, and so on.

The proliferation of improvement tools has certainly increased the complexity of the improvement planning cycle. Crosby's 14 Steps, Deming's 14 Points, Feigenbaum's 10 Benchmarks of Quality Success, plus hundreds and hundreds of others, are all similar but still all different. The result? More than 400 different improvement tools are now available for an organization to select from.

Difference between Planning and Problem Solving

We find there is a lot of confusion between planning and problem solving. North Americans are good problem solvers, but they hate to plan. Maybe we are such good problem solvers because we have so many problems to solve as a result of the poor job of planning we are doing. Planning sessions continuously flow over into problem-solving sessions. It is important to separate planning from problem solving if the three-year plan is to be completed in an expeditious manner. Planning is upper management's responsibility. Problem solving is the responsibility of middle management, first-level management, and the employees. Look at the difference between the two:

Planning	Problem Solving
Define direction	Define solutions
Identify change areas	Implement changes
Assign resources	Use resources
Identify needed action	Take action
Highlight symptoms	Find root causes
Look at big picture	Focus on single issues
Short-term cycle	Long-term cycle

Individual Environmental Improvement Three-Year Plans

The EIT should look at each vision statement and develop a plan to transform the organization's environment over the next three years in keeping with the vision statement. This environmental improvement plan must provide a logical transition from the as-is state to the desired future state as defined by the vision. Transition is defined as an "orderly passage from one state, condition, or action to another." An effectively planned-for transition

- Is not abrupt.
- Does not create morale problems.
- Does not have schedule slippage.

- Is not uncontrolled.
- Is not unplanned for.
- Does not create customer complaints.
- Accomplishes desired results without rework.

The EIT will then generate a list of today's problems related to the environmental process that is being planned for, and a list of roadblocks that will impede the change of state. When this is complete, the tools that impact the environmental process under study will be reviewed. For example, as mentioned earlier in this chapter, in the management support and leadership category, about 44 of the 400 improvement tools are directly applicable in helping bring about this transformation.

The appropriate improvement tools and the list of problems and roadblocks are then analyzed to determine which tools are used to correct which problems. In many cases, different tools are effective on the same problems. The EIT must study these interrelationships to determine which tool provides the best combined results in their particular environment. Once the EIT has selected the appropriate tools, an implementation plan for each tool will be prepared and an individual assigned the responsibility for ensuring the plan is implemented. At this point in the planning process, priorities are not given to individual tools unless there is some type of interdependency.

After the individual environmental improvement plans are completed, the EIT should then review the performance improvement goals to identify which measurements are affected by the specific environmental improvement plan. The EIT should then evaluate how much improvement the specific environmental improvement plan will have related to the affected performance improvement goals. Although a number of environmental improvement plans can impact one measurement, the total sum of the impacts should add up to at least the minimum goal for each measurement. If this is not the case, the individual environmental improvement plans need to be improved.

The EIT should also evaluate each of the specific environmental improvement plans to ensure that they will be conducive to the "desired behavior and habit patterns" previously developed. If the individual environmental improvement plans do not meet this test, they will need to be modified.

Step 6—Develop a Combined Three-Year Plan

When the EIT has completed developing the individual three-year improvement plans, they are now ready to combine the plans and prioritize the activities. A number of things should be considered when the individual plans are combined, not the least of which are the performance improvement goals that were developed earlier. The executive team should review the individual plans to define which activities impact each of the performance improvement measurements and schedule the activities so that the performance goals will be met. Other things that should be considered in scheduling the activities in the three-year plan are as follows:

- Available resources
- Other activities going on within the affected area
- Holidays and vacation periods
- Seasonal and/or new product workload fluctuations
- Interdependencies
- Organized labor involvement
- Organizational Change Management timing

If, when all the constraints are considered, the combined improvement plan will not bring about the desired improvements as defined in the performance improvement goals, then either the goals or the plan should be modified.

The single biggest mistake most organizations make is in trying to implement the improvement process too fast. Great care should be taken to balance the improvement effort and resources required with the other activities going on within the organization. Most organizations want to overcommit to the improvement effort at this point in time. It is much better to be conservative during the first year rather than too aggressive. It is our experience that organizations already feel that they have a workload that is 110 percent of their workforce capability.

When the improvement process starts, there is an increase in workload. In some areas, the increased workload can go up as much as 30 percent. The total workload typically does not drop down to below its original value for 12 to 18 months. To offset this short-time, peak workload, consultants and temporary employees should be used. As employees are freed up from their present jobs because of the improvements made in the processes, they should be redeployed to replace the consultants and temporary personnel.

A major portion of the three-year improvement plan is the supporting OCM plan that will help ensure the smooth implementation of the individual process changes. Special focus should be placed on the OCM plan because it is such an important part of the three-year improvement plan, and it is often overlooked.

Step 7—Develop a Rolling 90-Day Implementation Plan

Now that the organization has agreed on a combined three-year improvement plan, it is time to put theory into action. The EIT should now use the combined three-year improvement plan to create a rolling 90-day implementation plan. The rolling 90-day implementation action plan is used to provide the organization with an agreed-to, short-range schedule for implementing the combined three-year improvement plan. This schedule will be divided into weekly segments, but specific target dates are often added to the plan (e.g., the EIT will meet on the first and third Tuesday of every month from 9 A.M. to 12 noon; or, the final report is due February 3).

To accomplish this, any activity that starts during the first three months of the combined three-year plan should have a detailed, day-by-day implementation plan developed for it. This plan should be prepared by the individual who is assigned responsibility for that activity by the EIT. These plans are then combined into a rolling 90-day implementation plan.

Every 30 days, 30 days are dropped off the front end of the rolling 90-day implementation plan, and 30 days are added to the end of the plan. The activities included in the additional 30 days reflect the activities scheduled in the same time period in the combined three-year improvement plan, only in much more detail.

Step 8—Implement the Improvement Plan and Measure the Results

The problem that we have had in the West is not what we do; it's how we implement it. Almost all the improvement tools that individual organizations have tried are good under the right conditions. Unfortunately, in most cases, although we did the right thing, we did it very ineffectively, thereby minimizing the potential gains from the activity. Literally billions of dollars have been wasted in the West training employees to do things that they are not using today. The key to successful implementation of the three-year improvement plan is an excellent change management process. To ensure that the improvement activities are successful, the OCM activities must be an integral part of the three-year improvement plan. (See Appendix V for more information on Organizational Change Management.)

Do not blindly implement the improvement plan thinking it is perfect. It is very important that you measure the results to be sure the organization is getting the desired return on investment. Be sure the organization is meeting the improvement goals it set in Step 3 of Phase VI. If the goals are not being met, it may be necessary to adjust the improvement plan or the organization's commitment to the improvement plan. The improvement plan should be made part of the organization's strategic plan and the targeted gain should be reflected in each department budget. A good balanced scorecard is a key factor that helps to ensure the success of the continuous improvement process.

Keeping the QMS in Line with the Changing Organization

There is no doubt about it. Conflicts will arise between your QMS and your Total Improvement Management (TIM) efforts. TIM will push the organization to empower your employees, reduce checks and balances, bureaucracy, cycle time, and so on. In short, TIM will push the organization to provide more value to all the organization's stakeholders. However, the ISO 9000 standards focus on the external customer. This may seem to be a conflict of interest. In truth, they work well together. The ISO 9000 standards do not tell you who should do things or how they should be done. It allows the organization to use a great deal of freedom and creativity in implementing its TIM process. We see the ISO 9000 standards as the watchdog that helps keep the TIM process on track and keep it from slipping backward. It only takes a little additional care and time to be sure that changes made to improve the organization's processes are reflected in the supporting documentation and the way the organization functions. QMS and TIM do not conflict—they complement each other.

Summary

The piecemeal approach to improvement usually produces results, but not the best results. To become a winner, or to stay a winner, organizations need to define how they want the organization's environment to evolve over the next five years, by preparing a series of vision statements that define the desired future state. Once the organization's direction is defined, it can design the improvement process that will uniquely meet its transformation needs. Organizations can no longer react to the latest improvement fad. They must consider all of the options available to them, then patiently implement them over a period of time.

In today's turbulent environment, where demands for change are continually accelerating, there will be losers, survivors, and winners. Throughout this book we have presented many ideas that can help your organization become more successful. However, these improvements will not bring substantial value to your organization unless they can be implemented successfully. To implement those solutions, your organization must be able to manage change. It is your organization's ability to manage and implement change that will determine whether you will be a loser, survivor, or winner. The most critical issue of managing change is the ability to manage the people who must change, helping them to become more resilient and adaptable in the process.

It may be better to be lucky than good, but being prepared to take advantage of opportunities makes a person or an organization lucky.

—H. James Harrington

References

1. Ernst & Young Technical Report TR 93.004-1 HJH
2. Ernst & Young Technical Report TR 93.004-2 HJH

Makeup of ISO/TC 176 as of January 1996

Participation Table

P-	O-	Member Body	P-	O-	Member Body
x		Algeria (INAPI)		x	Iran, Islamic Rep. of (ISIRI)
x		Argentina (IRAM)	x		Ireland (NSAI)
x		Australia (SAA)	x		Israel (SII)
x		Austria (ON)	x		Italy (UNI)
x		Belgium (IBN)	x		Jamaica (JBS)
x		Brazil (ABNT)	x		Japan (JISC)
x		Canada (SCC)		x	Kenya (KEBS)
x		Chile (INN)	x		Korea, Rep. of (KBS)
x		China (CSBTS)	x		Malaysia (SIRIM)
x		Colombia (ICONTEC)	x		Mauritius (MSB)
x		Cuba (NC)	x		Mexico (DGN)
	x	Cyprus (CYS)		x	Mongolia (MISM)
x		Czech Republic (COSMT)	x		Netherlands (NNI)
x		Denmark (DS)	x		New Zealand (SNZ)
x		Ecuador (INEN)	x		Norway (NSF)
x		Egypt (EOS)	x		Philippines (BPS)
	x	Ethiopia (ESA)	x		Poland (PKN)
x		Finland (SFS)	x		Portugal (IPQ)
x		France (AFNOR)		x	Romania (IRS)
x		Germany (DIN)	x		Russian Federation (GOST R)
x		Greece (ELOT)		x	Saudi Arabia (SASO)
x		Hungary (MSZH)	x		Singapore (SISIR)
	x	Iceland (STRI)		x	Slovakia (UNMS)
x		India (BIS)	x		Slovenia (SMIS)
x		Indonesia (DSN)	x		South Africa (SABS)

Participation Table

P-	O-	Member Body	P-	O-	Member Body
x		Spain (AENOR)		x	Ukraine (DSTU)
x		Sri Lanka (SKSI)	x		United Kingdom (BSI)
x		Sweden (SIS)	x		Uruguay (UNIT)
x		Switzerland (SNV)	x		USA (ANSI)
	x	Syrian Arab Republic (SASMO)	x		Venezuela (COVENIN)
x		Tanzania, United Rep. of (TBS)		x	Vietnam (TCVN)
	x	Thailand (TISI)	x		Yugoslavia (SZS)
x		Trinidad and Tobago (TTBS)	x		Zimbabwe (SAZ)
	x	Tunisia (INNORPI)	x		Estonia (EST)
x		Turkey (TSE)	x		Hong Kong (HKG)

P- = Voting Members
O- = Correspondent Members

Liaisons with other organizations, at the end of the year

Abbrev.	Name of organization	Category A	Category B
AMS/QMSC	Arab Management Society QMSC	x	
APO	Asian Productivity Organization		x
ASQC	American Society for Quality Control	x	
CEFIC	European Chemical Industry Council	x	
CI	Consumers International	x	
EOQ	European Organization for Quality	x	
FIDIC	International Federation of Consulting Engineers	x	
IAEA	International Atomic Energy Agency		x
IAQ	International Academy for Quality	x	
OIML	International Organization of Legal Metrology	x	
RILEM	International Union of Testing and Research Laboratories for Materials and Structures		x
WASP	World Association of Societies of Pathology (Anatomic and Clinical)	x	

ISO/TC 176 Structure as of January 1996

SC	WG	Title
SC 1		Concepts and terminology
	WG 1	Development of ISO 8402
	WG 2	Consistency of use of concepts, terms and definitions in ISO/TC 176 standards
	WG 3	Harmonization of terms and definitions with other bodies
SC 2		Quality Management Systems
	WG 8	Quality in project management
	WG 10	Revision of ISO 9000
	WG 11	Revision of ISO 9001, 9002 and 9003
	WG 12	Revision of ISO 9004
	WG 15	Quality principles and their application to management practices
	WG 16	Revision of ISO 9000-2
	WG 17	Revision of ISO 9000-3 Supporting technologies
SC 3		Supporting technologies
	WG 1	Measuring equipment
	WG 3	Economic effects
	WG 4	Continuing education and training
	WG 5	Inspection and test records
	WG 6	Statistical techniques
	WG 7	Guidelines for auditing Quality Management Systems (Revision of ISO 10011)

SC = Subcommittee
WG = Working Group

APPENDIX II

List of ISO 9000 Series as They Are Released by Country

Country	ISO 9000	ISO 9001	ISO 9002	ISO 9003	ISO 9004
Argentina	IRAM-IACC-ISO E9000	IRAM-IACC-ISO E9001	IRAM-IACC-ISO E9002	IRAM-IACC-ISO E9003	IRAM-IACC-ISO E9004
Australia	AS 3900	AS 3901	AS 3902	AS 3903	AS 3904
Austria	ONORM EN 29000	ONORM EN 29001	ONORM EN 29002	ONORM EN 29003	ONORM EN 29004
Belgium	NBN-EN 29000	NBN-EN 29001	NBN-EN 29002	NBN-EN 29003	NBN-EN 29004
Brazil	NBR/ISO 9000	NBR/ISO 9001	NBR/ISO 9002	NBR/ISO 9003	NBR/ISO 9004
Canada	CAN/CSA-ISO 9000	CAN/CSA-ISO 9001	CAN/CSA-ISO 9002	CAN/CSA-ISO 9003	CAN/CSA-ISO 9004
Chile	NCH-ISO 9000	NCH-ISO 9001	NCH-ISO 9002	NCH-ISO 9003	NCH-ISO 9004
China	GB/T 19000	GB/T 19001	GB/T 19002	GB/T 19003	GB/T 19004
Colombia	NTC-ISO 9000	NTC-ISO 9001	NTC-ISO 9002	NTC-ISO 9003	NTC-ISO 9004
Denmark	DS/ISO 9000	DS/ISO 9001	DS/ISO 9002	DS/ISO 9003	DS/ISO 9004
Finland	SFS-ISO 9000	SFS-ISO 9001	SFS-ISO 9002	SFS-ISO 9003	SFS-ISO 9004
France	NF-EN 29000	NF-EN 29001	NF-EN 29002	NF-EN 29003	NF-EN 29004
Germany	DIN ISO 9000	DIN ISO 9001	DIN ISO 9002	DIN ISO 9003	DIN ISO 9004
Greece	ELOT EN 29000	ELOT EN 29001	ELOT EN 29002	ELOT EN 29003	ELOT EN 29004
Hungary	MSZ EN 29000	MSZ EN 29001	MSZ EN 29002	MSZ EN 29003	MSZ EN 29004
India	IS 14000	IS 14001	IS 14002	IS 14003	IS 14004
Israel	SI 2000	SI 2001	SI 2002	SI 2003	SI 2004
Italy	UNI/EN 29000	UNI/EN 29001	UNI/EN 29002	UNI/EN 29003	UNI/EN 29004
Japan	JIS Z 9900	JIS Z 9901	JIS Z 9902	JIS Z 9903	JIS Z 9904
Korea, Rep. of	KS A 9000	KS A 9001	KS A 9002	KS A 9003	KS A 9004
Mexico	NOM-CC-2	NOM-CC-3	NOM-CC-4	NOM-CC-5	NOM-CC-6
Netherlands	NEN-ISO 9000	NEN-ISO 9001	NEN-ISO 9002	NEN-ISO 9003	NEN-ISO 9004
New Zealand	NZS 9000	NZS 9001	NZS 9002	NZS 9003	NZS 9004
Norway	NS-ISO 9000	NS-ISO 9001	NS-ISO 9002	NS-ISO 9003	NS-ISO 9004
Philippines	PNS 1000	PNS 1001	PNS 1002	PNS 1003	PNS 1004
Poland	PN-EN 29000	PN-EN 29001	PN-EN 29002	PN-EN 29003	PN-EN 29004
Portugal	NP EN 29000	NP EN 29001	NP EN 29002	NP EN 29003	NP EN 29004
Russian Fed.		GOST 40.9001	GOST 40.9002	GOST 40.9003	
Singapore	SS/ISO 9000	SS/ISO 9001	SS/ISO 9002	SS/ISO 9003	SS/ISO 9004

List of ISO 9000 Series as They Are Released by Country (Cont.)

Country	ISO 9000	ISO 9001	ISO 9002	ISO 9003	ISO 9004
South Africa	SABS/ISO 9000	SABS/ISO 9001	SABS/ISO 9002	SABS/ISO 9003	SABS/ISO 9004
Spain	UNE 66 900	UNE 66 901	UNE 66 902	UNE 66 903	UNE 66 904
Sweden	SS-ISO 9000	SS-ISO 9001	SS-ISO 9002	SS-ISO 9003	SS-ISO 9004
Switzerland	SN EN 29000	SN EN 29001	SN EN 29002	SN EN 29003	SN EN 29004
Turkey	TS-ISO 9000	TS-ISO-9001	TS-ISO 9002	TS-ISO 9003	TS-ISO 9004
United Kingdom	BS 5750: Pt 0	BS 5750: Pt 1	BS 5750: Pt 2	BS 5750: Pt 3	BS 5750: Pt 0
Vietnam	TCVN 5200	TCVN 5201	TCVN 5202	TCVN 5203	TCVN 5204
Yugoslavia	JUS-ISO 9000	JUS-ISO 9001	JUS-ISO 9002	JUS-ISO 9003	JUS-ISO 9004
Zimbabwe	SAZS 300: Part 5	SAZS 300: Part 1	SAZS 300: Part 2	SAZS 300: Part 3	SAZS 300: Part 4
CEN*	EN 29000	EN 29001	EN 29002	EN 29003	EN 29004
COPANT**	COPANT-ISO 9000	COPANT-ISO 9001	COPANT-ISO 9002	COPANT-ISO 9003	COPANT-ISO 9004

*CEN = European Committee for Standardization
**COPANT = Pan American Standards Commission

List of Typical ISO 9000 Registrars

ABS Quality Evaluations, Inc.
16855 Northchase Drive
Houston, TX 77060-6008
Phone: 713-873-9400
Fax: 713-874-9564

American Association for Laboratory Accreditation (A2LA)
656 Quince Orchard Road, #304
Gaithersburg, MD 20878-1409
Phone: 301-670-1377
Fax: 301-869-1495

American European Services, Inc.
1054 31st Street, NW, Suite 120
Washington, DC 20007
Phone: 202-337-3214
Fax: 202-337-3709

AT&T Quality Registrar
To reach AT&T Quality Registrar, call 800-521-3399 (Union, New Jersey)
or contact one of the following:

John Malinauskas, AT&T
650 Liberty Avenue
Union, NJ 07083
Phone: 908-851-3058
Fax: 908-851-3158

David Swasey, AT&T
2600 San Tomas Expressway
Santa Clara, CA 95051-1366
Phone: 408-562-1370
Fax: 408-562-1366

Bellcore Quality Registration
6 Corporate Place
Piscataway, NJ 08854
Phone: 908-699-3739
Fax: 908-336-2220

British Standards Institution Quality Assurance

In the U.S.: **British Standards Institution, Inc.**
8000 Towers Crescent Drive, Suite 1350
Vienna, VA 22182
Phone: 703-760-7828
Fax: 703-760-7899

In the U.K.: **BSI Quality Assurance**
P.O. Box 375
Milton Keynes MK14 6LL
Phone: 0908-220-909
Fax: 0908-220-671

Bureau Veritas Quality International (NA) Inc.
North American Central Offices
509 North Main Street
Jamestown, NY 14701
Phone: 716-484-9002
Fax: 716-484-9003

Canadian General Standards Board
Quality Management Systems Division
222 Queen Street, Suite 1402
Ottawa, Ontario KIA 1G6
Canada
Phone: 613-941-8657
Fax: 613-941-8706

CGA Approvals—Canadian Operation of International Approvals Services
55 Scarsdale Road
Don Mills
Toronto, Ontario M3B 2R3
Canada
Phone: 416-447-6468
Fax: 416-447-7067

Intertek Services Corporation
9900 Main Street, Suite 500
Fairfax, VA 22031
Phone: 703-476-9000
Fax: 703-273-4124 or 2885

Kema Registered Quality, Inc.
4379 County Line Road
Chalfont, PA 18914
Phone: 215-822-4281
Fax: 215-822-4285

Lloyd's Register Quality Assurance, Ltd.
33-41 Newark Street
Hoboken, NJ 07030
Phone: 201-963-1111
Fax: 201-963-3299

Moody-Tottrup International, Inc.
350 McKnight Plaza Building
105 Braunlich Drive
Pittsburgh, PA 15237
Phone: 412-366-5567
Fax: 412-366-5571

National Quality Assurance USA
1146 Massachusetts Avenue
Boxborough, MA 01719
Phone: 508-635-9256
Fax: 508-266-1073

Professional Registrar Organization, Inc.
42000 West Six Mile Road
Northville, MI 48167
Phone: 810-344-9700
1-800-793-4408
Fax: 810-793-4408

Quality Management Institute
1 Robert Speck Parkway
Mississauga, Ontario L4Z 1H8
Canada
Phone: 905-272-3920
Fax: 905-272-3942

Quality Management Systems Registrars, Inc.
13873 Park Center Road, Suite 217
Herndon, VA 22071-3279
Phone: 703-478-0241
Fax: 703-478-0645

Quebec Quality Certification Group
70, rue Dalhousie, Bureau 220
Quebec, Quebec G1K 4B2
Canada
Phone: 418-643-5813
Fax: 418-646-3315

TUV Rheinland of North America, Inc.
12 Commerce Road
Newtown, CT 06470
Phone: 203-426-0888
Fax: 203-426-3156

Underwriters Laboratories of Canada
7 Crouse Road
Scarborough, Ontario M1R 3A9
Canada
Phone: 416-757-3611
Fax: 416-757-1781

Underwriters Laboratories, Inc.
1285 Walt Whitman Road
Melville, NY 11747-3081
Phone: 516-271-6200
Fax: 516-271-8259

See *ISO 9000 Almanac,* published by
Irwin Professional Publishing, Burr Ridge,
Illinois, copyrighted 1994 and edited by
Eric D. Peters for additional lists of reg-
istrars.

List of Typical ISO 9000 Implementation Consulting Firms

American Institute for Quality & Reliability
P.O. Box 41163
San Jose, CA 95160
Phone: 408-275-9300
Fax: 408-275-9399

American Supplier Institute
15041 Commerce Drive South
Suite 401
Dearborn, MI 48120-1238
Phone: 313-271-4200
Phone: 800-462-4500
Fax: 313-336-3187

Brewer & Associates, Inc.
2505 Locksley Drive
Grand Prairie, TX 75050
Phone: 214-641-8020
Fax: 214-641-1327

BSI Quality Assurance
10521 Baddock Road
Fairfax, VA 22032
Phone: 703-250-5900
Fax: 703-250-5313

Center for Quality & Productivity
Route 252 & Media Line Road
Media, PA 19063-1094
Phone: 215-359-5367

Charles R. "Chuck" Carter & Associates
6400 Barrie Road, No. 1101
Edina, MN 55435-2317
Phone: 612-927-6003

Columbia Quality Management International
P.O. Box 506
Orefield, PA 18069
Phone: 215-391-9496
Fax: 215-391-9497

Coopers & Lybrand
1100 Louisiana, Suite 4100
Houston, TX 77002
Phone: 713-757-5200
Fax: 713-757-5249

Donald W. Marquardt & Associates
1415 Athens Road
Wilmington, DE 19803
Phone: 302-478-6695
Fax: 302-478-9329

Eastern Michigan University Center for Quality
34 N. Washington Street
Ypsilanti, MI 48197
Phone: 313-487-2259
Fax: 313-481-0509

EBB Associates, Inc.
Box 8249
Norfolk, VA 23503
Phone: 804-588-3939
Fax: 804-588-5824

Eckersberg & Associates Consultants
819 Bowling Green Road
Homewood, IL 60430
Phone: 312-799-6880

Ernst & Young LLP
55 Almaden Blvd., 4th Floor
San Jose, CA 95113
Phone: 408-947-6587
Fax: 408-947-4971

Fed-Pro, Inc.
5615 Jensen Drive
Rockford, IL 61111
Phone: 815-282-4300
Fax: 815-282-4304

H.W. Fahrlander & Associates
640 Downing Drive
Richardson, TX 75080-6117
Phone: 214-783-1216
Fax: 214-783-6043

Harrington Group, Inc.
3208-C E. Colonial Drive, Suite 253
Orlando, FL 32803
Phone: 407-275-9841
Fax: 407-281-4941

Harrison M. Wadsworth & Associates
660 Valley Green Drive Northeast
Atlanta, GA 30342
Phone: 404-255-8662
Fax: 404-250-1493

The Ironbridge Group
9200 Indian Creek Parkway, Building 9, Suite 201
Overland Park, KS 66210
Phone: 800-ISO-9001 (476-9001)
Fax: 913-491-9389

James Lamprecht, ISO 9000 Certified Consultancy and Training
1420 N.W. Gilman Blvd., Suite 2576
Issaquah, WA 98027-7001
Phone: 206-644-9504
Fax: 206-557-8905

John Kidwell & Associates
116 Skimmer Way
Daytona Beach, FL 32119
Phone: 904-756-2504
Fax: 904-788-1472

Kastle Consulting Group
P.O. Box 207
Englewood, OH 45322
Phone: 513-890-6416

Lloyd's Register Technical Services, Inc.
One Corporate Plaza
2525 Bay Area Blvd., Suite 690
Houston, TX 77058
Phone: 713-480-5008
Fax: 713-480-5313

Mathers & Associates
48 Alpha Mills Road
Mississauga, Ontario, L5N 1H6
Canada
Phone: 905-821-2139
Fax: 905-821-7636

Organizational Dynamics, Inc.
25 Mall Road
Burlington, MA 01803
Phone: 800-634-4636
Fax: 617-273-2558

Perry Johnson, Inc.
3000 Town Center, Suite 2960
Southfield, MI 48075
Phone: 313-356-4410
Fax: 313-356-4230

Philip Crosby Associates, Inc.
3260 University Blvd.
P.O. Box 606
Winter Park, FL 32793-6006
Phone: 407-677-3000
Fax: 407-677-3055

Powers Consulting, Inc.
6107 Knox Avenue S.
Minneapolis, MN 55419
Phone: 612-861-4794

QCI International
P.O. Box 1503
Red Bluff, CA 96080-1503
Phone: 800-527-6970
Fax: 800-527-6983

Quality International Limited
2716 Orthodox Street
Philadelphia, PA 19137-1604
Phone: 800-524-5877

Quality Management International Limited
55 Morley Circle
Saint John, New Brunswick E2J 2X5
Canada
Phone: 506-633-2060
Fax: 506-633-2060

Rath & Strong, Inc.
92 Hayden Avenue
Lexington, MA 02173
Phone 617-861-1700
Fax: 617-861-1424

Robert Peach & Associates, Inc.
541 North Brainard Avenue
La Grange Park, IL 60525
Phone: 708-579-3400
Fax: 708-579-1620

Rochester Institute of Technology
Center for Quality & Applied Statistics
P.O. Box 7887
Hugh L. Carvey Building
Rochester, NY 14623-0887
Phone: 716-475-6990
Fax: 716-475-5959

Roger Hunt Management Consulting, Inc.
3220 Schoolhouse Drive
Waterford, MI 48329-4331
Phone: 313-673-7675

Stat-A-Matrix Institute
2124 Oak Tree Road
Edison, NJ 08820-1059
Phone: 908-548-0600
Fax: 908-548-0409

W. A. Golomski & Associates
20 E. Jackson Blvd., Suite 850
Chicago, IL 60604-2208
Phone: 312-922-5986
Fax: 312-922-4070

See *ISO 9000 Almanac,* published by Irwin Professional Publishing, Burr Ridge, Illinois, copyrighted 1994 and edited by Eric D. Peters for additional lists of ISO 9000 consultants.

The Organizational Change

Management Methodology

Mark B. Hefner
National Director—Organizational Change Management Ernst & Young LLP

C. Keith Cox
Staff Consultant Ernst & Young LLP

Abstract

The really successful improvement process has two essential ingredients: a better concept, and effective implementation. The major problem facing most organizations today is the way they are implementing their major improvement processes. This report explains how to use the Organizational Change Management (OCM) methodology to reduce and/or eliminate the resistance to change within your organization. If used correctly, OCM will have your employees saying, "How can I make this change work?" instead of telling management why it won't work.

> Only 5% of the organizations in the West truly excel. Their secret is not what they do, but how they do it. They are the ones that manage the change process.
> —*Dr H. James Harrington*

Introduction

A critical component of an integrated Total Improvement Management (TIM) methodology is a structured and disciplined process for managing and

315

implementing change. The adoption of a TIM philosophy will create a great deal of organizational change that will have a major impact on organizational members' current beliefs, behaviors, knowledge, and expectations. To make this challenge even more daunting, the changes brought about by TIM will impact people who are probably already overwhelmed with the increasing acceleration of change in their professional and personal lives. Therefore, all organizational members must realize that organizational change can, and must, be managed. Change cannot be viewed as a one-time event or a passing phase. Change must be seen as the manageable process that it is (see Figure V.1).

For TIM to bring about real, sustainable business improvements, it is imperative that managers at all levels of the organization have the ability and willingness to deal with the tough issues associated with implementing major change. They must be capable of guiding their organization safely through the change process. This involves convincing people to leave the comfort of the current state, move through the turbulent, new way of doing things (the transi-

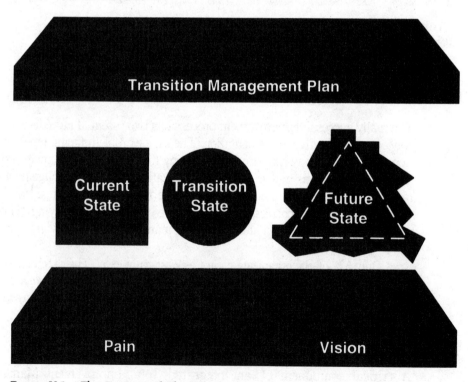

FIGURE V.1   The Process of Change

tion state), to arrive at what may be an unclear, distant future state. Specifically, these three states are defined as follows:

1. *Current state*—The status quo, or the established patterns of expectations. The normal routine an organization follows before the implementation of TIM.
2. *Transition state*—The point in the change process where people break away from the status quo. They no longer behave as they have done in the past, yet they still have not thoroughly established the "new way" of operating. The transition state begins when TIM solutions disrupt individuals' expectations and they must start to change the way they work.
3. *Future state*—The point where change initiatives are implemented and integrated with the behavior patterns that are required by the change. TIM goals and objectives have been achieved.

The focus of OCM implementation methods is on the transition between these various states. The journey from the current state to the future state can be long and perilous, and if not properly managed with appropriate strategies and tactics, it can be disastrous.

Over the last 20 years, we have been involved with ODR, Inc., in an ongoing field research project focused entirely on change management. The primary purpose of this project has been to identify the distinguishing characteristics of those managers/organizations who were highly successful at implementing major change, and those who were not. As a result, we have been able to identify some of the "best practices," as well as common "pitfalls" of implementing major change projects. Prior to an in-depth look at some of the more critical best practices of OCM, it is important for us to first set the proper context from which the best practices were identified.

Working Definition of OCM

What is the definition of successful implementation of major organizational change? To determine which organizations were successful at implementing major change projects and those that were not, it was necessary to develop an operating definition of "success." The definition created is as follows: "*Successful implementation equals achievement of the stated human and technical and business objectives on time and within budget.*" Granted, this is a very restrictive definition of success, but to truly identify the best practices of what it takes to make change happen successfully, it was critical to identify those actions that were taken by organizations that achieved this definition of success, and to identify those actions that resulted in a less than acceptable (i.e., unsuccessful) change project. The philosophy of TIM and the identification of improvement projects will bring little value to the organization unless fully implemented. The remainder of this chapter will be dedicated to highlighting those best practices which an organization should follow to increase the likelihood of successfully implementing improvement projects. It will also discuss the most common pitfalls that would cause implementation failures.

OCM Best Practices

Determining When a Change Is Major

We can apply our first best practice to any improvement project that is being implemented by first identifying the pitfalls. Many organizations have a tendency to assume that every change or improvement project requires the same level of implementation effort. In essence, they tend to repeat their past implementation history; they budget for cost and time requirements for both the technical and human objectives as if all change projects were the same. The best practice that should be applied here deals with accurately determining when an improvement project is going to be a major change for the people impacted within the organization. If it is a major change, then it is worth some special implementation effort and some special allocation of implementation resources. According to Daryl Conner, president and CEO of ODR, Inc., there are some guidelines, in terms of when or how to determine whether a major project needs special implementation effort.

Factors to Consider

Essentially there are three factors to consider:

1. *Is the change a major change for the people in the organization (human impact)?* A major change is any change that produces a significant disruption of an individual's normal expectation patterns. For management to determine whether a change initiative is considered major, 14 specific factors should be examined. These factors that disrupt expectation patterns are as follows:

Amount	The greater the number of alterations that are required by the change, the greater the level of disruption.
Scope	The larger the range or span of the organization affected by the change, the greater the level of disruption.
Transferability	The more difficult the change is to communicate to and be understood by the targets (the individual or group that must change), the greater the level of disruption.
Time	The less amount of time that the targets have to implement the change, the greater the level of disruption.
Predictability	The more likely the targets will not be able to anticipate the effect of the change on them, the greater the level of disruption.
Ability	The more targets feel that they don't have or can't attain the knowledge and skill necessary to implement the change, the greater the level of disruption.
Willingness	The less motivated the targets are to implement the change, the greater the level of disruption.
Values	The more the targets must change strongly held beliefs about the way that they are operating, the greater the level of disruption.
Emotions	The more targets must change the way they feel about people or operating procedures, the greater the level of disruption.
Knowledge	The more new information targets must learn, the greater the level of disruption.
Behaviors	The more modifications targets must make to their daily routines, the greater the level of disruption.
Logistics	The more significant the changes to the targets' job procedures, the greater the level of disruption.
Economics	The more extensive the changes to the operating procedures regarding budgets, expenses, and/or funding, the greater the level of disruption.
Politics	The more targets must change their methods of influencing others, utilizing power, working in a team, and so on, the greater the level of disruption.

One, or any combination of these factors, can cause a change to be considered major in the eyes of the targets. Management must have a handle on the way their employees are perceiving even what seems like the most insignificant of changes.

2. *Is there a high cost of implementation failure?* What is the price associated with failing to implement a specific improvement project (cost of failure)? It is imperative for management to understand the consequences of failing to successfully implement any change. Not only will resources be wasted on a problem that is not solved or an opportunity that is not exploited, but there may be other implications such as morale suffering, job security threatened, and the organization losing confidence in its leadership.

3. *What are the risks that certain human factors could cause implementation failure (resistance)?* Questions that need to be answered include: Is senior management truly committed to this project, how resistant will the organization be, and does this change "fit" with our culture, among others. Once again, ignoring any of these human factors can cause a project to fail. Later in this chapter there are specific best practices that address a majority of these factors.

These three factors must be considered for every improvement project identified. If (1) the change is a major disruption from the status quo (especially for the people who actually have to assimilate this change), (2) there is a very high cost to the organization if the change fails, and (3) there is a very high risk that the change could fail (especially due to some of the human and cultural variables), then this change project can be considered a business imperative. Senior management must be able to recognize these business imperatives, which require a dedicated effort in managing the human and technical objectives to achieve success. Therefore, to leverage this best practice, each improvement project resulting from the adoption of a TIM philosophy should be assessed with regard to these three factors. Hence, an accurate determination can be made of the level of disruption change causes the organization, and how much time, effort, money, and resources will be required to ensure successful implementation.

Building Resolve to Manage Change

Next, we can discuss pitfalls and best practices with regard to building the resolve and commitment necessary not only to initiate an improvement project but also to sustain that project all the way through to completion. One of the common pitfalls that we have seen many organizations make is strong, zealous initiation of improvement projects, only to have them flounder from lack of resolve to sustain the project through to completion. Obviously, then, the best practice in this case is to build the necessary commitment to sustain the change with senior and middle management, thereby enabling the organization to manage the change process over time.

Achieving "informed commitment" at the beginning of a project is one of the main issues in any change project. A basic formula can be applied that addresses the perceived cost of change versus the perceived cost of maintaining the status quo. As long as people perceive the change as being more costly than maintaining the status quo, it is extremely unlikely that the resolve to sustain the change process has been built. The initiator of the change must move to increase people's perception of the high cost of maintaining the status quo and decrease their perception of the cost of the change, so that people recognize that even though the change may be expensive and frightening, maintaining the status quo is no longer viable and is, in fact, more costly. This process is referred to as "pain management."

Pain management is the process of consciously surfacing, orchestrating, and communicating certain information to generate the appropriate awareness of the pain associated with maintaining the status quo compared with the pain resulting from implementing the change. The "pain" the initiator is dealing with is not actual physical pain. Rather, change-related pain refers to the level of dissatisfaction a person experiences when his or her goals are not being met or are not expected to be met because of the status quo. This pain occurs when people are paying or will pay the price for an unresolved problem or missing a key opportunity. Change-related pain can fall into one of two categories, current pain and anticipated pain.

Current pain revolves around an organization's reaction to an immediate crisis or opportunity, while *anticipated pain* takes a look into the future, predicting probable problems or opportunities. It is very crucial that management understands where their organization is located on this continuum of current versus anticipated pain. This understanding enables management to better time the "resolve to change." This resolve/commitment, which must be built and sustained, can occur during either the current or anticipated time frames. If this attempt to build resolve is formed too early, it won't be sustained; if it's formed too late, it won't matter. Management has a wide variety of pain management techniques from which it can choose. Some of these techniques being used by *Fortune 500* companies include: cost/benefit analysis, industry benchmarking, industry trend analysis, and force-field analysis, among many others. When this process has been accepted by senior and middle management, a critical mass of pain associated with the status quo has been established, and the resolve to sustain the change process has also been established. It is only then that management can begin to manage change as a process, instead of an event.

Any project that results from the TIM philosophy will, by necessity, cause change in an organization. The application of this best practice is critical in beginning to mobilize support and understanding for the reasons for change, to help them let go of the status quo and move forward to a very difficult state, known as the transition state. Managing people through the transition state to project completion requires resolve not only to initiate change but also to sustain it over time, with management continually communicating the necessity for change and supporting the actions required to bring it about.

Identify and Orchestrate Key Roles

Identification of key roles in the change process is vital to successful implementation of change projects. Many scholars have studied the field of change management and have formulated different names for the five key roles. The names that we will use are as follows:

1. *Initiating sponsor* is the individual or group with the power to initiate or legitimize the change for all the affected people in the organization.
2. *Sustaining sponsor* is the individual or group with the political, logistic, and economic proximity to the people who actually have to change. Often we talk about initiating sponsors as senior management, and sustaining sponsors as middle management, but that's not necessarily the case. Often sponsors can be someone in the organization who has no real line power but has significant influence power as a result of relationships with the people affected by the change, past successes of the individual, knowledge, or power.
3. *Change agent* is the individual or group with responsibility for implementing the change. Change agents are given this responsibility by the sponsors. Agents do not have the power to legitimize change. They do not have the power to motivate the members of the organization to change, but they certainly have the responsibility for making it happen. They must depend on and leverage sponsorship when necessary.
4. *Change target* is the individual or group who must actually change. There really is nothing derogative associated with the word *target*. In fact, it's really more of an indication of where the resources that are allocated to any specific project must be focused to achieve successful change.
5. *Change advocate* is an individual or group who wants to achieve change but who lacks sponsorship. The role of change advocates is to advise, influence, and lobby support for change. Identifying the mem-

bers of an organization who must fulfill these roles, and then orchestrating them throughout the change process, is a best practice that organizations can leverage to greatly increase their likelihood of success with any specific improvement project.

Once these roles are identified, management should maneuver those key roles to optimize each of them throughout the change process to achieve successful implementation. To be effective in that task, management must understand the intricacies of each role, how they interact with each other, and how they work in an organization. The first thing that needs to be understood is that in all major change projects, key roles will overlap. When this occurs, the individual(s) should always be treated as a "target" first (i.e., surface pain, manage resistance, build commitment). An example of this would be if a divisional president would sponsor Management By Objectives (MBO) for his division. He might also serve as a change agent by promoting MBO's use to midlevel mangers and could be considered a target if he uses MBO himself.

Impact of Change on the Organization

Another important point management must understand is the interaction of these key roles in the three most basic organizational structures. These three basic structures in most organizations are linear, triangular (e.g., staff), and square (e.g., levels of business). (See Figure V.2.)

All these structures are usually found in an organization and can be useful; however, each one can become dysfunctional. The linear structure is the simplest to understand. A sponsor delegates implementation responsibility to a change agent who implements down to the target. The triangular structure is more complicated because the change agent and target report to the same sponsor, but the target does not report to the change agent. What tends to happen in this situation is that the change agent often will try to use his or her own legitimizing power to implement the change. The target, however, usually knows who "the boss" is, so the sponsor-change agent relationship must be clarified. The appropriate action in this situation is for the sponsor to play "watch my lips" with the target to ensure he or she understands that the change is the sponsor's idea and no one else's.

The final basic organizational structure, the square, can also be very dysfunctional. The problem here is that a sponsor, or a sponsor's change agent, will try to implement a change on a second sponsor's employees/targets. What sponsor #1 is usually unaware of is that these targets will rarely respond to change directives unless those directives are received by those who control the

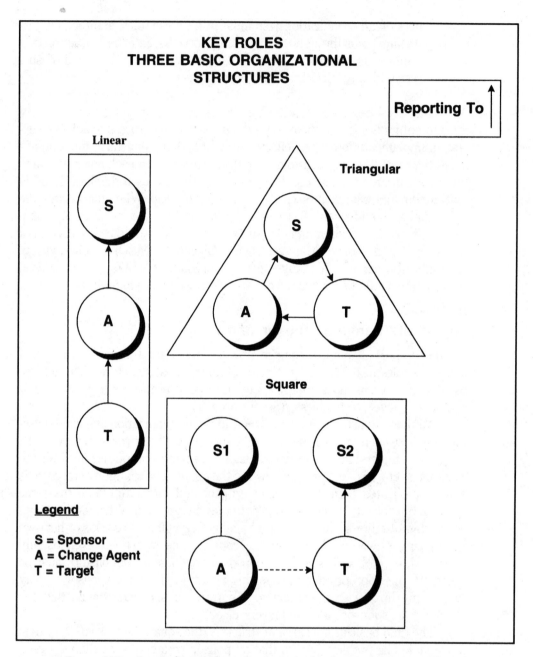

consequence management. The proper solution is for sponsor #1 to become an advocate to sponsor #2 in order to bring him or her on board with the change initiative. If this tactic fails, appealing to a higher authority to intercede is necessary.

Management needs to comprehend that these types of problems involved with the triangular and square structures are associated with a high risk implementation failure. Therefore, with a solid understanding of what the key roles are and how they affect change in an organization, sponsors, both initiating and sustaining, will help to identify these roles and fill them. It is then up to management to establish an optimum performance level and orchestrate and manage that performance.

Build Sponsorship to Support and Sustain Change Objectives

One of the common pitfalls associated with implementing major change among the sponsorship group is an assumption that once the decision has been made and communicated regarding what must be implemented, no further involvement on their part is necessary. Top management tends to ignore the importance of the other key roles, relying instead on employee compliance with orders from above. They are often dismayed to find that after six months, their directives still are ignored. In fact, if major change is involved, sponsor involvement and commitment is most important. The best practice that we have helped organizations apply to successful change initiatives is the accurate and timely identification of initiating and sustaining sponsors, exactly what their roles entail, and installing an architected, proactive approach to building the sponsorship necessary at each level to support and sustain the change through to completion. This process has been referred to as the building of cascading sponsorship.

Cascading sponsorship is an effective way to eliminate the corporate black hole. *Black holes* are those places in organizations where change decisions enter but are never heard from again. These typically occur when there is a manager who does not sponsor the change and, therefore, the targets beneath him or her do not adopt the change. Initiating sponsors can do little to maintain the change at lower levels of the organization because they do not have the logistical, economical, or political proximity to the targets. The result is that change cannot succeed if there is not a network of sustaining sponsorship that maintains the integrity of the implementation as it moves down through all levels of the organization; hence, cascading sponsorship.

Essentially, the way cascading sponsorship works is by starting with the initiating sponsor and working down through the different levels, specific to any improvement project. Sponsors prepare the change agents to fulfill their roles, giving them the necessary skills to manage not only the technical aspects of the engagement but the human aspects as well. The success of any improvement project starts at the top and ultimately rests on the shoulders of the sponsors. Sponsorship is the most critical risk factor in any change project. To have an effective network of sponsors, organizations implementing major change need to adhere to the following five critical principles:

1. Sponsorship is critical to successful change, so all sponsors must demonstrate, publicly and privately, unsurpassable commitment.
2. Weak sponsors must be educated or replaced, or failure is inevitable.
3. Sponsorship cannot be delegated to change agents.
4. Initiating and sustaining sponsors must never attempt to fulfill each other's functions. Initiating sponsors are the only ones who can start the change process, and sustaining sponsors are the only ones who can maintain it.
5. Cascading sponsorship must be established and maintained.

Sponsors must also be sure not just to speak rhetoric about being committed to the change; they must openly demonstrate it. Sponsors need to develop a clear vision of the future state at the strategic and tactical level, and surface the appropriate amount of pain to move toward that vision. Sponsors need to become educated to understand the effect the change will have on the organization, and empathize with what the targets are being asked to change about the way they operate. Sponsors not only need to be prepared to allocate necessary organizational resources (e.g., time, money, people, etc.) for successful implementation; they must also be prepared to personally pay the price for success. Finally, sponsors need to develop a reward structure that recognizes those who facilitate the implementation process and discourages those who attempt to inhibit the acceptance of change.

Preparing Change Agents in the Required Skills

We are living in a turbulent environment, where change is accelerating dramatically in three ways: volume, speed, and complexity. This means that we can no longer manage as we have in the past. A possible pitfall in this area is that sponsors assume, often incorrectly, that those identified as change agents and advocates possess the skills necessary to successfully deal with human, as well as technical, implementation problems.

In today's unstable environment, it is necessary to have finely honed skills for managing and implementing technical and human change. These skills are in very high demand, and special training is often necessary. The best practice for organizations is to build the capacity to manage change. To accomplish this objective, the change agents must come into the engagement with a different perspective. Part of the development of these skills is also a bit of a shift in mind-set.

When you look at agents historically, you will note that they tended to have more of a technical expertise mentality. Their primary focus and objective was to be sure that the change, whatever it might be, was technically sound and that if people weren't able to use it, then it wasn't the agents' fault. That mind-set must shift to a mind-set that follows the idea of facilitators of change—the mind-set that says change agents need to be responsible for managing not only the technical aspects of the change but also the human aspects of the change. This mind-set also dictates that the change agent should focus on the process as well as the content issues, with technology being designed to accommodate human interests, needs, and values.

Truly effective change agents should be skilled in a complex combination of characteristics that can be brought to bear on a given change project. Successful change agents must have the ability to work within the parameters set by the sponsor and understand the psychological dynamics regarding how individuals and organizations can modify their operations. Change agents must optimize their performance by placing emphasis on the technical, and especially the human, aspects of the change. Change agents must be skilled in dealing with resistance. To understand that resistance, it is critical for change agents to be able to identify, relate to, and respect the targets' and sponsors' diverse frames of reference. Change agents must also be the "cheerleaders." They must constantly strive to build commitment and synergy among targets and sponsors while being aware of and utilizing power dynamics and influence techniques in a manner that reflects a capacity to achieve results in an ethical way. The bottom line is that a change agent must be professional, setting aside a personal agenda for the good of the change.

Success ultimately is judged by achievement of both the human and the technical objectives. That mind shift needs to occur if change agents are going to more effectively manage the human aspects of implementing major change projects. The change management skills within the organization are critical to the success of any change project. This change of perspective must occur if change agents are going to successfully manage the implementation of change projects. However, even the most skilled change agents in the world cannot successfully implement major change by themselves. The other roles in the change process, specifically the advocates, must have their skills finely honed and be prepared to use them.

Preparing Advocates in the Required Skills

To be a successful advocate, as with change agents, a special mind-set is required. Successful advocates must focus their attention on the sponsor(s) of the change and position the change as being beneficial to the sponsor(s). Advocates must seek the approval of those in power and avoid at all costs wasting time/energy with people who can't say yes. Effective advocates are results oriented and are willing to accept nothing less than successful change. They are unwilling to simply adjust to the unacceptable status quo. Advocates must be confrontative and assertive and when faced with poor or declining sponsorship, they must be prepared to either educate the sponsor, replace the sponsor, or ultimately prepare to miss deadlines and projected budgets. ODR, Inc., states that the advocate simply needs to follow these five basic steps to be successful:

1. Precisely define the change that needs to occur and how success would be measured.
2. Identify the key targets that must accommodate the change.
3. With each key target or target group identified, determine the initiating and sustaining sponsor(s) who must support the change.
4. Evaluate the current level of sponsor commitment.
5. Develop "pain management" strategies to increase and gain the appropriate sponsor commitment level.

When everyone in the change process knows their role(s) and has the skills necessary to fulfill those roles, successful implementation will be completed on time and within budget. Without the correct perspective and skill base, especially for change agents and advocates, the chance for successful implementation is nearly eliminated.

Enable Sponsors, Agents, Targets, and Advocates to Work as a Synergistic Team

The next best practice that we can discuss deals with the idea of synergy—building synergistic work environments and synergistic work teams. Synergy is a very important concept when implementing change projects. *Synergy* occurs when two or more people, working together, produce more than the sum of their individual efforts. Much has been said about empowerment, participative management, cross-functional teams—all are very good ideas and necessary, but none are likely to be successful without a basic synergistic environment. A common pitfall is that management promotes the idea of synergistic output and synergistic teams, yet most fail to achieve them. The advised best practice is to enable sponsors, agents, and targets to work effectively as a synergistic team throughout the change process.

Integral to synergy is allowing people to work in a synergistic environment. Synergistic environments are open, there is no fear, there is two-way communication, and people in those environments really do feel as if they can have some influence over the outcome of any specific project or business issue. In synergistic work environments, people tend to produce a greater total output than the sum of individual efforts, which generates more benefits to the organization than the amount of resources that are consumed. It promotes a higher future shock threshold that aids people to more easily adopt and assimilate change because of this openness.

To really build this kind of environment and this kind of teamwork, it is necessary to first meet the two prerequisites of synergistic work teams:

1. There needs to be a very powerful common goal shared by sponsors, agents, targets, and advocates for the change. This must be a common goal that everybody is motivated to achieve; therefore, selecting goals, how goals are communicated, how well they are communicated, and what incentives are offered to achieve any of these goals is very important.
2. Goal achievement requires a recognition of interdependency: sponsors, agents, targets, and advocates must recognize that the goal cannot be achieved without working together. As long as one member feels that he or she can achieve the goal without another member, synergy will not occur. Synergy does not require that people like each other or that people necessarily have a history of good relations. What it does require is that there is a common, powerful goal that motivates people in the same direction and that they recognize the need to work together to achieve success.

Therefore, the best practice here is primarily to focus on making sure that those prerequisites exist. Once the existing prerequisites are confirmed, a team and a process can be built so that people can really capture the potential synergy. With the prerequisites for synergy met, a group or organization can begin its journey through the four phases of the synergistic process and team development. It is important to note that all teams must go through this process—there are no shortcuts. However, the length of time a team has already been in existence can affect the duration of time it spends in each phase of the process.

These synergistic relationships are generated through a four-phase process:

I.   Interacting
II. Appreciative Understanding
III. Integrating
IV. Implementing

Each phase is interdependent on the others, and individuals or groups on an implementation team must demonstrate the ability and willingness to operate to the characteristics associated with each phase.

Interacting—For people to work together effectively and synergistically, they first must interact with one another. If this interaction is going to be meaningful, people must communicate effectively. At first, this task is not easy and one usually filled with conflict. This is referred to as a group "storming." The inevitable misunderstandings individuals are bound to have go unresolved. This causes anger, frustration, blaming, suspicion, alienation, hostility, and, possibly, withdrawal. In an attempt to stop this destructive cycle, and a total breakdown of the team development process, teams must move on to group "norming." Here, the group decides on some basic ground rules as to how it is going to operate. Most importantly, the group must

- Agree upon a common goal.
- Acknowledge interdependence regarding the successful accomplishment of this goal.
- Effectively communicate to each other with directness, low distortion, and high congruence.
- Actively listen to both the facts and feelings expressed in communication.
- Communicate in a manner that generates trust and credibility with each other.

Once a group has satisfied the aforementioned conditions, it is ready to move into the "Appreciative Understanding" phase.

Appreciative Understanding—As important as effective communication is for successful change, something more must occur. Group members in a synergistic team effort must value and utilize the diversity that exists among the members. This is a continuation of the norming process that occurs in team development. Valuing a different point of view can be difficult for individuals because of the emphasis our culture places on rational, linear, left-hemispheric thinking processes that encourage critical analyses. This thought process can produce an "I'm right, you're wrong" attitude, whereas synergy dictates that people should support each other and look for the merit in another's viewpoint. To ensure synergy, team members should

- Create an open climate where differences can be surfaced appropriately.
- Delay initial judgments about each other's ideas, beliefs, feelings, attitudes, behavior, or concerns.
- Actively empathize with each other and view the perspective of others as legitimate for them.
- Value diversity and identify positive characteristics about one another's viewpoints.

These actions will eliminate the need for a win/lose atmosphere.

Integrating—Even though a team has passed through the first two phases of the synergistic process, it is not yet sufficient to produce synergistic outcomes. Synergy is the result of communicating, valuing, and merging separate, diverse viewpoints. Once again, accomplishing this integration is extremely difficult because our culture does not teach and reward the skills needed. For team members to work through the norming process of team development and move on to "performing" the final phase, they need to develop the skills necessary to make integration possible. Specifically, team members need to

- Tolerate ambiguity and be persistent in the struggle for new possibilities.
- Modify their own views, beliefs, and behavior in order to support the team.
- Generate creative ways of merging diverse perspectives into new, mutually supported alternatives.
- Identify issues, concepts, and so on that cannot or should not be integrated.

When teams can successfully complete these tasks, they are one step away from synergistic results.

Implementing—Even the best plans and solutions are useless unless they are fully implemented. The bottom line for synergy must be the successful implementation of change initiatives. The culmination of synergistic events should be well-thought-out, change-oriented action plans. The final phase in the synergy process is designed to build on all the momentum that the previous phases have built and to direct that energy into completing the task at hand. At this point in the team development process, teams actually begin to "perform." The key to success in this phase is basic management skills. As individuals' capacity to grow beyond themselves (synergy) is increased, it must be managed like any other valuable resource. The following actions in this phase are necessary for successful implementation:

- Establish specific, measurable goals/objectives/action plans regarding change implementation.
- Monitor implementation progress and supply the necessary reinforcement to ensure success.
- Implement the change in a manner that respects the needs of all parties (timing, interruptions, cost, effort, etc.).
- Modify the implementation plan (throughout the change process) to ensure its relevancy to current realities.

Most implementation problems are the result of nonsynergistic behavior. This behavior can be attributed to human nature and bad habits. Fortunately, if a team follows the guidelines developed to create synergy and effective team development, successful implementation will be the result.

View Resistance as a Natural Reaction That Must Be Expected and Managed

Resistance is any opposition to a shift in the status quo and is a common response to change. Resistance occurs because people are control oriented, and when their environment is disrupted, they perceive that they have lost the ability to control their lives. This resistance will begin as soon as major change is initiated and can be expressed overtly or covertly. The amount of resistance generated will vary from person to person because each individual has his or her own unique frame of reference that influences how the person views, the change. An individual's frame of reference is comprised from his or her values, emotions, knowledge, and behavior. Organizational resistance usually takes the form of a key sponsor not supporting the change because of his or her frame of reference. Although similar to individual frame of reference, organizational frame of reference is comprised of logistics, economics, and politics.

One of the common pitfalls with regard to resistance is that sponsors who are driving change tend to think of resistance as inexplicable. They view resistance as a mysterious force that affects people. They think that resistance is avoidable, believing that if it does occur, it is really a result of somebody's failure. Typical responses are: "What's wrong with that person?; What's wrong with that group?; Why won't they support our change effort? There must be something wrong with those people." That perspective on resistance is a major barrier to successful change. Other perspectives that can become major barriers to change include the following:

- An unclear corporate vision that causes confusion on how changes should be interpreted
- A poor implementation history that makes people perceive this change as simply "the flavor of the month"
- No consequence management to accompany the change
- Too little time to implement the change
- Lack of synergy; and many others

When these implications are understood, management will see that they cause disruption to people's expectations, producing resistance. The best practice applicable to resistance is to first view the phenomenon as a natural and understandable human reaction to disruption and that, as a result, we respond to resistance as an inevitable part of managing a major change. The greater the change, and the more disruptive it is to the status quo, the stronger the resistance will be. This is true not only of changes that are perceived as negative but also of changes that are perceived, initially, as positive. The reason is that any change, positive or negative, brings about unknown implications. Resistance must be expected, budgeted and planned for, and managed in order for change objectives to be successful. To effectively manage resistance, one must first understand the reasons for resistance.

To add perspective to the process of managing resistance to change, explore options available when managing resistance. Expect resistance and manage it through a prevention approach or through a healing approach. It is important to recognize that there is a price associated with managing resistance to change. Resistance will always be the companion of major disruptive change, regardless of whether people view it as positive or negative. Acceptance of this fact implies the recognition and acceptance of the price tag. There is no choice in whether or not you pay for resistance if your change project is going to be successful. The question is: How are you going to pay? There is a choice between paying for prevention—which incorporates planning and allocating resources in advance for managing resistance, building plans to overcome the phenomenon, and building commitment to change objectives—versus healing payments, which are the later maintenance costs associated with changes that were forced on targets.

People accept change not because they believe in it but because they must. To ensure compliance, there is a later and greater cost to pay. Included in a compliance system is the burden to the organization of hiring additional supervisors and managers to ensure that employees are doing what they are told. Resistance that is managed by healing is manifested in higher turnover, lower productivity, low morale, pessimism, and distrust of management. These costs can be significant. Resistance always has a price tag. A conscious decision must be made whether that invoice will be paid in advance or after the fact.

With a clear understanding of resistance and how it can be paid for, management can take a number of actions to manage it. The first step that must be taken is to determine whether the resistance is an ability deficiency or a willingness deficiency. If it is an ability deficiency, management should proceed as follows. First, the needed knowledge and skills must be identified. Second, education and training programs should be developed to address the deficiency. Next, the education and training should be delivered to the designated sponsors, agents, and targets. Then the learnings should be reinforced. Finally, the desired behaviors and skills need to be modeled.

If it is a willingness deficiency, management should proceed as follows. First, the reason for the change should be effectively communicated to the targets so that they understand why they are being asked to change. Second, the targets should be evaluated to see whether they have accepted the change. Third, any inconsistencies with what is necessary to motivate people in the direction of the change objectives (i.e., clear vision, committed sponsorship) should be identified. Next, the current rewards, recognition, performance measures, and compensation should be analyzed. Then plans for rewards, recognition, performance measures, and compensation that will support the change objectives should be developed. Finally, the new consequence management system should be communicated, implemented, and enforced.

Although the prescriptions to manage resistance appear to be "cut and dried," one must remember that the introduction of major change and the resistance that follows it are fueled by very emotional responses. However, these emotional responses fall into predictable patterns that have been researched and, like resistance, can be managed. The first pattern, the emotional response to a positively perceived change, has five stages an individual goes through:

1. Uninformed optimism
2. Informed pessimism
3. Hopeful realism
4. Informed optimism
5. Completion

Individuals move from believing the change at hand will be easy to a point where pessimism sets in as they realize the change will be considerably more complicated than first anticipated. At this point, individuals may choose to "check out," either publicly or privately. *Checking out* refers to dissatisfaction and a withdrawal of one's investment in the change. During this period, change agents should increase opportunities for public expression of pessimism. Attempts to suppress negative reactions only lead to increased target frustration and private checking out. Once an individual has passed through informed pessimism, they begin to "see the light at the end of the tunnel." They now have renewed confidence in the ability to complete the change and integrate it into the normal work routine.

The second pattern, the emotional response to a negatively perceived change, has eight stages a target must pass through:

1. Stability
2. Immobilization
3. Denial
4. Anger
5. Bargaining
6. Depression
7. Testing
8. Acceptance

The first four stages of this model are a natural progression. The change is introduced and the target is in disbelief. He or she then refuses to believe that the change is really going to happen. When the target finally realizes the change cannot be stopped, a period of anger sets in, followed by bargaining. It is at the bargaining stage where change agents must be cautious. Targets will make every attempt to delay the change or get back to the status quo. The change agent must use confrontative reality testing (i.e., the clear and firm affirmation of the change). The target will inevitably get depressed but as time goes on, they will learn to live with the change, eventually accepting it.

With actions in place to manage resistance and the emotional response to change, additional follow-up activities need to be initiated to ensure successful implementation. Management should be sure to continually provide the targets with information to keep them informed of the progress of the change. Management needs to mark the ending of the change and celebrate the successes. The past status quo should be treated with respect and never denigrated. Most important, the change needs to be reinforced, and its implementation cycle should be minimized.

Recognize the Levels of Commitment That Are Required

Commitment is the cornerstone of successful change implementation, but it is fraught with pitfalls and obstacles. One of the most common pitfalls observed here is underestimating the initial level of commitment necessary for the change to be successful. In looking at any specific change project, there needs to be some level of commitment at some level of the organization for it to be successful. Many changes, however, require very little commitment, whereas others require a great deal of commitment at every level of the organization. The best practice is to recognize the initial level of commitment required from key people in order for the change to succeed. Once that level of commitment is identified, proactively pursue building that commitment throughout the organization at every level. An operating axiom requires (1) knowledge of the level of commitment required to achieve your change objectives, and (2) only asking for the level of commitment necessary to achieve your change.

The commitment model that management should work from consists of three developmental phases (see Figure V.3). Each phase consists of specific

Phase 1.	**Preparation**	
	Stage 1.	Contact
	Stage 2.	Awareness
Phase 2.	**Acceptance**	
	Stage 3.	Understanding
	Stage 4.	Positive Perception
Phase 3.	**Commitment**	
	Stage 5.	Installation
	Stage 6.	Adoption
	Stage 7.	Institutionalization
	Stage 8.	Internalization

FIGURE V.3   The Commitment Model

and identifiable stages that cannot be avoided. At each stage in the model, there will be reasons why resistance is generated. Change agents should use the appropriate actions at each stage to build commitment.

The first phase, *Preparation,* forms the foundation of either support or resistance to change. The first stage in the commitment model is the *Contact* stage. Here, the target will either become aware of the change or they will be unaware because contact was not perceived by the targets. Once contact has been acknowledged, the targets will move to the *Awareness* stage where they realize that their jobs will be modified. This does not mean that people understand the full impact of the change. If understanding is achieved, the targets move to the next phase. If not, they are left in confusion and progress is halted.

Phase 2, *Acceptance,* marks people's passage over what is called the disposition threshold. The targets' new awareness enables them to make decisions about accepting or rejecting the change. The third stage, *Understanding,* is critical. Targets now become more familiar with the ramifications of the change and begin to form an opinion about it. Negative perceptions will lead to resistance. Once targets accept and support the change, they will move to the next stage, *Positive Perception.* At this point, people must decide whether they are going to support implementation. If the targets refuse to support the change, then resistance is increased, and change agents must raise pain and manage the resistance. If a positive perception of the change is developed, the person has reached the point of action (installation). A formal decision to install and use the change is made. The target has now reached the *Commitment* phase and passed the commitment threshold.

In the next stage, *Installation,* targets demonstrate truly committed action by installing the change. However, this decision does not mean the maximum level of commitment has been reached. In fact, the possibility of reversibility should be stressed. If the change is not aborted and long-term usage commences, the *Adoption* stage has begun. During this time, the change is still in a trial period despite the enormous amount of commitment it took to reach this point. If, after extensive usage, the change is successful, the target will reach the seventh stage of the commitment model, the *Institutionalization* stage. The change has been around a long time and become part of the everyday routine and corporate culture. Reversibility is no longer a possibility at this point. It takes time to institutionalize a change and the organizational structure should be aligned accordingly. At this level all the targets regard the change as standard operating procedure, yet this does not necessarily mean they have to believe in the change.

The final stage of the commitment model is just that, *Internalization.* Here, the targets have reached maximum commitment because the change reflects their own beliefs as well as those of the organization. Once the level of commitment has been decided, management should use communication to assist in reaching that level. However, when using communication to build commitment, the following considerations should be taken by management:

- Who must receive the message (internal/external)?
- What do the targets need to know?
- What is the desired likely response?
- How should the message be delivered (media)? How often?
- Who should deliver the message?

Once these questions have been answered, achieving the desired level of commitment will be easier. The one thing that management must know is that building commitment is a time-consuming, expensive process and the investment should only be made to build a level of commitment necessary for the change to be successful—no more and no less.

Understand the Strategic Importance of the Organization's Culture

Adoption of a TIM philosophy will, in and of itself, have some cultural implications. For some organizations it may be a minor cultural modification, but for many, the adoption of a TIM philosophy will be a major cultural shift. In either case, the current culture is a huge issue that must be addressed for change projects to be implemented successfully. Because culture is difficult to understand and hard to measure and manage, it is relatively easy to ignore. Commonly, organizations ignore it or do not treat corporate culture as a key variable when implementing a major change initiative. Obviously the best practice is just the opposite. Senior management must understand the strategic importance of the overall culture to the change initiative and work hard to understand and manage the impact that culture has on the successful implementation of improvement projects.

Corporate culture is the basic pattern of shared beliefs, behaviors, norms, values, and expectations acquired over a long time by members of an organization. If an improvement project or a change initiative is consistent with that set of behaviors, beliefs, norms, values, and expectations, then the culture is actually an enabler or facilitator of that change. The culture will help that change to be successful. However, a change project may be fundamentally counter to the culture. One thing we are very clear about is that whenever there is a discrepancy between change in culture and existing culture, existing culture wins. So to apply this best practice to any change initiative, we need to understand whether culture is an enabler to change or a barrier. If it is a barrier, we must identify why it is a barrier, what the existing cultural barriers are, and proactively modify the change or modify the culture, or some combination of both, in order for change objectives to be successfully met. Only three options are available:

Option 1 Modify the change to be more consistent with the culture of the organization.

Option 2 Modify or change the culture to be more consistent with the achievement of the change objectives.

Option 3 Ignore options 1 and 2 and plan the change initiative to take significantly longer and cost significantly more than what you may have originally budgeted. (This is not really an option.)

The question that management wants to know is, "When is culture an issue?" The answer is that culture is always an issue when a strategic decision requires a major shift in the way management and/or employees operate. The most strategic decisions are likely to require a significant realignment of the culture when the changes caused by those decisions are implemented. It is at these times, as when any major change is introduced, when the sponsors, change agents, advocates, and targets will want to follow the best practices that have been described.

Summary

In today's turbulent environment, where demands for change are continually accelerating, there will be losers, survivors, and winners. Throughout this book you will receive many ideas on identifying what improvements your organization can make to be more successful. However, these improvements will not bring substantial value to your organization unless they can be implemented successfully. To implement those solutions, your organization must be able to manage change. It is your organization's ability to manage and implement change that will determine whether you will be a loser, survivor, or winner. The most critical issue of managing change is the ability to manage the people who must change, helping them to become more resilient and adaptable in the process.

References

1. Ernst & Young Technical Report TR 93.004-1 HJH
2. Ernst & Young Technical Report TR 93.004-2
3. Daryl Conner, *Managing at the Speed Of Change,* published by Random House in 1994.

(*Note:* The authors would like to thank Daryl R. Conner of ODR, Inc. for the use of some of his concepts in this section on Organizational Change Management.)

APPENDIX VI
ISO 9000 Books and Audio/Video References

ISO 9000 Reference Books

Audit Standards: A Comparative Analysis, 2nd Edition
American Society for Quality Control
Education & Training Institute
Phone: 800-952-6587
Cost: $19.95 Nonmember; $17.95 Member
Length: 80 pages

Documenting Quality for ISO 9000 & Other Industry Standards
American Society for Quality Control
Education & Training Institute
Phone: 800-952-6587
Cost: $24.95 Nonmember; $21.95 Member
Length: 200 pages

Eight-Step Process to Successful ISO-9000 Implementation
American Society for Quality Control
Phone: 800-952-6587
Author: Lawrence A. Wilson
Cost: $35.00 Nonmember; $31.50 Member
Length: 350 pages

Guidebook to ISO 9000 & ANSI/ASQC Q90
American Society for Quality Control
Education & Training Institute
Phone: 800-952-6587
Cost: $53.95 Nonmember; $45.95 Member
Length: 138 pages

How to Write Your ISO 9000 Quality Manual
Perry Johnson, Inc.
Phone: 313-356-4410

ISO 9000 & Strategies to Compete in the Single European Market
Goal/QPC
Phone: 508-685-3900
Cost: $125.00
Length: 675 pages

ISO 9000 Book: A Global Competitor's Guide to Compliance & Certification
George Washington University (CEEP)
Continuing Engineering Education Program
Phone: 800-424-9773
Cost: $26.95

ISO 9000 Equivalent: ANSI/ASQC Q90-1987 Series Quality Management & Quality Assurance Standards
American Society for Quality Control
Education & Training Institute
Phone: 800-952-6587
Cost: $52.95 Nonmember; $44.95 Member

ISO 9000-3: Software Quality Assurance
American Society for Quality Control
Education & Training Institute
Phone: 800-952-6587
Cost: $35.00

ISO 9000: A Comprehensive Guide to Registration, Audit Guidelines & Successful Implementation
Oliver Wright Publications
Phone: 800-343-0625
Author: Greg Hutchins
Cost: $37.50
Length: 288 pages

ISO 9000: A Global Competitor's Guide to Compliance & Certification
Association for Quality & Participation
Phone: 513-381-1959
Cost: $26.95 Nonmember; $24.26 Member

ISO 9000: Handbook of Quality Standards & Compliance
American Society for Quality Control
Education & Training Institute
Phone: 800-952-6587
Cost: $69.95 Nonmember; $59.95 Member
Length: 287 pages

ISO 9000: Preparing for Registration
American Society for Quality Control
Education & Training Institute
Phone: 800-952-6587
Publisher: Marcel Dekker, Inc.
Cost: $45.00 Nonmember; $40.50 Member
Length: 254 pages

ISO 9000 and the Service Sector
American Society for Quality Control
Phone: 800-952-6587
Author: James L. Lamprecht
Cost: $35.00 Nonmember; $31.50 Member

Overview of the ISO 9000 Standards & ISO 9000 Facility Registration
National Electrical Manufacturers Association NEMA
Phone: 202-457-8400
Cost: $40.00 Nonmember; $25.00 Member

The Audit Kit
American Society for Quality Control
Phone: 800-957-6587
Author: Kent A. Keeney
Cost: $44.00 Nonmember; $39.50 Member
Length: 210 pages

The ISO 9000 Auditor's Companion
American Society for Quality Control
Phone: 800-957-6587
Author: Kent A. Keeney
Cost: $27.00 Nonmember; $24.00 Member
Length: 49 pages

The ISO 9000 Essentials
Canadian Standards Association
Phone: 905-272-3920
Author: Dwayne D. Mathers, et al.
Cost: $38.00 Canadian dollars
Length: 134 pages

ISO—9000 Audio/Video References

H. James Harrington's ISO 9000 Step by Step
SystemCorp Inc.
Phone: 1-800-665-3003
Author: H. James Harrington
Cost: $995.00
Media: CD-ROM

ISO 9000: Executive Briefing
American Society for Quality Control
Phone: 800-957-6587
Narrator: Ian Durand
Cost: $195.00
Length: 25 minutes
Media: Videotape and Audiotape

ISO 9000 International
Quality Standard
American Society for Quality Control
Phone: 800-957-6587
Narrator: Ian Durand
Cost: $595.00
Length: 55 minutes
Media: Videotape and Audiotape

ISO 9000: Opportunity
Within Revision
American Society for Quality Control
Phone: 800-957-6587
Author: Richard B. Clements
Cost: $19.95
Length: 90 minutes
Media: Audiotape

ISO 9000: Tips and Techniques
American Society for Quality Control
Phone: 800-957-6587
Author: Richard B. Clements
Cost: $19.95
Length: 90 minutes
Media: Audiotape

ISO 9001 In Action
SystemCorp, Inc.
Phone: 800-665-3003
Cost: $195.00
Length: 40 minutes
Media: Videotape

LearnerFirst How
to Implement ISO 9000
American Society for Quality Control
Phone: 800-957-6587
Author: Lawrence A. Wilson
Cost: $795.00 Nonmember; $695.00 Member
Media: Interactive Computer Program

The Executive Guide to ISO 9000
American Society for Quality Control
Phone: 800-957-6587
Author: Reality Interactive, Inc.
Cost: $129.00
Media: CD-ROM

Understanding ISO 9000
American Society for Quality Control
Phone: 800-957-6587
Cost: $985.00
Length: 150 minutes
Media: Videotape

What Is ISO 9000,
And Why Do I Care?
Excellence in Training Corp.
Phone: 800-747-6569
Cost: $450.00
Length: 33 minutes
Media: Audiotape

List of ISO Self-Evaluation Questions

1. Are your organization's quality policy, objectives, and commitment for quality
   - defined?
   - documented?
2. At all levels of the organization, do you ensure that the quality policy is
   - communicated?
   - implemented?
   - understood?
3. Do you have a document that defines the responsibility, authority, and interrelationship of personnel doing work affecting quality?
4. Have you identified the resource requirements for quality activities within your organization? Are the resources for each quality activity documented?
5. Does the management representative have the defined authority to ensure that the quality management system requirements are
   - established?
   - implemented?
   - maintained?
6. Are all personnel aware of the management representative's
   - authority?
   - responsibility?
7. Are the reviews of the quality management system carried out at defined intervals?
8. Are the reviews recorded and maintained?
9. Have you established, and do you maintain a documented quality management system as a means of ensuring that the product conforms to specified requirements?

10. Do you effectively implement documented procedures consistent with the requirements for the chosen international standard?
11. Do you define and document how requirements for quality will be met?
12. Do you establish and maintain documented procedures for contract review activities?
13. Is each accepted tender, contract, and order reviewed to ensure that requirements are adequately
    - defined?
    - documented?
14. Do you have a procedure for resolving accepted order requirements for quality requirements that differ from their tender?
15. Does your contract review procedure ensure that you have the capability to meet contract or accepted order requirements?
    - Is this documented?
16. Do you have a document that defines how an amendment to a contract is made?
17. Does this document define how this amendment will be communicated to functions concerned within your organization?
18. Do you maintain records of contract review activities?
19. Do you establish and maintain documented procedures to control and verify the design of the product to ensure that specified requirements are met?
20. In preparing plans for each design and development activity, do you
    - define responsibilities?
    - assign activities to qualified personnel with resources?
    - update the design as it evolves?
21. Are the design input groups defined and is the necessary information
    - documented?
    - transmitted?
    - reviewed regularly?
22. Do you have documented procedures to
    - identify design input for customer, statutory, and regulatory requirements?
    - resolve incomplete, ambiguous, or conflicting requirements?
    - incorporate contract review activities?
23. Do you plan and conduct formal documented reviews of the design results with representatives of all functions involved in the design process?
24. Do you have documentation to ensure that design output
    - meets input requirements and is reviewed before release?

- contains or references acceptance criteria?
- identifies crucial design characteristics?

25. Has design verification been made to ensure design stage output meets the design stage requirements?

26. Has design validation been performed to ensure that the product conforms to defined user requirements or desires?

27. Have all design changes been identified, documented, reviewed, and approved by authorized personnel prior to implementation?

28. Do you have documented procedures to control all documents that relate to the quality management system in your organization, including to the extent applicable documents of external origin, such as standards and drawings?

29. Do you have documented procedures to control document approval and distribution?
Do you have a master list of current documents?
Do you promptly remove obsolete documents?

30. Are changes to documents reviewed and approved by the same functions or organizations that originally reviewed the change? Is the nature of the change identified?

31. Do you have documented procedures to ensure that purchased product conforms to specified requirements?

32. Do you have documented procedures for the evaluation and selection of subcontractors?

33. Have you defined the extent and type of control exercised over subcontractors?

34. Have you established acceptable records of subcontractors?
Are these records maintained?

35. Do your purchasing documents contain data that clearly describe the product ordered? Do you review and approve purchasing documents for adequacy of the specified requirements prior to release?

36. Do you have documented procedures for verification and release of products that require verification at the subcontractor's premises?

37. When specified in the contract, does your customer verify the product at the subcontractor's premises?

38. Do you understand that customer verification does not absolve you from the responsibility to provide acceptable products?

39. Have you established and do you maintain documented procedures for the
- verification of customer-supplied products?
- storage of customer-supplied products?

- maintenance of customer-supplied products?

40. Do you record and report to the customer any customer-supplied product that is lost, damaged, or is otherwise unsuitable for use?
   Does the customer understand that verification by the supplier does not absolve him or her of the responsibility to provide acceptable products?

41. Do you establish and maintain documented procedures for identifying the product from receipt and during all stages of
   - production?
   - delivery?
   - installation?

42. Do you establish and maintain documented procedures for traceability where and when this is a specified requirement?

43. Is the unique identification of the product recorded?

44. Do you identify and plan production, installation, and servicing processes that directly affect quality?

45. Do you have documented procedures defining the manner of production, installation, and servicing where the lack of such procedures would adversely affect quality?

46. Do you ensure the use of suitable equipment for production, installation, and servicing?

47. Do you ensure that processes are in compliance with reference standards/codes, quality plans, and/or documented procedures?

48. Do you monitor and control process parameters and product characteristics during production, installation, and servicing?

49. Do you approve of processes and equipment as appropriate?

50. Do you have criteria for workmanship?

51. Do you carry out suitable maintenance of equipment to ensure process capability?

52. Do you have processes whose results cannot be fully verified by inspection and test of product?

53. Do you have processes that require qualified operators and continuous monitoring?

54. Are your documented procedures for inspection and testing activities
   - established?
   - maintained?

55. Do you ensure that an incoming product is not used or processed until it has been inspected or otherwise verified as conforming to specified requirements?

56. Do your inspection and testing procedures take into account the amount of control exercised at the subcontractor's premises?
57. Do you positively identify and record all products that are released prior to testing, to permit immediate recall and replacement?
58. Do you inspect a product as required by your quality plan and/or your documented procedures?
59. Do you hold the product until all tests and reports are completed prior to its release, except when it is required for urgent production purposes?
60. Do you have a quality plan or documented procedure that ensures that prior to releasing the product
    - all final inspection and testing are completed?
    - required specifications are met?
    - associated data and documentation are available and authorized?
61. Do you establish and maintain records that show that the product has been inspected and/or tested?
62. Do you establish and maintain documented procedures to control, calibrate, and maintain inspection, measuring, and test equipment?
63. Are inspection, measuring, and test equipment used in a manner to ensure that the measurement uncertainty is known and is consistent with the required measurement capability?
64. When test hardware or test software are used as suitable forms of inspection, do you
    - check them to prove that they are capable of verifying the acceptability of the product?
    - recheck them at prescribed intervals?
65. Do you establish the extent and frequency of calibration checks and maintain records as evidence of control?
66. Do you supply, when requested by the customer or the customer's representative, technical data to verify that the inspection, measuring, and test equipment are functionally adequate?
67. Do you determine the measurements to be made and the selection of the test equipment as having suitable accuracy and precision?
68. Do you identify all inspection, measuring, and test equipment that can affect quality?
69. Do you calibrate and adjust all inspection, measuring, and test equipment at prescribed intervals against valid international or national standards?
70. Do you define the calibration process?

71. Do you identify inspection, measuring, and test equipment to identify the calibration status?
72. Do you maintain calibration records for inspection, measuring, and test equipment?
73. Do you assess and document the validity of previous inspection and test results when equipment is found to be out of calibration?
74. Do you ensure that environmental conditions are suitable for the calibrations, inspections, measurements, and tests?
75. Do you ensure that the handling, preservation, and storage of inspection, measuring, and test equipment is proper to maintain the accuracy and fitness for use?
76. Do you safeguard inspection, measuring, and test facilities from adjustments that would invalidate calibration settings?
77. Do you identify suitable means for identifying inspection and test status indicating conformance or nonconformance with respect to inspection and testing?
78. Does the means chosen to identify inspection and test status indicate the conformity or nonconformity to specified requirements?
79. Is the identification of inspection and test status maintained through production, installation, and servicing to ensure the use of an acceptable product?
80. Have you defined and documented the responsibility and authority required to ensure that a nonconforming product is neither used nor installed?
81. Do you have documented procedures for the identification of nonconforming product?
82. Do you have documented procedures for the treatment of nonconforming products?
83. Do you have documented procedures for the evaluation of nonconforming products?
84. Do you segregate (when practical) a nonconforming product?
85. Do you have documented procedures for the disposition of nonconforming product and/or material?
86. Do you have documented procedures to notify all functions concerned or affected by the disposition of nonconformity of the decision?
87. Have you defined responsibility and authority for the review and disposition of a nonconforming product?
88. Do you have documented procedures covering rework, repair, regrading, or rejection of a nonconforming product?

89. When required by the contract, do you obtain a waiver (concession) from the customer before using or repairing a product that does not conform to specified requirements?

90. Do you reinspect the repaired or reworked product according to the quality plan and/or documented procedures?

91. Do you have documented procedures for implementing corrective and preventive action?
Is corrective and preventive action in line with the seriousness of the problem?
Do you record changes to procedures due to corrective and preventive actions?

92. Do you have documented procedures for the effective handling of customer complaints?

93. Do you have documented procedures for investigating the cause of nonconformities relating to the product, process, and quality management system and for recording the results?

94. Do you have documented procedures for determining the corrective action needed to eliminate the cause of nonconformities?

95. Do you have documented procedures to define the corrective action needed to eliminate causes of nonconformities?

96. Do you have documented procedures for the application of controls to ensure that the corrective action is taken and is effective?

97. Do you have documented procedures for implementing preventive action to eliminate the causes of potential nonconformities?
Do you make use of appropriate sources of information?

98. Do you establish and maintain documented procedures for the handling, storage, packaging, preservation, and delivery of materials?

99. Do you provide handling methods that prevent damage or deterioration?

100. Do you control product flow in storage areas and check the condition of the product at appropriate intervals?

101. Do you control packing, packaging, and marking processes to the extent necessary to ensure conformance to specified requirements?

102. Do you apply appropriate measures for preservation and segregation of a product when it is under your control?

103. Do you arrange for the protection of product quality after inspection and testing? Where contractually specified, do you extend this to include delivery?

104. Do you have documented procedures for the identification of quality records?

105. Do you have documented procedures for the collection of quality records?
106. Do you have documented procedures for the indexing of quality records?
107. Do you have documented procedures for the filing of quality records?
108. Do you have documented procedures for the storage of quality records?
109. Do you have documented procedures for the maintenance of quality records?
110. Do you have documented procedures for the disposition of quality records?
111. Do you have documented procedures for planning internal quality audits?
112. Do you have documented procedures for implementing internal quality audits?
113. Do you schedule internal quality audits on the basis of status and importance of the activity to be audited?
114. Do you bring audit results to the attention of the personnel having responsibility for the area being audited?
115. Do you have follow-up audit activities to verify the implementation and effectiveness of the corrective action taken?
116. Do you establish and maintain documented procedures for identifying training needs for all personnel performing activities affecting quality?
117. Do you establish and maintain documented procedures for providing the training of all personnel performing activities affecting quality?
118. Do you retain training records?
119. Do you clarify servicing responsibilities among suppliers, distributors and users?
120. Do you plan service activities (whether carried out by the supplier or by a separate agent)?
121. Do you control the measuring and test equipment used in field servicing and tests?
122. Do you provide the customer with suitable documentation concerning product servicing?
123. Do you provide for adequate backup, such as technical advice and support, and spares or parts supply?
124. Do you provide competent servicing personnel?
125. Do you train service personnel?
126. Do you provide feedback of information that would be useful in improving product or servicing design?

127. Do you identify the need for statistical techniques required for establishing process capability and product characteristics?
128. Do you identify the need for statistical techniques required for controlling process capability and product characteristics?
129. Do you identify the need for statistical techniques required for verifying process capability and product characteristics?
130. Do you have documented procedures for the application of identified statistical techniques?

Index